# THE ANATOMY *of* CHOICE

HARSHALI SINGH

Readomania

Readomania Publishing
A division of Kurious Kind Media Private Limited
466, DDA SFS Apartments, Pocket 1, Sector 22, Dwarka,
New Delhi – 110077
books.readomania.com
email: support@readomania.com
Facebook: facebook.com/iamreadomania
Twitter: twitter.com/iamreadomania

First Published in 2018 by Readomania



ISBN: 978-93-858547-4-3

Typeset in Palatino Linotype by Shine Graphics

Printed and bound at Thomson Press India Ltd.

*Readomania*

India has traditionally been the land of storytellers and a lot of us have an inherent skill of creating good plots, good stories and good narrations. With a little encouragement and support, many more authors will be widely read and attain a place in the sun. This is the essence of *Readomania*—an initiative that nurtures emerging stars of the literary world.

It would not be an exaggeration to say that *Readomania* is the talent hunt in fiction. It goes a step beyond by not just identifying the talent but also nurturing it and showcasing it to the world. In the process, we have created a powerhouse of content.

*Readomania* has four principle interest areas – traditional print publishing, online library of short stories and poetry, literary events and products.

The print publishing works towards delivering good quality content to the readers. We publish good authors in meaningful anthologies, novels and works of narrative non-fiction. Our books stand out for their perspectives, the plots, the language and most importantly their ability to enrich lives.

Take a break, read something nice, write something beautiful. Read our books or visit us at www.readomania.com and enjoy a whole new world of literature.

*To everyone who chooses sanity instead of the chaos that their hearts crave.*

*I feel you.*

# Prologue

*This reclusive twilight brings with it February winds that howl, choked full of untethered emotions. I bear them as best as I can…these wintry, slate-grey skies. This numbing cold makes me want to shield the ones I love. The ones who huddle behind my lonely fogged windows or sit next to a roaring fire warming their cold, aching bones…they reminisce about the happy days gone by.*

*More than anything else, this solitude makes me long for her sunny warmth that illuminates my heart. Some people have that effect. She is one of them.*

*My bright star, my bumbling Bee, my Bhavya.*

*Noorie, who rests close by, celebrated in death, as she never was in life, sings hauntingly sad ghazal's these days.*

*What ails her, I wonder.*

*Every year as the north winds make my foundations shiver, her melodious, heart-wrenching voice full of grief makes these months unbearable.*

*I stand as I have stood for many decades, concrete and firm. One of the six daughters of the family that inhabit me now calls me Anwar. Fittingly, I suppose.*

*The family that occupied my echoing interiors before the partition of this country had a child. My namesake. He played in my greens until the very end.*

*Those were terrible times.*

*I eavesdropped in horror at the unspeakable atrocities that were talked about. The big living room, home to many a discussion. Some even effected within my walls. I am witness to rivers of tears and walls of pain and anguish that I have absorbed through the years as people have come and gone leaving behind only empty rooms to an onlooker, but, to me they are crammed full of reminiscences, some good and some unspeakable.*

*I am the Haveli with the hundred doors.*

*In the years that I have weathered the living in this old colony of Naugraha, witnessing old Delhi's lanes grow narrower, the outcroppings and illegal constructions almost choking the lanes where once horse carriages rode confident in their self-possession.*

*It all seems lost in the grains of time.*

*We were nine Havelis, once.*

*Slowly the families moved away, leaving nothing but memories of a bygone era fresh in the blows that we have withstood…blows of ignominy and changing dynamics of the times. My counterparts slowly grew silent, their voices reduced to mere whispers and musings about their families. I was saved from this sad fate by the good fortune of geography. The only reason I survived, one would say.*

*The family that thrives here now is a large one and I have always felt it is the large ones, which are the most interesting.*

*Arun, the head of the Sharma family, came as a boy full of spirit and grit. Happy as a child should be. His father's heavy handedness and his own dreams crushed under the passage of time made Arun the man he is today, passive and resigned.*

*His wife, the devout Uma, who walks with a limp due to a past illness, is full of gumption and an emotional strength that I would be hard-pressed to recollect seeing in some men, who have crossed my threshold.*

*The children came in quick succession. Aruna, the eldest daughter, then Bhavya and finally, Charu.*

*I had thought they had given up but Uma always wanted a son and despite Arun's misgiving, they tried one last time.*

*The success of bearing a male child, the heir, had lasted on Uma's face for many years. Not that she loved her daughters any less, but it is just one of those things I have come to understand as I silently watch this spectacle before me. Women crave to give their families a male child. At least the women whom I have known….*

*And so Dheeraj, the son after three daughters, became the heir apparent, set to inherit the saree shop that his father had inherited from his father-in-law. The settlement for marrying Arun's mother.*

*Now some would say, 'So much trouble for a saree shop,' but you see therein lay the complication or in Dheeraj's case, the obstacle.*

*For a few years, everything seemed right after Dheeraj's birth. The children grew up happy and a strong bond was forged within my walls as time ebbed and flowed. And then came the announcement… after four children, Uma was pregnant again.*

*Oh! What a vicious fight it was between Arun and Uma. The children huddled together scared, expecting the worst. Their fears were unfounded, of course. Uma managed to convince Arun, once again.*

*God's gift, she said.*

*Arun only saw it as another mouth to feed.*

*It was too late to withdraw from that decision as life threw another challenge their way. I heard Uma contemplating an abortion the day they found out it was not one child, but three. It was Arun this time who mollified his panicked wife.*

*And, so the already big family became enormous with the advent of the three angels, as they are lovingly called by their indulgent family.*

*Etti came first; a second later, it was Fanny, and then came Gina.*

*Tonight, my heart beats hard, as if there is a weight on it. She always has that effect on me. Time slows down with her around… her voice breaks as she talks to me. Hear her story, for she longs for someone to know her, hear her. Noorie's voice.*

*A soft breeze that haunts, reminds me of the days that I have lived and loved. Some over too soon and some days that stretch to eternity… days that bind instead of releasing.*

*I wait, as I have waited for eons, ever hopeful, for the ripped part of my soul to find me…to complete me.*

*Where is he...my love? The only one who understands...who loves me despite...myself? Why has he not joined me this morning as I ready for my riyaaz? My still heart beats like nervous fingers on a tanpura.*

*The sun shines on the decaying walls that surround me, built to bind me, to constrict, to tie me down in death as they tried to do when I lived. And, I take pleasure in the knowledge that they remain unaware, unknowing of my flight in spirit, similar to the one I took in life. Beautiful portraits parade before my eyes as I recall the days of grandeur, the mehfils and mushairas in the Haveli next door, an excuse to meet.*

*The excitement of the weekly invitation, the breathless rush to finish the ghazal before the night sky tuned indigo. His tread as it whispered on the marbled floor and his dark eyes as they scorched my skin when he gazed at my bejewelled form...raise goosebumps on my inanimate form even now, as they did then.*

*Oh! Those nights...a hundred flickering candles imitating our stuttering breath even as the velvety bedspread enveloped our sensitised, glistening skin in its warmth.*

*Would I have done the same had I known that my life would end here, I sometimes ask myself. I remember Ammi asking if all this intrigue and hiding was worth the pain it eventually would and did cost and I remember saying...*

*'Anything for love.'*

*My eyes take in the blackened walls of this old and dead house in which I rest, yet my mind remembers the glory of its yesteryears when the Haveli and this domed mansion complemented each other.*

*Chaand and Chaand Raat, we were once called.*

*What has now become my mausoleum was once a haven that my love built for me. The ones who objected and were blinded by the sparkle of our love desecrated the beautiful black-onyx stone that made my house unique. They thought dulling the exterior would hide the love that lived inside.*

*How wrong they were!*

*The Haveli and I are spared the ravages of time, the Haveli passing through time thriving in that passage and I, standing still. Frozen. All I can do is roam the walls of my cavernous resting place, this all-consuming loneliness relieved every morning with his advent.*

*Unseen, I endeavour to remind him of our love through the music he loved so much. As he rises to leave, I want to push at this veil of time and show myself, to stop him, ask him to stay for a moment more.*

*Alas! I cannot for I am Noorie.*

*A famed tawaif, the courtesan with a voice of gold to the world. But a simple girl with a heart that sings when I behold the one that I love. For him, I had agreed to sully the name of my family, to go down in history as a prostitute and yet I could not conquer myself or was it that he could not look beyond his own distrust?*

*What does it matter now? I tell myself.*

*If this is our destiny, to be so close and yet so far then I shall accept it with grace as I have done everything else that I had to endure.*

*As I feel the first rays of the early morning sun filter through me, I clear my throat waiting for him to enter the inner sanctum of the chamber. No one comes here except him. I have not allowed anyone else to cross these walls until now.*

*So, I wait for us to be joined, never to be separated again…ever. This time with a promise, to forgive, to accept his flaws, as I had not been able to then.*

*Where is he?*

*As Noorie awaits her mate, I await the arrival of my bright star, my Bhavya. The most loyal and courageous person of this family, she has the heart of a lion.*

*But, every coin has two sides, one that shines and the other that remains shadowed.*

*Is that why my foundations shiver, as if to warn me of testing times to come? Does my stone heart tremble with hope for her well-being or a foreboding of a difficult future…an advent of trouble?*

*This is Bhavya's story.*

# 1

## *Solecism—A Mistake*

(Language: English, Origin: Greek)

The emerald-blue waters of Bali sparkled behind her closed eyes as her consciousness entered the twilight state of being untethered in that gap between wakefulness and sleep. She sighed in sleep, longing for the warm, tropical wind, swaying palms, moonlit beaches and freedom from the confines of the expected. Her thoughts dissolved into the gently lapping jade waters of her memories of their vacation, to Indonesia. The trip had been a celebration, their third year together as lovers, as partners or so they told themselves.

Trying to escape herself, Bhavya curled into a ball of frustration unable to block the slide of her mind's eye into the past. She remembered the rush of excitement when the tickets came, the fervent packing, the mad rush of anticipation and drunk on that happiness they had tried to rekindle what had been dying within, the spark of love that remained elusive even as its memory remained fresh and alluring.

In the bid to find it, she had given in to and eventually celebrated Tenzin's need to experiment.

Bhavya turned to her side, her exhausted body trying to find comfort. The reality of her presence in her own bed faded as her mindscape took her back to Bali and her own culpability in the choice she had finally made. She now constantly struggled with the consequence of the choice.

Falling deeper into the abyss of her subconscious, she watched the days of leisure they had spent together. The thin veneer of trying too hard, fraying and yet both she and Tenzin had clutched it tightly, not willing to accept defeat at the hands of destiny. The roaring flame of need and carnal urgency had simmered down to a steady awareness. It was then that Tenzin had brought in the idea of adding another partner, to indulge in a threesome if the opportunity presented itself.

Shocked for an instant, she found that the thought intrigued her. His idea of putting theory into practice titillated her, buoyed their spirits and their conversations. The why's and how's were discussed and she spent countless hours debating it with Tenzin, unable to comprehend how right it was for a man to watch his partner taken by another.

In solitude, she doubted herself as was her way. Was she open to allowing another woman into the equation? Was she not enough that Tenzin had wanted to add another element? He had not said that it would be a woman or a man, had he? She could recall the extra urgency that had been evident even in their conversations of having another man put his hands on her while Tenzin watched and participated. Undoubtedly, it had made her insides tingle, the pictures that formed in her mind, leaving her excited and breathless.

She had elicited a promise from Tenzin that she would be open to it but could back out at any time; it was her way to safeguard herself first.

On deeper introspection, she found a lack of a moral guilt that she would have expected from her devout upbringing. Shrugging her shoulders at its absence, she justified the act as a consensual way to turn up the heat in a relationship that was losing passion. The fact that he readily agreed had told her that he was not new to this desire.

So, heart pounding with anticipation, she had gone on the trip to celebrate their love, blind to the paradox of her thoughts.

*I love seeing you climb the peak, Bee; I want to see that from a distance with another man pushing you over that peak. I want to see my hands covering, mauling your breasts as he enters you. I want to see your mouth wrap around me as he starts moving inside you. Can you feel my fingers on your nub and him inside you? Tell me, Bee…tell me?* He had teased her. And, she had shouted and moaned and writhed picturing everything he said, her mind's eye flush with the images he created so well with his velvety words.

Like a picture flipbook, the pages opened slowly at first then faster and faster.

On the last day of their vacation as they sat laughing over their mutual failure to attract attention of either a male or a female partner, she noticed Kabir looking at her. He walked over to her when Tenzin went to get their drinks.

'Hi there, Kabir,' he said, completely unselfconscious of approaching a stranger.

'Hi, Bhavya…Bee,' Bhavya said, taking his proffered hand. She assessed the man before her in one look. Where Tenzin was a silver fox, this Kabir was a dark, wiry jaguar. Leashed strength, long, blue-black hair tied in a candid man bun. Eyes the colour of dark Guinness, dripping youth, watched her weighing him with a laugh in their dark depths.

'You from India?' he asked after a few moments had passed leaning forward, his hands on the bolster next to her.

'Yes.'

'Vacationing?'

'Anniversary celebration.' She lied smiling, not wanting to divulge the status of their relationship.

'Oh wow, congratulations! I am just happy to talk to someone with an Indian accent.' He said, looking out at the water, giving her a chance to check him out as she had caught his eyes lingering over her bikini-clad body earlier.

Behind her dark sunglasses, she took in his bare chest with well-defined abs. She also saw Tenzin pause, then sit at the bar, watchful.

*What...what am I supposed to do?* 'What about you?' she asked instead.

Kabir told her that he was a lonely artist, living and travelling through Indonesia since the last three months and was homesick. She listened to him with growing interest, realising he was easy to talk to, with a ready laugh. A man who was not scared of following his heart.

Tenzin had cautioned her not to divulge too much about their lives in Paris so she had kept him talking. Aware of himself and comfortable with it he made her relax and it was some time later that she realised that the sun was about to set and though she refrained from telling him about her life with Tenzin, Bhavya was comfortable telling him about herself.

*Should I ask him straight out or should I test waters? What if he is an undercover cop looking to find people who are engaging in such activities? What will my parents say if I am arrested?*

She could not hear his words clearly over the million doubts that were raising their hooded heads.

*Why does it fall on me to hook a guy?* She thought frowning. She looked at Tenzin, angry at being left alone with a task that she was not sure how to accomplish.

Sensing her ire, Tenzin walked over and started a conversation with Kabir all cool and easy, and Bhavya suddenly felt excluded.

'It seems we have ignored the lady far too long,' Kabir remarked. 'I should leave you guys alone.'

'Or...why don't you join us for a drink in our room? I hope you are of age?' Tenzin slid in smoothly.

Both men looked at each other and a knowledge passed between them.

'Is the lady willing?' Kabir asked, after a moment's pause, looking straight at her.

'Are you?' Bhavya countered, pretending that her heart was not ready to jump out of her chest.

'Yes, Ma'am,' he said with a grin on his face.

'Good! Let's go!'

'Bee, are you sure?' Tenzin whispered, taken aback at her answer.

*You wanted this and now, after bringing me almost half way, you act surprised. Men are idiots!*

'I was born sure, you know that...' she said, knowing that Kabir was listening in.

'You can't fool around with something like this,' Tenzin said, taking her arm as Kabir moved a little distance away looking innocent and unperturbed at the ripples he had created.

'Are you trying to talk me out of this? I thought you wanted to do this!' she asked, feeling silly and adamant.

*He is making it look like this was my idea and I am pushing him into this.* Bhavya thought, angry at the drama Tenzin was creating.

'I...I...it's a fantasy but I never thought...' he said, uncertain.

'Well, Mr Tenzin Jamyang, be careful what you wish for.'

'Hey! Guys, if you aren't sure it's fine.' Kabir said, trying to play the peacekeeper.

'I am sure,' Bhavya almost yelled.

Tenzin straightened and nodding handed him the key to their room.

'See you in ten minutes, Kabir,' he said before walking towards the elevators.

After a mute ride up to the fifty-second floor, she saw herself walk into the room that Tenzin and she had shared for the past four days. Silent and unsure, wanting to question Tenzin about the sense in this decision she looked at herself in the large mirror in the washroom. A woman with large, surprised eyes on a face with a prominent jawline stared back at her. She untied the bun she had scrunched her hair into. Her teeth worked her lower lip making it turn a deep red as she questioned herself, then fluffing her hair to fan her face she splashed water on her cheeks. As an afterthought, she dabbed her favourite perfume behind her ears, on her wrists and between her breasts, wondering if it was necessary.

She turned to exchange the kaftan that she had worn over her bikini with the scrapes of black silk that hung behind the door. The full-length mirror reflected a lean body, smooth skin and long, willowy limbs. She looked at her body critically, wondering what Kabir, if he came, would think. She was older than him and he was obviously experienced. Comparison was inevitable.

The swipe of the key card signalled that he had entered, the slosh of the drink that Tenzin poured, the heat in their eyes as she walked into the room in her negligée, her heart fluttering and pounding simultaneously.

*What do I do now*? She had wondered, ready to bolt.

Tenzin, adept at reading her confusion, held her close, the music allowing them to move slowly, relaxing her, rubbing her back. Steady kisses, pecks that soothed and excited, keeping her confused. He turned her around, his front to her back. It was then that Kabir stepped in, facing her, touching her.

Unknown hands, arms and chest brought with them some fear and excitement mixed with anxiousness. She felt both the men. Surrounded, not stifled, two pairs of hands explored, uncovered and rejoiced. One confident and knowing, the other hesitant and exploring new-found freedom. Millions of goosebumps rose all over her as her clothes melted away.

A strange magic occurs when you remove the armour of clothes making yourself vulnerable before another. In harmony with their rhythm, Kabir did not feel odd or different. She could not fathom if it was his confidence, his gentleness or his ability to accept himself, as he was, that made him attractive to her.

*Can I take this plunge into brutal, unforgiving nothingness and be drowned in the pleasure that came with the unknown?* She thought, submerging herself in the deep colours of pleasures. She allowed herself to experience intoxication at the hands of another, one that was not her partner.

She felt Tenzin move away, watching her as she entwined with Kabir on the bed that she had shared with only Tenzin until this minute.

In a moment of clarity she wondered if she was making the right choice before an insistent pair of lips claimed her attention not letting her think any further.

She remembered the night in flashes like snapshots in her head—glistening, salty skin, fingers that dug deep... clawed...sought, pushed for more. Lips that found peaks and valleys, engulfed and squeezed out more. Gasps and sighs, a symphony, a language onto itself, understood and reciprocated.

A jumble of limbs when Tenzin joined them, the king-size bed seemed too small for the heaving, pushing, lithe bodies. Demands were met, dark fantasies fulfilled. There was a freedom in being used as it was in using a body for pleasure. Everything was allowed, nothing refused. Doubts assuaged and overcome.

Some would call it freedom...others sin. Bee simply called it a freeing, a breaking away from the tightly held and hidden want.

Their masks ripped off, they looked at each other with feral eyes, feeding, ripping, biting, hunting for that elusive, peak paramount.

She did not feel guilty for finding pleasure in the thought or the eventual deed but the confusion stemmed from what came next.

Bhavya pulled herself out of the sensual daze, her breath panting, knowing she would not get any sleep now. She lay listening to the ticking clock as her eyes cleared and reality demanded acknowledgement.

*We could have gone anywhere else, never met Kabir, never dealt with this possessive side of Tenzin,* her sleep-hazed thoughts made their presence felt.

*Would it have made a difference?* The voice of reason intoned.

Even now, after four months had passed, her mind sought answers. Maybe it was the loneliness with Kabir leaving Paris that was causing this soul searching or maybe it was the affirmation of the doubt that had assailed her for the past few weeks.

It was time for that talk she had been putting off.

# 2

## *Deracinate—To pull up something by the roots*

(Language: English borrowed from French)

'You have shattered me,' he said quietly.

She spun around, her eyes wide and brimming with hurt. Her hair settled around her angular face as she looked at him, staggered by this turn of events. Her hands circled her waist, hugging herself, suddenly cold in the cosy, warm study.

'I have shattered you Tenzin...you...the unbreakable? Are we not equally culpable? We are both responsible for the distance that separates us. And, it has only been growing since the past year. Is that not why we decided to take a vacation, to rekindle the spark that we had been steadily losing?'

When Tenzin only looked at her silently, she rushed to continue.

'And, frankly, is that all that matters, who's at fault? Not the reasons, not how we should go forward but who is responsible?' Agitated now with his insistence on holding on to the cause of this misery, Bhavya yelled.

'It matters to me...or are my feelings not of consequence? Everything has always been about you, your wants, your dislikes, your passions...well, these are *mine*. It was supposed to be a one-time thing, something to experiment with, and something to add spice. But, you made him a constant fixture in our lives. What should have been left in Bali, you brought into our present! How can you say this is not your fault?'

'No, you do not get to put this on my shoulders. What about your ex-girlfriend safely tucked away in Leh?'

'My ex-girlfriend is an employee....'

'I can't do this anymore. Everyday there is a new list of things I am not doing right. One day it is tidying up the flat and another day it is where I was, who I met, what time I am coming home...something, anything every single day. We barely go out; we barely do anything new....'

'And, so you need him to do all that? When are we going to settle down?'

'If by settling you mean like dust, into a mundane routine...uh...I hope never. You know me too well to expect that out of me. And you knew all along that I was meeting him.'

'Yes, but now I am asking you to stop. And, not telling me where you were going is not a way to develop trust.'

'Trust? Are we going to make this about trust? Look at the way you are behaving...is it any wonder that I don't want to be marr....'

'What...say it?'

'Don't try to control me. I knew you would get angry. Tenzin, I did not choose this connection, it happened, now we have to figure out a way to make it work.'

He remained silent.

'Tenzin, he is my friend and nothing more.' She tried placating him.

'Really?'

'He gets me, completes my sentences and understands my need to fly....'

'I know. I have heard it all before.'

'Do you think we are still having sex?' She questioned.

'No...no, I don't but even though you are not unfaithful in body you are unfaithful emotionally...mentally. You need him to complete you. I am not enough...I cannot deal with this feeling of inadequacy anymore. Do you think

I am blind to the way your eyes shine when you talk to him or laugh at his quips? I don't want to put myself in this situation.'

'What do you want from me? I love you, is that not enough? Wanting me to leave him, cut off all ties, is that fair? You ask me to leave my friends because you are unable to deal with your own insecurities as a man.' She stressed, angry at the unfairness meted out by him.

'Why this ego, Bee? Why do you refuse to see how bull-headed you are being?' He asked, his head tilted as if looking at an exceptionally hard puzzle.

'I could ask you the same thing. Look, Tenzin, I haven't done anything wrong, I haven't slept with him after that night in Bali. So, if you need me to separate myself from him you will have to say it.'

'I won't. Why should I? That distinction you will have to make.'

'Well, it goes both ways.'

'Bee, do you really want to leave me for him?' He asked, his eyes flabbergasted, grasping her hand as if to hold her.

'See, that's where you are wrong. I am not leaving you for him; I am leaving for myself, my self-respect.'

He let go of her hand and stood looking at her adamant eyes.

'You never did understand, Tenzin. For me, trust equals love and you don't trust me anymore.'

When he opened his mouth to reply, she raised her eyebrow enquiringly and he could not give her empty platitudes.

The deep sigh that he exhaled was the direction she needed.

Acceptance.

She looped the strap of her tote over her shoulder, gripped the handle of her traveller tighter and turned to walk out of the life she had painstakingly built and compromised for. Her heart felt like it would burst out of her chest, as she started walking towards the front door. Her knees shook, there was drumming in her ears and she was dizzy, and yet, she did not look back.

Bhavya Sharma turned the handle of the front door of her palatial apartment in Paris, the one she shared with Tenzin, where she had spent the last three years of her life and walked out of the life of her dreams.

*How can I walk away after all this time? What will everyone say? Why does this always happen, why can I never commit, what stops me? Why do I keep looking for more? What is that 'more' that I am looking for? What if Tenzin is right and nothing will ever be enough....*

This battle was internally fought with nary a whisper of her troubled thoughts reflected on her composed face. This was her way after all, never show...never tell.

Resolute in keeping her mind numb until she reached her safe haven...her home, she closed her eyes blocking all further commiserations with herself.

The squalling child or the loud and rude music could not break her. The mantle of reserve that she gripped like her mother's old, red shawl seemed to be holding her together through the ten hours it took her to reach the airport at New Delhi. It held firm for the three hours it took her to finish the immigration formalities and to claim her bags.

Paris became a misty dream that she had awoken from, a dream she could not remember with clarity. Her mind was groggy with too many thoughts, seemingly too heavy for her thin shoulders, as she finally got into the taxi. She gave the address of the *Haveli*, her home, and was promptly lulled to sleep by the taxi's slow pace.

The taxi driver kept a watch over his young, emaciated passenger wondering what could have happened to make the young girl with lost eyes look agonised. Her soft, gamine features in repose were vulnerable and yet the strength in her chin was unmistakable. She was a contradiction, one who stacked her luggage without waiting for his help or wringing her hands but then promptly falling asleep as if all her reserves of strength were depleted.

'Madam.'

There was no response.

'Madam*ji*!' He called out again.

'Hmmm...' Bhavya woke taking her time, letting her senses absorb all that they could before they were bombarded with the harsh realities of life.

What greeted her was a sight that she had been longing to behold. The *Haveli*, her home, stood glowing, surrounded by the greenery that was her mother's doing. Newly painted, its white walls contrasted beautifully with the green of the hedges and the bright pink of the bougainvillea flower. The green and brown of the doors and windows were also new. It stood proud and handsome amidst the tangled chaos of the nearby Chandni Chowk.

*Can an edifice of stone miss its dwellers when they are away?* She wondered, looking at it even as a memory floated up from a time when the blush of love was rose pink and laughter was the language they had used to communicate.

She pressed her eyelids closed. She had seen another side of him that day. The first day...she had pulled him along to celebrate Tara's birth, springing him on her family, a shock to all of them. She remembered giggling about it later with Aruna, her elder sister, as they caught up with the adventures that had taken place in the other's life since Bhavya had left for Paris after Aruna's wedding. The sisters had sat on the floor whispering under Aruna's favourite window with Tara tucked in her mother's arms trying to catch the moonbeams that filtered in through the swirly, cerulean grille.

Where had her life taken this wrong turn, when did she lose her way? Was it when she entered into a relationship for which she was not fully prepared? If she was brutally honest with herself, she had to accept her role in the breakdown of their relationship. She had tried so hard to keep his exuberance alive and yet despite all her efforts had failed to make him happy.

He accused her of trying to change him while it was he, who wanted her to change.

'Madam, I need to…' the taxi driver broke her reverie.

'Oh, yes, sorry! Here, keep the change.'

'It's too much.'

'No, no, you waited while I….'

'*Koi nahi,* Madam*ji,* don't worry, sometimes coming home takes adjustment. Don't worry, *sab theek hoga*. Have faith,' he said helpfully and then, with a small twinge of regret at his inability to do more left his passenger standing on the road. His eyes traced her bent head as she squared her shoulders and lifted her bag with one hand.

The sun rose, turning the red of her shawl into a beacon, warming the chilly morning as he watched out for her in the rear-view mirror till he turned the corner.

*Allah be praised! My Bhavya is back. I was worried for naught.*

*But wait…Why does she stand before me, solitary…upset… hard, as if holding herself in by sheer will.*

*She had left here more than a year back with stars shining in her eyes.*

*Now here she is…alone.*

*What could have caused the lines around her mouth to deepen…her eyes to become damp?*

*As I watch her an ominous shiver runs through my stone walls. Her disquiet settles all around me as I wonder what causes her to stand this way…taut with a potential to wreak havoc.*

# 3

## *Déjà vu*

## A feeling of already having experienced the present situation

(Language: English, Origin: French)

Bhavya quietly moved towards the waist high gate and found it locked.

'No place for you here as well...' she whispered, feeling shut out, excluded.

Her fingers worried the lock of hair near her ear, tucking it behind the same dainty ear for probably the hundredth time since starting from Paris.

A few years back she would have jumped the gate, in fact she remembered doing just that, vaguely. Then she had returned home, the prodigal daughter, for her elder sister Aruna's wedding to Bhuvan, *how long ago was that... five years, four....*

Today, again, she stood at the gate seeking sanctuary as dawn crept over the aqua-blue sky, thinking the same thoughts, overrun by the same doubts she had then.

*I keep repeating the same patterns, making the same mistakes. I had better learn whatever lesson the universe is trying to teach me, soon.*

*Do you regret leaving him?* Her heart asked.

Bhavya thought for a moment, maybe even less, the answer firming her wavering mind.

*No, I need time to figure out what I want first. If I am ready to take the next step and what is the next step going to be?*

Her doubts silenced, she looked at the *Haveli* shining in welcome, calling to her and then at the gate.

*No upgrade to this excuse of security, how do they not know this?* She thought as she cut across the grass of the front lawn, her eyes wanting to capture everything at once, walking unhurriedly towards the imposing façade of the *Haveli,* her home…no…it was her parents' home.

Leaving it had been as painful as leaving her family. It was like a soft ache that she carried within her wherever her feet might land.

*From the hovel-like barsati I inhabited in Chandigarh to the apartment in Paris…I always longed for this place. It seems this is the place I will grow old in too,* Bhavya thought gazing at the spruced-up ziggurat.

The *Haveli* stood like a pearl in the muck of the nearby Chandni Chowk. She was glad her father had not succumbed to the craziness of covering every inch of land as the others had done around them. Her home and the mausoleum of Noorie Begum were the only two structures left that even remotely resembled the architecture of the bygone era.

She had often wondered what had stopped her father from renting out the many empty rooms but that would have meant change and therein lay the answer to her question. Her thoughts in a spiral, she questioned herself and even that which was familiar.

Walking up to the front door, she raised her suddenly trembling fingers towards the doorbell to wake up the storm that would certainly engulf her. She felt absurd standing there in thin, ripped jeans and a loose top, shivering, and most likely looking like a loon. Her mother's red shawl, her favourite, her constant and only companion, covered her pointy shoulders.

*I am not ready for this…not yet…there is time…* Lowering her arm, her breath torrential, she backed away… She dropped down on the wooden swing near the door, her legs stretched out, her feet crossed at the ankles. The back-

and-forth motion was familiar and soothing…she looked out into the visibly changing sky. She rested her head at the carved back letting herself find the balance she knew she would need before facing her parents.

After all, the reason for her return today would render all her earlier transgressions insipid before her family.

*This time I have outdone myself,* she thought with a lopsided, self-deprecating smile.

It was asking for too much from parents to understand first, the need to engage in a threesome when one is in a relationship…of sorts and then to leave the said relationship for a reason that was difficult to put in words.

Possessiveness and suffocation were accepted truths in any relationship that had a dominant and a subservient. She just did not want to fill the role of the latter.

There was no physical violence as had been the case in Aruna's first marriage that would allow her parents to understand the need to leave. There was no marriage in her case, which was another social red-mark against her.

After grudgingly giving their nod to her and Tenzin, her parents had constantly pushed her towards marriage… but she had been unable to take that final step.

Her father had barely spoken to her when she called home. His rancour was not with Tenzin, whom he liked and found sensible. He did not know how to talk to her knowing she was living with him without the sanction of marriage.

She knew the resultant argument would lead to the reopening of her past relationships that she had not had the good sense to hide from her father. Tenzin's age and religion would be commented upon as would their disappointment and shame in her actions.

*What should I do…should I tell them everything or should I just ask for some time to think, to be?*

'What is there to hide? I did not have an affair or do something that he was unaware of; in fact, he was the one who suggested it.' Bhavya sniffed, tired of feeling like a victim.

*Yes, but because you wanted…more…and then later a lot more….*

*You are building a mind story, Bee. They will rally around you as they have always done in the past. Plus, you stand at their doorstep again asking them to understand that which you know is too exacting for them to even accept. Give them time and stop twisting yourself up,* her inner voice tried its best to calm her drumming heart.

'I am doomed,' she groaned, then looked at the sky trying to stem the bubbling lava of emotions that was threatening to burst out of her as she sat contemplating her life.

She concentrated on the aegean blue that was now on its way to a lovely azure and she knew before long it would turn into sparkling lapis, finally turning a soft Maya blue of the late morning. Her troubled eyes took in the splendour of the majestic greens that stretched for some distance, at least till the shortfall of a boundary wall.

The diverse colours before her attracted her and she could name so many of them, the chartreuse, fern, olive, juniper, the green of the basil that was so different from the green of the mint. Even though she knew many people could not make out the variance in the different hues of colours, she always could discern the different shades.

It was an OCD almost, to be able to name the different colours.

*Everybody deserved a few quirks, after all, they are what make us unique,* she almost smiled, remembering Tenzin's words when she had teased him about his penchant for looking for unique words to simplify emotions.

*'So…what is your favourite colour?'*

*'Cerise,' she answered, deadpan.*

*'I beg your pardon...What is that?'*

*'A shade of red,' she clarified, used to the un-awareness.*

*'Shade...of red...why couldn't you just say red then?'*

*'Because it's not red alone....'*

*'What are you talking about? You're crazy.' He laughed, aloud. She could not recall him doing that in the past year that she had known him. It was such a happy...slightly rusty, unused sound.*

*Then after sometime as they were walking back, he asked, 'Bee, can you explain the colour?'*

*'What do you mean?'*

*'I mean, can you describe it?'*

*'I could try but...' she said as the street lights flickered on.*

*'Try, please.'*

*'Okay, can you visualise power...passion...fire?'*

*He shrugged.*

*'That feeling you get when the one you love places a hand over your heart?'*

*He nodded, looking at her making her blush.*

*'Or, when you hear her laugh trickle out as you twirl her all of a sudden,' she said, reminding him of the impromptu waltz, he had taught her some weeks ago ending with the grand twirl.*

*'The smell of my perfume,' she whispered, as he lifted her hand and nuzzled her wrists.*

*Taking his hands, she pressed them to her cheeks, 'It's the heat of my cheeks when you look at me as you are doing now.'*

*'Red, that's my favourite colour too, from now on.'*

*'Which red?' she asked, playfully.*

*'What?'*

*'So there's crimson like the rose, there is ruby, blush is lighter, brick is...' she started enumerating, laughing at his dumbstruck face.*

So much laughter.

*Why was she thinking of him? What was the use?*

Her eyes snapped open when she heard the bolt being unlocked from the inside.

*Time to face the music.*

The Bhavya who got up from the wooden swing was a different one from the one who had sat down. She walked up to the door, to face whatever would come…because that was her way. Standing before the slowly opening door she looked nonchalant and confident, her mask firmly in place.

No one could tell that it hid not one but two stuttering heartbeats.

# 4

## *Desire Path*

## A path created by natural means, simply because it is the 'shortest or most easily navigated' way

(Language: English)

'Arre...Bee, when did you arrive and why are you standing on the porch?' Arun, her father asked. She could see surprise and irritation at her foolhardiness fighting for space in his eyes.

'I just came...' she started.

'It is cold, *beta*, and you are only wearing this thin shawl...where is Ten-sing?' he rolled right over her cleverly thought-out explanations.

She stood perplexed, not sure which emotion to deal with first. Hearing his name brought an ache and then there was the giggle that always worked up her throat whenever she heard his name from her father's lips. She could see Tenzin rolling his eyes, pinching his nose and his signature, I-am-defeated, sigh, on hearing his name being twisted out of recognition.

Her eyes overflowing she launched herself in her father's arms. She wondered whether it was due to the suppressed laughter or the avalanche of feelings crashing on her ill-equipped self that she let loose.

'Da...Dad...Dad...' she cried, her tears unstoppable.

All she could grapple with and find strength to endure, she had used up in the journey to her family. All her reserves depleted, she now lay down her mask in relief even as her thoughts whispered:

*Is there any safer place than your father's enveloping arms?*

Arun stood, warring with shock and a strange relief.

*She still needs me, she still needs me,* his mind chanted.

Holding his sobbing daughter, he was caught between her distress and his misgivings. What could have caused his proud daughter to cry?

'Bee, what is the matter? What happened?'

When she just burrowed deeper into his chest seeking comfort, he pulled away.

'Okay…okay…stop crying, go inside, Ma is in the kitchen…I will see you in a little while…I…I need to go for my walk,' he said, patting her shoulder awkwardly.

'Wh…what…Dad, you are going for your walk?'

'Yes, I will see you in some time.'

When she looked at him, her eyes wet, rounded with surprise and accusations, he felt a prickling of guilt which made him more brusque that usual.

'Go in now and stop crying…everything will be alright,' he said, disengaging himself from his clinging daughter.

He walked the length of the driveway, careful not to step on the grass and walked towards Noorie's mausoleum and peace.

*How can he leave me like this? He actually just left…not even wanting to know what is wrong…I will never be this callous towards my children…ever….*

Bhavya stood dumbstruck, her tears drying up as her mind worked to process yet another notch against her father. Her shoulders squared as she promised herself watching him stride away…*I will not tell them anything…* she decided. *I can deal with this on my own.*

Meanwhile, Arun walked slowly towards the mausoleum, his usually brisk pace was replaced with a stooped, worried step. He kept wondering as he took measured steps about the reason Bhavya would have broken down in such a way.

*I should have taken her inside, what made her weep like that? Why do I keep falling short with her? Should I go back and see what the matter is? I should have asked her.*

*No, no, she will tell Uma, and Uma will know what to do…I would have just said something wrong and hurt her more.*

*I swear if that Ten-sing has done something to hurt my daughter, I am going to break his legs.*

He walked up to the glistening onyx stone of the mausoleum, entering the inner sanctum. No one was there at this time except him; it was too early for anyone else. He sat heavily on the cold, stone bench, his bones creaking and making him smile. He closed his eyes and waited for the music to begin.

*What will she sing today…I hope it is a ghazal…I like those the best.*

Bhavya looked at the open door. Her body was stiff and disquiet at her father's indifference.

*What is wrong with Dad, he couldn't miss his walk for one day?* The thought kept repeating itself in her mind as if trying to convince itself of the anti-climax.

She stepped into the foyer looking for her mother and found her where she knew she would be.

*'Ma,'* she called out softly, unable to move a single step forward.

That one word had Uma, her mother, lifting her head in alarm.

# 5

## *Saudade*

## A nostalgic longing to be near again to something or someone that is distant or that has been loved and then lost

(Language and Origin: Portuguese)

'Bee, what are you? Come here.' Uma hugged her daughter. 'You are so cold. Why can't you wear proper clothes? It's time to retire this shawl.' When her daughter buried her long, cold nose into her neck and breathed deep, Uma knew she needed to tread carefully.

She gathered her tall daughter close, rubbing her back, soothing a hurt she did not know the reason for. Uma's small, unadorned hands moved down her daughter's back smoothing the corded muscles, relieving them of their rigidity. They replaced the stress that seemed to have gripped her brave and strong second born with a mother's warmth.

Both held on to each other.

When Uma's polio-mangled leg cramped, making her wince audibly in pain, Bhavya stepped back, guiding her mother to the ever-present stool in the kitchen.

'Sorry, sorry,' Bhavya said, then turned around and without another word started adding tea leaves to the boiling water. Uma smiled watching her daughter who would not have moved a finger a couple of years back, now working the kitchen like a pro. Her mother's heart swelled with pride at her daughter's accomplishment and yet there remained a small twinge.

Even as the aroma of the tea filled the kitchen, the two women still did not speak. Filling the tea in the cups Bhavya turned and met her mother's direct gaze.

'Ma…I want to live here….'

The silence that followed was filled with the ticking of the grandfather clock. It patiently marked the empty minutes she spent fidgeting with the events that wanted to tumble out.

'Can I?' Bhavya asked timidly, breaking the spell of the silence that had descended on them like a pall.

'What happened? Has Ten-sing done anything to hurt?'

'No, no, Ma…nothing like that. You know I can give as good as I get. You know me too well to worry on that regard. Ma, look at me…I just want to stay for a while…I need some space.' Bhavya quickly interrupted her mother, her voice strong, desperate to reassure.

She had watched her parents take each torturous step along with Aruna towards overcoming, the physical and mental torment she had suffered at the hands of Rafi, her first husband. She never again wanted to see the look of utter helplessness in their eyes. Her sister's first marriage and her own titular role in its destruction and its aftermath had made her wary of loving anyone to the exclusion of everything else.

*'You do not allow me access to your innermost thoughts….'*

*'Why should I?'*

*'So that I know what you think, what you feel….'*

*'I talk all the time and we decided keeping our lives separate. Remember, your rules? Now, suddenly you need to keep tabs on my comings and goings…why?'*

*'Yes, but rules change. You avoid talking about things that affect you expecting me to understand, to change.'*

*'And, you don't talk at all….'*

*'Ask me anything?'*

'Bee?' her mother's voice pulled her back to the present.

'Hmmm...Ma, sorry what was I saying? Yes, may I stay till I can clear these cobwebs that my mind is overrun with?' Uma stood up and hugged her daughter, then held her at arm's length.

'Don't be silly, one slap you will get. This is your house; you can stay for as long as you want.' Uma gentled her brisk tone watching Bhavya's lowered eyes.

'Bee, *meri jaan*, don't run home to escape from your problems but take the time to figure out the solution and know that your family is there for you, always.'

'Even Dad?'

Shocked into silence, it took Uma a moment to reply.

'Yes, even him. Why do you think he would not understand?'

'I...no, he just....'

'Bee, he may come across as hard but he worries about all his children. Why do you always look at the glass half-empty? Rest now. Take the time you need. Come; let's have our tea before the hordes descend on you. Should I call Aruna for a visit? Are you okay with that?'

'Yes Ma, actually I will call her...but don't tell anyone that I want to stay.'

'Okay, whatever you want.'

Without any inkling of what was distressing her second daughter, Uma was left at sea as to how to help her fight the conflict that she was engaged in.

Her mouth near the rim of the cup and her eyes hawk like, she asked, 'How is Ten-sing?'

She watched her daughter jerk.

And that unconscious movement was more telling than words could ever be.

## 6

## *A Chiliad—A Thousand Things*

(Language: Late Middle English, Origin: Greek)

A tall, lean man stood looking out of the glass window. From the fifth floor of the apartment building, he could faintly see the Eiffel Tower.

*The reason why you had made your home here, giving in to her love for romance, even at the cost of comfort.*

*I never could say no to Bee, not from the first day,* he thought.

He stood remembering the days, weeks, months that they had spent exploring the cities in France. The million questions she asked about Versailles, Nice, Toulouse, Lyon...*exhausting even the tour guides we hired,* he thought with a sad smile.

*I never did understand her need to fill the silence with words, what was the point? Silence was better, safer,* he thought now.

Was this his flaw, his silence? His need to absorb and observe rather than express and discuss. She had done enough of the latter for the both of them. The more she pressed him to talk the more reticent he became. He knew he could have told her to back off but why should he? She should have understood! Plus, he wasn't doing anything new. She had known what she had been getting into when she agreed to marry him.

She said she could not deal with his coldness anymore. She proclaimed it with such alacrity that he was starting to question himself. He knew he was cautious, most times pragmatic, maybe even reserved compared to her childlike exuberance.

As a child, he had to distance himself, remain detached and unaffected so that he would never again feel abandoned, until Bhavya.

He had given in to all of her demands, had worked towards fulfilling all her wishes, her dreams so she would never feel the absence of...hope. And, yet, here he stood, left with only the string of precious moments he had spent with her in this house.

These were crystal clear, the past years unable to make his memory of her laughter and her anger, hazy. They shone bright like a rare diamond in his mind, to be angled just right in times of despair to catch that elusive last sunbeam of hope.

He needed that crutch of optimism today and so he let his mind journey back in time to the first moment he had laid eyes on her only to fall headlong in...lust.

He remembered, sitting behind his oakwood desk, surrounded by the glass wall of his cabin, wondering how to keep the branch office open so the company could continue with their plan to expand overseas.

Then, suddenly the air was enthused with more energy...more life.

A frown on his broad forehead Tenzin Jamyang, the new CEO, looked up from the downward-sloping graph of the company accounts to check the reason for this change in the vibrating air.

He saw her then, a shimmering illusion, the tall girl, her hair already escaping the pins that were valiantly trying to hold them back. A green scarf tied jauntily around her neck over a black, sleeveless top and jeans, she stood with her elbow on the cubicle frame bending close to the pony-tailed guy.

What was his name...Gautam...Gaurav or something?

A feeling of envy snaked through him first, followed by the need to possess this woman whose face he was yet to see. He wondered at both the emotions that he could feel coursing through him. The envy and the lust, for he was not a man given to excess of any kind, neither physical nor emotional. He liked the word moderation; living by it was a compulsion.

He kept staring at her, waiting for her to look up. She did and then burst into his life with a loud laugh that ran through him with the speed and intensity of a lightning bolt.

He sat stunned, his heart galloping, a look of utter bemusement on his face. She sauntered to his door. It barely took a minute but those 60 seconds gave him the opportunity to wipe all expression from his face. He was once more the boss and she, his employee. A loud knock and the door opened with a flourish to announce her arrival.

'Good morning, Sir.'

He just nodded, acknowledging her presence and watching her frown at his silence.

'I am Bhavya Sharma, just back and ready to start on a campaign if you have any.'

'Yes, I know, long leave, Miss Bhavya, I hope all is well.'

'It is now,' she said, eyes lowered.

*There is something here, hidden from the world,* he thought.

'Good.'

'So…' she started.

'As to starting work on a new project, I shall ask the manager to appraise you on the pending accounts, let's first clear the backlog and then start on the new ones. Alright, good day to you.' He said before looking intently at the blinking cursor on the screen as if that alone would solve all the problems of this world.

She stood there, shock at her dismissal written clear on her face and then snapped her mouth shut. She closed the door of his office with a crisp precision, which gave

Tenzin an inkling that she would have rather liked to bang it closed, making him smile.

From the corner of his eye, he saw her walk to her desk, which only made the pony-tailed boy leave his work to go to her. He spent the day watching her interact with everyone, and then berated himself for this crazed behaviour.

Over the next few days he kept away from her, though keeping her in his periphery became an obsession.

He was unaware of her short fuse then. That unawareness did not last long.

Even now as he replayed that day, he could not help but grin. Every chair in the presentation room had been occupied…for it had been Bhavya on point. The interns made sure to sit in on her presentations knowing that it would be an entertaining show.

He remembered her passion as she laid out the facts and figures, the reasons and the clip that would play to highlight the affordable township for the elderly. It was only when the cocky son of the builder asked her when were the girls in short dresses going to be featured that she lost all semblance of control.

Tenzin had felt his heart drop as he watched her narrow her eyes, square her shoulders and smile, the rabid smile of a mad dog, teeth gleaming.

'Bee,' he heard Gaurav whisper, warningly.

'Oh! My dear, did you want girls to prance around half naked in the old age home then?' she bent forward, and Tenzin saw the boy's eyes drop to her chest as he silently nodded.

The room went silent knowing something was about to take place.

With a deadly smile, she whispered, 'How about you, would you like to feature in the ad? We could have you prance around, sing a song if you like, you would appeal to a...certain...section of the audience. What do you think, *Sir*?'

She raised her angry eyes to his, daring him to reprimand her, the collective gasp of the rapt audience not helping her cause. Tenzin acknowledged her anger with raised eyebrows but otherwise remained silent.

It took a moment for the boy to make sense of the set down, so lost was he in her husky voice and visible cleavage.

When he did, however, there was hell to pay.

Later, when Bhavya knocked on the door, a groan escaped him. He was not in the frame of mind to deal with her, not then.

They had almost lost the account but he had finally managed to smooth the boy's ruffled feathers, at a cost of course.

He knew she was waiting for him to shout at her. His daylong silence and cold shoulder had only made her more agitated. Everyone at the office was waiting for the showdown between the star employee and the boss. And that was the very fact why he was not giving in to his urge to accommodate them. Ignoring her had accomplished what shouting at her would not have.

He could have said...should have said he was busy like all the other times but the lure proved too much. He needed to bask in her passion for just a minute.

'Come in,' he said and sat straighter.

She stood shaking before him, talking a mile a minute explaining; giving justifications. And, all he heard was the first word she had uttered:

'Tenzin.'

His name uttered in that tone took the connotation of velvety nights of sin, her honeyed voice bringing to his mind the touch of a sultry, balmy breeze. He wanted to hear her say it as she climaxed, as she begged him to let her experience the thrill of fulfilment. He could sense it, almost taste it, the hunger that clawed.

He could feel himself harden and clenched his fist on his knee ashamed at his thoughts. His restrain was slipping out of his fingers like sand and he stood watching helpless.

He was a theorist, happy to think deeply before taking the smallest step forward, a strategist who never did anything impulsively. Then, why did he want to leap across the desk and have his way with her? He felt like the worst kind of pervert. And, this realisation of his weakness made him rude and curt with it.

'Ms Sharma, stop, I did not ask you for explanations. Please make sure that you are able to control your base emotions next time in front of the client. Is that clear?'

'Base emotions,' she parroted, 'but you heard....'

'Yes, I heard. He is an ass but are you any better? You were as crude as he was offensive. Putting him down for his stupidity so that you can shine is nothing but a child's reaction. Grow up.'

'Gro....'

He raised a hand to stop her chagrin, an added insult.

'It will not be tolerated in the future. Is it clear?'

'Crystal,' she said through clenched teeth.

'Good. Dismissed.'

'Dismiss...what the fu....'

'I will advise you to stop right there, I am not your... family to take your bad temper lightly. Consider this a warning; I shall not be this lenient the next time.'

Bhavya had stood looking at him, her body rigid with anger and affront, then turned and walked out of his office.

This time she banged the door, loudly, behind her.

*She always made me smile...always.* Tenzin wanted to share this memory with her. But, she was gone, leaving him to pick up the pieces of their life, alone, running away.

*What can I say that will make her see sense? Should I call her?* He wondered.

Everything and its cousin had been discussed. In his mind it was a simple logic, if something is creating a rift or a roadblock in your peace…remove it from the equation. What was so challenging about understanding this?

Whatever the end result, he knew that the past had to stay where it belonged, it couldn't be allowed to enter their present.

*Why is she being so adamant about remaining in touch with Kabir? Was he really that important, even more than me? Were they in love? She always tested me and expected me to jump through hoops to prove my love for her and the one time I expect the same of her…she can't do it. Why? Is she choosing him over me?*

Introspection had been the backbone of his childhood and youth in the monastery in Leh. Through meditation, he had experienced true emptiness, a non-conceptual and non-dualistic awareness of reality, of being perfect as one is.

But, somewhere along the way, he had found himself skipping it, short changing it. He did not know why. He felt the need of it acutely now when his mind was muddled with questions that he didn't have answers for. The only one who could answer them was Bee.

*I am screwed.*

# 7

## *Aphthongs—Silent Letters*

(Language: English, Origin: Ancient Greek)

She sat rocking on her wooden swing, eyes closed. The wooden sentry at their main door was a testament to what a new coat of polish and friendship could accomplish.

She had claimed the wobbly wooden swing soon after Uma had dusted off the old, rickety thing that she found buried under piles of junk in the basements. She had been determined that this would belong to her. She remembered Suresh Uncle spending days polishing it a rich mahogany brown while continuously sneezing, his eyes watering. Ma had been livid with him but he kept at it until it shone with new pride.

One afternoon, as she had watched Suresh Uncle dab his eyes for the nth time, the fumes having turned them a scary red, she questioned him, 'Why don't you ask *Chowkidar Bhaiya* to do this, Uncle?'

He had jumped at her voice, 'I did not realise you were even here, Bee.'

'Well?'

'Because I know her eyes will shine when she sees it devoid of all this muck and neglect. I know that she…your parents…will sit here and have their evening tea and will look at all the different colours of the sky and the gardens and the flowers that they have brought to life.'

'And you…what will you get out of it?'

'Happiness…and the knowledge that I could do something for your…I mean all of you. She is always doing things for everyone else, no?' He had said, his eyes deep. Though young, she had known that that look hid many secrets.

She made it a point to help him after that, an unspoken bond forged between a slip of a girl and a middle-aged man over a wooden swing. The ever-present glass of his favourite *Rooh Afza* that Ma supplied with clockwork precision, every four hours...albeit with a frown, relieved the hot afternoons.

She had been thrilled at the end result as was evident in her fluttering around it, much to everyone's amusement.

She had taken to sleeping on its cushioned seats. The cool wind in the summers, the spray of rain during the monsoons and the sun in the winters had pulled her out of the stifling room that she shared with Aruna with equal fervour. Dad had his tea with Ma on it maybe once or twice, but Ma and Suresh Uncle enjoyed the creaking of the hinges as they discussed everything, swaying peacefully on it.

*How many nights did I lay nestled in Ma's lap as I heard the hum of their voices lull me to sleep*? Bhavya thought with a nostalgic smile. *Slowly, it became mine by association....*

*Was it these links that made things and people connect with each other? Or did time and shared history play a part in enmeshing lives?*

*How does Tenzin see me? As an oddity, to be placed in one corner and enjoyed when he feels like or a woman with a mind of my own? Why did he stop trusting me? Is he right that I am commitment phobic?* The questions tumbled in her mind, repeatedly.

*I was committed in all my relationships...*she started to justify her stand.

*Bee...don't lie to yourself,* her inner voice interrupted her thoughts.

With her eyes still closed, she huffed and admitted defeat. She knew she always had a plan B, always had one foot out of the door, always left a window open to jump out of a spiralling relationship, if need be.

*Who can blame me? With so many relationships disintegrating around me, how can I not?*

*Could that be the reason that none of my relationships last?*

Charu had once said that she always ended things at the first sign of trouble or disappointment. That fear of abandonment made her run. Tenzin too had asked her why she kept running, to him, to her family, to Kabir....

*What is it that I want?* She questioned herself.

'Bah! They just overanalyse things; I leave because of my self-respect....'

*Self-respect or ego*? The voice inside asked.

*Why should I waste time on a relationship that will eventually self-combust, they all do,* she argued with herself.

She knew she was not easy to live with. Her family had no choice but to accept her. But, why would someone who barely knew her, make the effort? Even now, she had come back after a failed live-in relationship and they refrained from asking questions even though she knew there were a thousand swimming in their minds as they looked at her. The how's and why's that they would feel compelled to justify before people.

*Or, don't I matter enough to warrant worry...Bee is strong she will know what to do. Have I been written off in the resilient image I created before my family too?* She thought, swinging again on her mental pendulum of doubts, one moment sure of her decision and the other insecure.

Her reflections were interrupted by the sound of a car turning into the gateway. She had been waiting to hear it for the past couple of hours. She stood up excited to meet her elder sister, Aruna, and her family.

'Hi, Bee...Bee!' Tara her niece called out. Just starting to speak, she waved her small, chubby arms from the car as Bhuvan, Aruna's husband, manoeuvred it around the driveway. Tara leapt out of the car as it came to a halt even as Aruna warned her to slow down. She ran to her aunt who swooped her up in a tight hug.

'Hi munchkin, let me look at you,' she said as she twirled the little girl making her laugh aloud in glee, dizzy and happy.

Bhavya raised her eyes to catch Bhuvan helping a very pregnant Aruna out of the car. The gentleness was evident in his smile as he stood giving her time to stretch her legs. His hand at her swollen belly brought a sharp pang of something akin to envy in her heart. It was a picture worth a thousand words....

A bright sunny day, a gleaming car, a pregnant woman standing with one hand under her swollen belly and the other on her man's shoulder as she looks up at him in adoration and love. The big man, slightly unkempt, bent towards her, protective and gentle. They say something to each other and laugh together.

*Some relationships do last, they may not be of a fiery passion but can glow softly with love, mutual respect and support for each other. One has to be willing to put the other before their own self occasionally and then permanence can thrive...*she heard her inner voice gently whisper; as the sound of their laughter filled the surroundings.

*Oh! Tenzin, why could we not get to this stage? Why was it so easy for me to walk away? It should not have been so after these many years together. Was it for lack of being tied to each other or were we just at the end of our patience with each other and this became a convenient excuse...to find newness.*

She hugged Tara as she watched Aruna and Bhuvan wrapped in themselves, ready to welcome a second child into their bubble of happiness. Tara wriggled down, her attention caught by the open door and ran into the house to meet everyone.

'Are you ever going to get here or do we break out the crane to carry you in, how many months is it? You are huge,'

Bhavya joked watching Aruna walk towards her with careful steps, hand clasped firmly in Bhuvan's.

'Ha ha ha, very funny, come here, I missed you, Bee. I am so glad you came.'

'And, why in the name of God would I miss this momentous occasion? After all, how will I get to spoil my niece or nephew from so far away?'

As both sisters hugged, the family came out of the house.

Aruna gazed at the triplets; Fanny and Gina were swinging Tara in between them making her giggle. Etti stood next to Gaurav, her shoulder touching his chest. She noticed the confusion in Gaurav's eyes as he stood looking at her. She smiled at the sly ploy. Dheeraj and Suresh Uncle, with tea cups in their hands, looked on indulgently, talking to Bhuvan. Her mother and sisters surrounded her, creating a cacophony of happy concerned voices making her glad for her large, boisterous family.

She looked at Bhavya who stood slightly apart, her hands anxiously pleating the edge of her shawl that was around her neck like a muffler today.

*What is bothering her, why has she come back so suddenly without informing anyone? Has the prospect of marriage scared her? I have to get her to talk.* Aruna thought while she continued to make small talk with her family, as they moved into the *Haveli*.

Aruna's unease turned to concern as she watched her energetic sister looking pale and growing quieter as evening turned to night.

Aruna knocked on the door of the room that she had shared with Bhavya when they were little. After three days of watching Bhavya untangle her thoughts, she had decided it was time to confront the issue at hand.

'Knocking to seek entry to your own room, Aruna?' said Bhavya as she opened the door.

'Well, that didn't take long.'

'What?' asked Bhavya, watching her sister run her fingers on the blue swirls of her favourite window.

'Falling back into the old routine of our childhood,' Aruna said, turning, leaning her back on the ledge of the window. They had fought and made up, had long conversations and cried silent tears, laughed and rejoiced before this window.

'You know what I mean,' said Bhavya, watching her sister.

'I know you look down upon women who marry for security...but Bee, I was lucky I found love too.'

'Yes, you are right. Sorry, I...I don't know why I was being callous...I...I am sorry. You have every right to live your life the way you deem fit.'

'That is true. You were always a snob anyway so...it is okay. Now that you are asking for forgiveness...can I ask you....'

'No!' Bhavya shot out hastily.

'Aruna,' Bhavya said after a minute of stunned silence, 'I need some time and I can't seem to get that. See, I came back because I need to sort some things out in my life. But, since I came back, everyone is extra polite, concerned, and looking at me with worry. If I see one more look of pity or hear one more, "don't worry", I will scream,' she said, her eyes ignited.

'What do you want, Bee? We can't be expected to remain impassive to your plight.'

'Plight? Why plight? I am not helpless, just confused, just unsure of where to go from here? That does not render me helpless, Aruna. Being without a man is not the end all for me....'

'You mean the way it was for me?'

'No, you are being overly sensitive. Look, we are as different from each other as day from night. Our paths are also bound to be separate. I envy your contentment however; I need to live my life.'

'Who has stopped you from living your life, Bee? No one was able to deter you about your decision to live with Tenzin even though it went against everything we stand for. But, we rallied around you because that was what you wanted. And now you come back and refuse to even tell us the reason. Don't you think that is pushing the envelope a bit much?' Aruna said, folding her arms on her rounded belly.

'Well, someone has grown a spine,' Bhavya looked at her waif-like sister with an amused smile.

'I am shaking inside, still getting used to saying what is on my mind. Coming back, what are you seeking, Bee, what do you want? You have a good job, you live in Paris, have a man beside you who makes no demands, lets you live your life as you want to and still you are unhappy? Why?'

'I don't know. I am as perturbed as you are, Aruna, I don't know what I want,' Bhavya said, turning her back to her sister. She could hear the doubt in her inability to handle the aftermath of the event she had set in motion by the choices she had made in Bali.

'Can we not talk about this now, Aruna? I am tired and you need to rest, too.' Bhavya said, her voice low, wanting this line of conversation to end before she blurted out the truth to Aruna.

'I am fine, pregnant but otherwise fine.' Aruna said, unable to leave her sister looking so forlorn. 'Did you hear about Charu?'

'What about her?'

'She is in Texas now,' Aruna informed.

'What is she doing there?'

'Our younger sister is being asked by diplomats to solve their cases for them, in a silent capacity of course, something to do with children going missing, obviously,' Aruna explained.

'Trust her to work relentlessly without even seeking credit for it,' said Bhavya.

'That's Charu!' Both the sisters echoed each other's thoughts before smiling.

They heard the grandfather clock boom the late hour.

'Go to bed, your lover must be waiting to hear what his crazy sister-in-law has gotten herself into now,' Bhavya said

'No, no, he is already asleep,' Aruna said, her eyes looking away blushing.

'Yeah right…' Bhavya laughed as Aruna swatted at her before walking away.

Bhavya lay, quiet and solemn, curled on the living room divan, her head in her mother's lap as Uma's fingers untangled the knots in her hair, suspiciously soothing.

Her eyes slowly closed as her mother's fingers worked like magic, relaxing her into sleep.

'Has she said anything to you, Ma?' She heard Aruna ask their mother.

'Any word from Tenzin?' Bhuvan added.

'No, he hasn't called and neither has she confided in me. It has just been a couple of days. I know I should ask her…question her for coming back but I don't want her to feel unwelcome, as if we are more concerned with the reason of her return than her. She was always a private child, always wanting to be seen as strong. I don't know what to do.' She said watching Bhavya's closed eyes.

Bhavya felt all their eyes on her and that made her feel small for this pretence.

'Gaurav, has she said anything to you?' Aruna asked.

Gaurav, who was now like family, had been Bhavya's associate at the Chandigarh office. After the convoluted dynamics of his family had blown up in his face resulting in him being thrown out, Bhavya had brought him to the *Haveli*. Her family had absorbed him within their fold tentatively at first. Soon, their fears had been soothed by his affable personality and he was entrusted with some responsibility at the saree shop to keep him gainfully occupied.

Bhavya knew he had not made any inroads to patch up with his own family since then, preferring to become a semi-permanent houseguest of her family instead.

'No, Aruna. I am sure all of you can tell that she is angry, but there is something else…she is hiding. Something…I can't be sure but I think…' said Gaurav.

'We should just give her time. She will figure out her own problems, I am sure,' Etti said in Bhavya's defence.

Bhavya felt undone by this outpouring of love. Everyone seemed united in their concern for her. Her eyes filled and dripped, a wet spot appearing under her cheek, on her mother's saree.

'Anyway, she will come around, my strong-willed Bee, *meri jaan*,' Uma crooned, knowing her two elder daughters stood at opposite ends of the spectrum. One at the cusp of happiness and the other…well…it did not bear contemplating.

'Ma Lakshmi, all I ask for is their happiness and health nothing less nothing more…just keep my children safe,' she whispered under her breath as she switched off the lights for the night. She limped to the porch, her leg dragging behind. She didn't correct her gait. There was no one to see. This was her time, her solitude. A time she shared with no one except Suresh sometimes. He sat on the other chair…waiting, two cups of steaming tea on the table before him.

'Trying to find answers in the depths of the teacup Suresh…*ji*?' she quipped.

'Hmmm…just thinking about *apni* Bee,' he replied, 'and can we drop the "*ji*" for these fifteen minutes?'

She looked at him and nodded so many things unsaid, latent in her eyes…and his.

They moved on to discuss what could be the matter with Bhavya, how happy Aruna looked and what a darling Tara was. They spoke of Dheeraj and his coming to terms with the loss of his dreams of becoming a chef. The triplets were discussed too, ready to step out into the world, to spread their wings, how Gaurav had become a part of the family, quite like Suresh himself.

All and every mundane issue a married couple with seven children would discuss at the end of the day. The only difference was that Uma's husband slept soundly in their bed, a few footsteps away as she emptied her heart to his…best friend.

# 8

## *Hyggelig*

## A feeling of openness, warmth and friendship

(Language: Danish)

The week passed in a blink. Aruna's visit, Tara's antics and the general catching up with a family that she had not met with in one year took precedence over her own problems. Now that Aruna had left and everyone had gone back to their own schedules Bhavya felt useless. She wanted to believe that was the reason for the delay as she dialled the number from a small piece of napkin on which he had written his home number and address.

*'Call me if you are ever in Delhi, I might be back at the same time. Won't that be surreal?'* he had laughed before leaving Paris.

Kabir, her... She didn't know what to call him for he straddled the fence between a lover and a friend.

She heard the bell ring and then suddenly he was there like a flash of a mirror catching the sun.

'Hi,' he said, his voice a mix of impatience and fun, as if he knew who was on the other end.

'Hi, this is Bha....'

'I know, Bee, where are you?'

'In Delhi.'

'Oh wow! When can we meet? Today, say today please. I was thinking of you. I do that every day, every minute. Come to my place. Please, say yes.'

His young voice made her sigh as she closed her eyes at the remembered warmth. The rush of pleasure at his exuberance, his excitement to meet her had a gurgle of happiness escaping her throat. The kind she had not felt for a long time. Before she could answer, Etti rushed in, 'Bee *di*, do you want to go shopping today?'

She shook her head.

Etti whispered, 'Who is it?'

'A friend I am planning to meet today,' Bee said, her face breaking into a sunny smile as she heard the whoop from the other end of the line. Etti frowned, then shrugged, leaving her sister curled on the bed whispering into the phone.

Bhavya found herself replacing the phone on its stand having agreed to meet at Kabir's house before she questioned her own hasty agreement. She knew she should give some thought to what she was going to say to him but now she would just have to see if the distance of months had made them strangers. Phone calls just did not have the same tangibility as sitting with a friend and talking about everything under the sun without worrying about hurt feelings.

There was excitement, certainly, and anticipation of meeting him. She also recognised that there was a pulsing fear that she was not in control of herself. Her mother's words rang in her head as they sometimes did at inopportune times.

'Decisions are the hardest to make, Bee,' she had said while helping her to pack for her first foray into the big, bad world, her first job in Chandigarh, 'especially when you have to choose between where you should be and where you want to be.'

At the time, she had not given the words a second thought. Now, Bhavya could hear the depth in the words her mother had armed her with without her knowledge.

She sat on the bed more confused than ever before.

Etti entered the kitchen looking to appease her hunger. She found her mother busy kneading dough for lunch.

'*Aalu-puri*, yum, is there an occasion that I have again forgotten, Ma?' she quipped.

Her brother Dheeraj, who was looking at the ladle, as if weighing it for gold, answered, 'Bee has come home, and so automatically everyday Ma will make what she loves best. We have been side lined now that her favourite child has come back.'

'Well, I have yet to decide who her favourite is, Aruna *di*, Bee *di* or Charu *di*.' Then confronting her brother she said, 'And, why are *you* cribbing, Dheeraj *Bhaiya*, you are the boy wonder of this family. Think of what I must be going through; always last in the list of favourites, schmoozed with two overachievers. My life is even more miserable than yours!'

'Wanna bet? A thousand bucks if Ma says she loves you more,' he said, playing along.

'Ma, what do you say?'

'I will share the money with you, all you have to do is agree,' Dheeraj whispered, making Etti fume and Uma laugh.

'I will slap both of you! Don't you know a mother loves all her children equally?'

Uma continued, 'All the five fingers of the hand are equal. If you get hurt on even one, the pain is the same. It is the same with children; all of you are differ....'

She turned around to find both her children miming her words. They fell into a fit of giggles when she huffed in mock anger.

'Ma, this is done, call me when you need to make the *puris*,' said Dheeraj, laughing before tugging at his sister's long hair, expertly dodging her swats.

'Why did you have this *dusht* son, were daughters not enough?' Etti asked her mother, sniffing at the potato curry her brother had left simmering.

'I take my blows on the chin, dear,' Uma bantered and then asked, 'Where is Bee, is she up?'

'Yeah, yeah but won't go shopping, she is talking to some secret friend.'

'What friend?'

'I don't know. She didn't say, though she is going to meet him today.'

'Why do you say him?'

'Because I know all her friends, we all do, not telling me the name means it's a guy and…she wants to keep that under wraps because she shooed me away. One plus one is two. Case closed; I shall take your applause now.'

'It could be Ten-sing,' Uma argued.

'Ma, come on, if it was Tenzin the whole house would have heard her. She is forever angry at him!'

'Hmmm…' said Uma, her frown lines pronounced.

'Anyway, you don't worry, Ma, they will sort it out. We can only support her, tell her that we stand beside her whatever she decides. No?' Etti said, wondering if she should have kept that deduction to herself.

'When did you grow up, Etti?' said Uma, her eyes misting at her daughter's wise words.

'When you were busy with everyone else, Ma,' she said before flouncing out of the kitchen saying, 'I am going to drag Gina with me to the movies. I will tell her, she can buy paints.'

Uma watched her daughter walk away, awed at her ability to drive in the knife smoothly. She went back to her kneading, her mind hinting at things she had no business thinking.

Unaware of her mother's thoughts, scooping up Dheeraj's car keys, Bhavya shouted a hasty 'Will be home by dinner' and drove away leaving Uma worrying and praying for good sense for her unsettled daughter. She had taught all her children that if you have to hide something from your family then whatever you are doing is wrong.

Not a stern mother, Uma trusted her children but she was a mother first and a friend later. She would ask the tough questions and drill some sense into Bhavya.

*Riddled with self-doubt and secrets she holds herself too tight as if her unaffected mask will crack if she tells me the truth. Every time her eyes slide away when she talks to me, my heart breaks just a little. This time I will not make the same mistake I made with Aruna, I will ask her whatever the cost to my own heart,* Uma thought, firming her resolve to confront her daughter once she came back.

'Be careful,' Uma cautioned hoping Bhavya had heard her words.

# 9

## *Raze—To Demolish*

(Language: Middle English, Origin: South Slavic)

Bhavya parked the car and took a moment to admire the tree-lined streets of Amrita Shergill Marg, in Central Delhi. The green shaded arch that spread as far as the eye could see represented the other end of the spectrum, as compared to the chaos of the lanes of Old Delhi.

She sat wondering if she was doing the right thing.

'What is wrong in this? I am going to meet my friend. Tenzin's words have made me doubt myself.' She said aloud as she ran a comb through her hair.

*Who you had sex with….*

*With Tenzin in the room, with his consent,* she thought frowning in the compact mirror as she pencilled in the kohl.

*Yes, but now…*the voice in her head began.

*Shut up, it isn't like I want to have sex with him, so how can I be accused of cheating?*

*Ummm…why are you here again?*

*Just to meet, talk….*

*And, will you tell him of the baby that you have kept hidden from everyone till now and the reason for the secrecy?*

*I will tell him about it, too.*

Her inner battle silenced, Bhavya walked to the room on the first floor of the red brick house and rang the bell.

'You are here!' The door opened and she was enveloped in the arms of an unselfconscious man. Kabir.

'I am really happy to see you, man!' He held her at arm's length and gazed at her with genuine happiness.

She looked at him, her mouth stretching into a grin, his transparent joy a balm to her smarting self-esteem.

Her eyes traced him, from his closely cropped hair to his chiselled face to his delicious body. Before her stood a man-child with laughing eyes, a devil-may-care attitude, a perfect mouth always ready with a smile or a joke; poignantly innocent, as only someone who never had to worry about the surety of a roof over their head could have.

Physically, he was the epitome of model-like dreamy looks. Working out was the only other thing he was passionate about, besides painting. His body defined in a white t-shirt, his jeans riding low, bare feet spattered with paint, he pulled off the poor artist look by the book. Only Bhavya knew that both those garments that covered him cost a bomb.

*He is so different from Tenzin's closed-barred expression that did not let a trickle of sunlight seep out. I had once loved the restrain that Tenzin personified. Now, I wish he was more open, friendly, lighter.*

*Is that not wrong on my part or is this realisation an omen… that it is better to rectify the mistake?*

*What am I thinking, since when did I start thinking that my relationship is a mistake?*

'Since you came back….'

'What?' Bhavya asked, startled out of her thoughts.

'Ever since you came back you did not contact me, should I be offended?' he asked and without waiting for an answer pulled her into his apartment.

Bhavya could only smile as she was led into a minimalistic room, which smelled of turpentine oil and was littered with canvases that leaned against the walls. Some finished, some still wet and some ready to be couriered.

'So, how have you been?' He asked from behind her.

'Alright.'

'You came to meet your family?'

'Yes, that too.'

'Have you been to all your old joints, college, school, friends?'

'Not yet.'

'How are things with Tenzin?'

Bhavya stood up, then turned to look at him, her eyes telling him everything.

'I have beer and coffee, maybe some *"bhodka"*,' he said, reminding her of the drink they had once shared with a man from Bengal in a small café in Paris. He could talk to everybody.

'Beer...no wait, tea?' She said grinning at the memory.

'Nope.'

'Coffee then.'

'Oh god! You are going to make me work. I know how you hate that instant stuff. Beaten coffee it is. Wait till I come to meet you in Paris, then I will take revenge. I shall insist you make me lunch,' he said, leaning his shoulder on the edge of the doorway. He grimaced as he stirred the coffee, milk and sugar in the mug for her.

'In your dreams, Kabir,' she said, laughing. She hated cooking; found it a waste of time. She cupped her chin in her hand, her elbow on her bent knee as her eyes darted from one beautiful canvas to another.

He grew silent, as did the clatter of the spoon against the mug. Her eyes lifted to catch him watching her. She saw his eyelids droop, the fun leave his face as he met her eyes with his direct, piercing gaze. He went from a friend to her old lover in an instant.

Bhavya felt her breath hitch. She knew he was remembering their time together in Bali. Though they had met a number of times in Paris, it had always been in a café, for a picnic near the Seine River, or taking in a show. This was the first time they were together without the comfortable blanket of people.

She watched him looking at her. A young man who could talk of anything under the sun without feeling bored, who listened to what she said, gave a thought to her opinions, wanted to know why she had them. He never shied away from a rip-rousing confrontation but was equally adept at not holding a grudge.

*He is perfect*. She realised she wanted to feel him against her, feel his whispered love words that had once marked her skin.

She did not stop him when he came towards her. The intent in his eyes was clear when he placed the mug on the table and walked with long strides to tilt her face up, holding her nape with one hand as he captured her lips forcefully.

Passion flared, as she knew it would and she wanted to give in to it.

'I am pregnant,' she murmured instead, against his mouth.

His lips stilled, the heat-glazed eyes cleared, and confusion shadowed his gaze.

'Explain.'

She pulled back.

'There is nothing to explain. I am four months pregnant. I may be—I reiterate—may be carrying your child.'

'Is this some kind of a joke?' he said leaning back, as if to put distance between her words and him.

Bhavya felt her heart crack, she literally heard it. It was not the loud sound of a crash but a soft break that would go unnoticed if one was not attuned to the sound.

'How could this have happened? We were all careful, are you sure?' He said, his forehead wrinkled and eyes worried.

'Nothing is a 100 percent certain...my friend,' Bhavya said sitting upright.

She looked at the ripped jeans that cradled his rock-hard thighs, the bare feet, the bulging muscles on his arms that became more pronounced as he repeatedly pulled his thick hair back from his forehead.

He was silent for a long, heart breaking moment. Bhavya could feel her heart beating. She did not know if it was expectation or acceptance.

'This can't be happening to me...' Kabir murmured. 'Are you planning to keep the baby?' He asked frowning, looking for a way out.

Bhavya could only nod in agreement.

'Are you sure, Bee?' He got on his knees before her and looked into her eyes earnestly before saying, 'People like us aren't meant to take care. You see, we ourselves take so much time to grow up that owning up to the responsibility of a little person who is completely dependent on us is too big to fathom. Be very cautious of your decision.'

*Tenzin would never do this, not worry about how things looked, say what was in his heart,* Bhavya thought, looking at Kabir.

*Neither would he try to convince you that you could not take care of your own child,* the infernal inner voice made an appearance.

'I am not asking you to take responsibility, Kabir.'

'I know, but I am clarifying that I can't. I still have to make something of myself. My profession demands focus. Bills, baby products, insurance...all this is not for me. I would come to resent you and the baby in no time.'

Bhavya nodded; at least he was being truthful. She had known that he would be unwilling to tie himself down, they were alike in that respect, but hearing him say the words made it all the more real and painful. She leaned her head on his shoulder not sure how she felt...relieved or hurt.

She sometimes wondered how it would be if she was with Kabir. Fun certainly but would he be able to give her the stability she needed to balance out her impulsiveness? Would he not grow bored of her and look for newness? Could she take that?

'Don't worry, Kabir, I am not expecting anything from you. I just wanted to tell you. It's a possibility but I don't know for sure.'

'Oh, okay,' he said, his voice still lost, unwilling to believe that he had managed to deflect that blow.

Bee wanted to mourn for the baby she carried when she saw the strong shoulders lower with relief.

*You sure can pick them, one is hoping that the baby is not his and the other will have you locked up albeit in a golden cage if the baby is his,* her thoughts taunted. The conclusion was so spot-on that it soured her mood. Feeling alone and deserted she started towards the door.

'Where are you going?'

'Home.'

'Have you told them about the baby…and who is the fath…?'

'No, no…I haven't, not yet,' Bhavya said her sorrow escalating. She turned away from the boy who she had thought was a man.

'Wait, but….'

'Not now, Kabir, let's talk later.'

'Hey! Are you angry?'

'No, you have nothing to worry about.'

He held her by the shoulders and looked deeply into her troubled eyes. Encountering only walls, he gave up and hugged her.

'Come and talk anytime. I am always here for you… dear friend.'

She nodded and hurried out trying to drown out the sound of her inner voice mocking her stupidity.

# 10

## *Werifesteria*
## To wander longingly through the forest in search of a mystery

(Language: Old English, Origin: Germanic)

*Another week wasted, just thinking, I should do something... take action...but what? At least Aruna's weekend visits with Tara give me something to do,* Bhavya thought as she paced.

*Will my baby also be as inquisitive as Tara or quiet like Tenzin or artistically inclined like...*Bhavya squeezed her eyes shut.

'Stop...stop, just stop thinking about this!' she muttered to herself as she dashed out of her room trying to escape her thoughts.

Sleepless she roamed the *Haveli,* her thoughts chasing her up to the first floor for she knew the porch would likely have her mother resting. Not wanting to intrude on her mother's alone time and wanting to avoid her questions; Bhavya took the stairs up to the rooms where she used to hide as a child.

Her hand swept the smooth wooden railing. The stairs were older than she was and still shone with care. Feeling broken in comparison, her mouth twisted into a parody of a smile.

*I could wake Gaurav up for some small talk; get my mind off my problems for some time,* she thought, moving towards his door.

She stopped in shock when she heard a quickly muffled giggle coming from his room. She stood there, her mind whirling with confusion.

Rethinking, retreating, she walked to the balcony that hugged the rooms on this floor, breaking the monotony of the walls that stood tall.

She loved the green-coloured wrought iron railing. Feminine and delicate, it was at odds with the masculine *Haveli*.

Bhavya now stood at a height, looking out into the darkness, wondering at her place in this cosmos. Her angular elbows bearing the weight of her body, she closed her eyes wishing for a chair. Then just sank to the floor.

She didn't know how long she sat there, wrapped in her red shawl, her eyes closed as she tried to view the past years with some semblance of logic, of acceptance.

*Where did I go wrong? Am I wrong in what I am asking for?* She kept thinking, questioning, finding fault.

*I did what we decided. The only liberty that I took was to stay in touch with Kabir despite knowing that Tenzin was uncomfortable with it. But, do I need his permission to decide who I shall befriend and who I shall talk to?*

A gust of wind had goose bumps rising on her arms not with fear but awareness, the kind that we feel when someone wraps their arms around us, in support and in understanding.

Her eyes dripped, slow tracks made their way down her pale, thin cheeks as she hugged her knees and tried valiantly to muffle the sound of her breaking heart.

Gaurav heard the sound as he was about to close the door behind a swiftly disappearing slim silhouette. He shook his head, his brow worried and crumpled.

*What am I doing? This is so wrong at so many levels. What will I say if anyone figures out...?*

The thought remained incomplete as he heard sniffling. Barefoot, he walked up to the balcony doors that he recalled bolting before a light tap on his door had blasted his good intentions sky high. He poked his head out, cautious and found his friend weeping on the floor of the forlorn, windy balcony.

What worried Gaurav was not that she wept but that she was trying to smother the sounds of her grief. The red shawl held over her pressed lips failing in its responsibility to muffle the sound that emerged through the weave of the wool. This quiet pain was unlike her and troubling. He slid down the wall next to her.

'Bee, talk to me. Please. It's been weeks since you appeared out of thin air. What is wrong?' he asked.

Bhavya raised her head looking at him with confused eyes. His bearded face was strange and unknown.

'Just tell me this then, has he hurt you?' he asked after a silent moment.

'Who?'

'Aurangzeb! Who do you think? Ten-sing.'

She guffawed, as he had wanted her to.

'No, no, he hasn't hurt me; we just...Please don't ask me...I can't just yet.'

She wanted to lay bare all her anguish, of Tenzin's demand and Kabir's reaction to the news and her own inability to decide what she wanted from life on his shoulders but she hesitated. Would he understand, would anyone?

Consenting adults or not, what they had done was not 'normal'. She knew her family would be scandalised with her for even thinking of it. Good girls did not do what she had indulged in. Tenzin would be spared from censor by most or maybe not but she...she would surely be branded an easy target, a loose woman.

'Okay...okay, but you know we are there.'

'We...hmmm...?' she asked, making light of the abyss of her uncertain future, a black hole that seemed to want to swallow her whole.

'I mean your family,' he stammered when she cocked her eyebrow at him, piercing him with her direct gaze, '…and of course I am always here.'

'There is something you aren't telling me, Gaurav.' Bhavya said looking at her suddenly fidgety friend.

She desperately wanted to change the direction of the conversation, wanting to hang on to the image of a self-sufficient woman for a little bit longer. She realised that the devil-may-care attitude of her youth had slowly eroded and weathered by the passage of time and experience. She cared…deeply…but did not want to own it yet. She would have to, eventually but she was procrastinating for now… in denial.

'What…what do you mean?'

'Nothing…just asking.'

She turned her head as she felt dawn approach, knowing that the colours that would spread out overhead would be the most beautiful of the day.

She lay down on the cold concrete, looking up at the changing sky as she felt Gaurav rise and quietly leave. The charcoal sky turned a velvety midnight blue which was now going smoky…Flint colour…a beautiful Holland blue…and then magically a Mystic blue….

It was time for Dad's walk.

*Maybe I will go with him*, she thought.

She walked down the stairs as the first chirping of the birds reached her. Her struggles still stood adamant, unsolved, unfought, another night wasted in introspection.

Uma entered the kitchen with a prayer on her lips, tying her hair to start steeping the first cup of tea of the day, for Arun. He always had a cup of tea before he left for his morning walk. She stood shocked at the entrance when she found Bhavya, already pouring the tea into the cups.

'*Arre,* Bee, why are you up so early? Are you feeling alright?'

A laugh escaped Bhavya.

'Are you seriously asking me why a grown-up woman is making tea in her own house in the morning? And on top of that if she is unwell...Ma, you are something. It is my house or is it not?'

'Of course, I am telling you...*lo* Aruna is here. You only ask this silly girl why she insists on asking me time and again if this is still her house.'

'Smells heavenly, Bee, I can't wait to have the first sip... Ma, can we get emotional later, pregnant woman here... wants her tea first.'

'Where is Bhuvan?' Uma asked.

'Still sleeping,' Aruna mumbled from behind the cup.

Bhavya raised her eyebrows and the sisters start talking to each other with their eyes.

*You're still having sex, wah wah,* Bhavya gestured, bowing her head in deference, her face imitating awe.

*Shut up, not really,* said Aruna, nose in the air.

*Are you able to...*Bee made a crude gesture with her fingers, her eyes laced with humour.

A thumbs up along with a similar gesture with more fingers was the answer she got, with a lot of wriggling eyebrows and an ecstatic face. The dejected Aruna of a few years back was nowhere to be found.

*Ewwww,* Bhavya conceded to her sister, covering her eyes.

'You girls need to stop talking about sex so early in the morning, it's giving me a headache,' Uma said casually, her back to her daughters.

The ease with which she had managed to bridge the distance between a mother and a friend set a benchmark for Uma's daughters to imitate later in life. Now, it sent both the girls into a fit of giggles and all the physical and emotional discomfort was forgotten for an instant.

Arun walked into this melee, his heart warming in the morning chill, hearing this epicentre of the *Haveli* ringing with laughter, the happiness reflected in the faces of the women who mattered to him the most.

'What's this about?' he asked. The ladies started off again after a moment's pause.

'Uma?'

'*Oh ho*, nothing just some silliness,' she said, grinning.

'Good...good, keep up this silliness,' he said, and then seemed more surprised when he found both his daughters doubling over with loud gaffes.

'What did I say now?' he asked.

'Nothing, you go, I will get your tea,' Uma said, smiling.

# 11

## *Natsukashii*

## Bringing back happy memories of the past

(Language: Japanese)

They walked, hand in hand, sisters by blood. Arun had long past walked on ahead. They dawdled, the meandering path giving them the time and quiet to think their own thoughts without interference.

'Do you remember the day you sprung Tenzin on us, the day Tara was born?' Aruna asked, suddenly.

'Hmmm…' said Bhavya.

'Tenzin was overwhelmed by us, no?'

'Hmmm.'

He had been unsure what he would do if he had to deal with so many people on a daily basis. His face had gone from amazement to shock as the noise levels rose, until Ma came out of the room to tell them to hush.

'Thankfully, Bhuvan had the brilliant idea of booking a suite for the delivery,' Bhavya said.

'Yes, but Tenzin was so stiff at the several pairs of eyes trained on him.'

Bhavya smiled.

'Until Ma took over, making short work of putting him at ease and the mushy guy that he is, he couldn't say no to Ma's invitation for dinner and to spend the night at the *Haveli*. And, Ma wouldn't stop talking about all of us. I still remember his expression….' Aruna went on.

Bhavya cringed. For a person who was used to a hard life, had the *Haveli* represented a family having illusions of grandeur, for him? It must have sounded so pretentious.

'…I remember how excitedly he got out of the car and insisted on walking up to the *Haveli*, taking in its magnificence. That certainly won Dad over. He is the happiest telling all and sundry about the *Haveli*, its past, its connections.' Aruna happily recollected not finding Bhavya's silences odd in the least.

'I have never seen Dad extend the invite for a stay so fast. And once Tenzin agreed he even promised to take him to Noorie's mausoleum the next morning. And Ma being Ma, kept on asking him what he likes to eat. Then Suresh Uncle waylaid him wanting to talk about the dipping exchange value of the Indian rupee. What fun it was!' Aruna said, her eyes on her sister, noticing her lowered head.

He had caught her eyes amidst the ruckus and smiled. Her heart had been ready to burst at that perfect moment. He was accepted as a part of the family, Bhavya recalled, her heart aching.

'Will you tell me what the matter is?' Aruna finally asked. 'Something so that I can help if possible….'

'There is nothing that can be done.'

'Have you fought with Tenzin?'

'I don't think one can call it a fight, I have left him, no I think he has left me…as in…we have decided it is better to part ways,' Bhavya said, looking at her feet.

'Bee…what are you saying? Look, don't react to whatever it is. Think, weigh the options, then take a decision. This is not a game. You have been together for what two years…three? Please take some time to decide what you want to do,' Aruna said.

'Four actually,' Bhavya muttered.

'Okay, please know that I want to shake you and ask you all the details and yet I will not because you have to be ready to talk about it before you can. Also, we are here, whatever you need, a shoulder, a bouncer, some space. I am here. It is not like you, Bee, to linger, at least not in the telling or the doing.'

'Some things are no easy to say, Aruna...even for me,' Bhavya said, feeling hemmed in.

They walked some distance, the worry and anguish that were subdued earlier now alive.

'Even to me?' The soft words were barely out before Bhavya turned to Aruna, annoyance coming off her in waves.

'Didn't you too choose to keep Rafi's vileness to yourself? Was I not close enough to you then?' Bhavya asked, her raised voice attracting attention.

'That was different,' Aruna answered unperturbed, used to her sister's tectonic mood shifts.

'Really, how? What was so different that you could not tell me that he was peeping into my room while I was undressing?' She asked, her face set, arms folded, waiting.

'Well, because I...I....'

'Yes, you what? You chose to tell all when there was no other way out. How many months did you keep this to yourself, Aruna? Had you told me that he was eyeing me, stalking me, I would have been better prepared to handle him. But, you let me make a fool of myself believing that he was someone I could trust!' Bhavya said her hurt palpable in her harsh words.

'I...I am sorry, Bee. I know I should have...all I can do is apologise,' Aruna said pained at the hurt she had inadvertently caused her sister under the misconception of protecting her.

Watching her sister grapple with her words, Bhavya regretted airing her anger. Taking a cleansing breath, Bhavya hugged Aruna.

'I am sorry too, Aruna. My words got the better of me.'

'You never said anything, laughing and joking when you came back for my marriage as if nothing had happened. I did not realise that I had hurt you this deeply,' Aruna tried to make amends.

'I should not have said anything.'

'Why do you do this?' Aruna asked.

'What?'

'Take one step forward and two steps back. Finish this, say what you really mean, what you really feel. I can take it and so can everyone else. It is not your job to protect us, Bee. If you need to scream like before...do that. I can take it and match you, my dear sister,' Aruna said, her hands on her hips.

'Oh my, someone's hormones are kicking in! And, by the way, you look like a damn penguin in that pose, an angry penguin but a penguin nonetheless,' Bhavya said, laughing.

'See, there you go again, making a joke of a serious thing. You know that it is your own fault?' Aruna said as they started walking again, slowly, holding hands again.

'Is it...what?'

'You pose to be really strong, thick skinned...whatever... who is not affected by what anyone does or says while I think you are the most fragile out of all of us.'

'It must be true since you are saying it,' Bhavya said after a while.

'Stop it.' Aruna shot back.

'You stop it...' Bhavya chuckled.

'No...you stop it, you silly goose.'

'Aruna...Aruna, that's enough walking for today, let's head back,' their father called out.

'Why do you always walk on this path, Dad?' Bhavya asked.

'What path?' Arun asked, looking around.

'Near the mausoleum of that prostitute...Noorie?' she asked.

'BEE!' Aruna cried and turned to her sister, scandalised.

'What...what? What did I say?' Bhavya asked, noting Aruna's red face and her father's uncomfortable countenance.

'Noorie was a courtesan, not a...' Arun finally replied.

'What's the difference?'

'The difference is in the respect you afford someone. Noorie belonged to a well-off Hindu family. After being... uhhh...despoiled by the prince, she found herself used, pregnant and alone. Her family had forsaken her but she did not lose her spirit. Gathering her meagre belongings, she went where she knew she would be accepted, the blot on her character not withstanding...or maybe because of it.'

'Where did she....'

'She was taken in by the people who live at the fringes of society, ostracised for no fault of theirs except that they are born into the life or are prisoners of their circumstances. Imagine the kind of life she would have lived for no fault of hers except being at the wrong place at the wrong time.'

Arun went on to tell his daughters about Noorie, in the shadow of her final resting place.

'Sorry, Dad, I had no idea,' Bhavya finally said.

'Be careful how you view another person, Bee, you don't know the path they have walked.'

'Hmmm...'

'How do you know so much about her?' Aruna asked.

'That is a story for another day,' he said. Setting aside their pleas for more of Noorie's life, he scolded them for delaying his morning routine as he herded his two eldest children home.

The gauzy, wet, kohl-lined eyes that were watching his retreating back filled with a yearning. They had waited centuries to hear these words.

The small hair on the back of Bhavya's neck rose and she looked back at the sunlit path and the lonely arch of Noorie's black tomb. A sadness and a longing swept within her that she shook off at her father's call and hurried to his side.

Bhavya, however, could not shake off her father's words that kept ringing in her head for the rest of the day. She kept thinking of Noorie and the circumstances that had led her to seek refuge at a whorehouse, the prince and his coterie that subjected her to torturous rape.

She was adept at reading between the lines of what her father had left unsaid.

'How was your walk?' Bhuvan asked Aruna as she folded their clothes into the small bag.

He had watched her chew her lip, worrying about something since she had returned from the stroll with Bhavya and his father-in-law in the morning. After a whole day of looking at her furrowed brow and preoccupied eyes, he had to ask her about what was bothering her.

'Huh...oh good, we talked,' she said.

'Did she tell you what the matter is?'

'No, she refused to talk about it. But Bhuvan, I have never seen her like this before. One minute she's angry, and the very next she is laughing and joking as if nothing has happened.'

'Well! She is certainly behaving like you. The Sharma sisters are more alike than they would have one believe,' Bhuvan laughed, relieved.

'Oh my god! You are right. She is pregnant, she could be...no? Hormonal changes could make her like this, constantly on edge, isn't it?' Aruna asked, excitedly gripping Bhuvan's hands.

Bhuvan didn't answer. How had Aruna made this deduction was beyond him?

'Yes, that makes sense. She is someone who will not know what to do if she got pregnant. Do you think she came back because Tenzin did not follow up on the marriage proposal? Or maybe she does not want to have the baby? Or maybe...I should just ask her,' Aruna said as she turned to go to her sister.

'Aruna, wait. Please just...if she is, she should be the one to tell you and everyone,' Bhuvan said

'Yes but....'

'I know you are worried about her, so am I, but if she needs time to figure out her path ahead should we not give her the space? It has just been three weeks,' Bhuvan said pulling her into his arms. 'What happened during the walk, did you two fight, is something troubling you?'

'I should have told her about Rafi,' she answered after a hesitant moment.

Bhuvan held her tighter, waiting for her to complete her thought.

'She feels betrayed...and she is not wrong. She always had trust issues, since we were young. She takes on the role of the knight very easily. All her boyfriends had major issues that she wanted to help them overcome. More recently there has been Gaurav and even Tenzin has a lot of baggage.'

'Did something happen to make her stop trusting people?'

'I don't think it was one thing. Small things she observed I think.'

'Like what?' Bhuvan asked.

'Like the lack of intimacy between our parents, the *Haveli* always being under threat, the family on the verge of expulsion. Once the police had come to the house and she hid in one of the first floor rooms so they would not take her away. Then the kidnapping of Charu happened. Bee felt responsible, took that really hard, even though Ma tried to tell her it was not her fault. And then Ma sent Charu to our grandmother in Surat. Bee felt she was being punished. She loves Charu a lot. For the longest time she joked about being adopted.'

'Is she?'

'*Uff*! No, no she just thought Baba loved me more and…her less. She could not understand why he treated us differently.' Aruna swatted his arm.

'Well, he does.'

'No, he does not…well…yes, maybe. I see that now; back then, I was too self-obsessed to realise it. I think they are too alike and hence the friction. Both refuse to bend.' Aruna tried to defend her father.

'Hmmm…' Bhuvan smiled.

'You really think I should not ask her?'

'Yes, let us give her one more week and then torpedo the truth out of her,' he said gently.

'Okay,' Aruna said, laying her head on his shoulder.

# 12

## *Abditory*

## A place into which you can disappear

(Language: English, Origin: Medieval Latin)

*A girl, almost a woman now, was running across fields of green. Her bare feet scarcely touched the ground, as she seemed to fly over the soft grass. Her long hair flew out behind her, not black not brown, lighter, as if she habitually played in the sun for far too long. A pink net veil that usually covered her head was held tightly between her fragile fingers, the shiny rhinestones on it catching the sun as if in anxiety. She raced away from a clutch of young boys who chased her, their evil intent shining in their eyes.*

*Her heart raced faster than her feet as she realised that she probably would not be able to evade them this time. Cursing her need for adventure and the misguided confidence of youth, she tried not looking at the inevitable. Her feet slowed and she rounded on the gaggle of laughing and jeering boys baiting her.*

*'Thank God, you realised running is of no use. I am tired.'*

*'Why are you doing this, Mehran? You are my brother's friend,' the girl gasped.*

*'Well, why did you think we allowed him to be our friend? Your nubile fire is what drew us like moths. Now, be a good girl and let us partake in your sweetness.'*

*They laughed as tears streamed down from her almond-shaped eyes. There was no help coming. Having slipped out to the marketplace without telling anyone of her whereabouts, she knew no one would be looking for her.*

*'Look at her perky breasts heaving, she is asking for it. Come on, what are you waiting for?' she heard one of the boys taunt the young prince.*

*'I shall be your first. You should be grateful,' said the girl's soon-to-be tormenter.*

*The laughter was making her dizzy even as her mind grappled with the realisation that there was no escape from where the fates had deemed to abandon her. Stopping to reason with them was a mistake, she realised.*

*Her head lowered in anticipation of humiliation and pain. Maybe, they would finish the deed and her as well.*

*But, I haven't even fallen in love yet, she thought.*

*Maybe after today there will be no reason to.*

*She walked backwards even as the prince she had admired from afar walked with a sneer on his mouth, his eyes enjoying her helplessness. His friends formed an arc closing in on the intended kill for that was what she was, this afternoon's entertainment.*

*As she lay on the dewy, green floor of the forest, the waves of pain having numbed her mind, she looked at the canopy of bright leaves that waved, as innocent and marooned as she. Concentrating on their silent call for help, she let her violators take away from her that which was hers, only hers, to give.*

*One after the other.*

*She didn't hear the sound of hooves, probably because of the ringing in her ears. Her tyrant's groans made her aware of another presence.*

*'Shehzade, the Shah has summoned you,' said a curt voice.*

*'Not now, Bahadur Khan,' the petulant reply came from the one who would one day rule over the people of this country.*

*'Now...come. And, you boys need to get back too or your mothers shall hear of this.' They all knew that the threat would be followed up on.*

*Mehran looked at his father's mansabdar with eyes squinted with anger. He knew of his hard and rigid moral code, he also knew of his proximity with his father. His intensions satisfied, he nudged at his friends to start moving back, giving one last look of satisfied greed at the doe-eyed girl he had finally had a taste of today. There would be more days like today he knew; he would just have to wait to slake his lust until then. Next time there shall be no interruptions, he thought, as he was surrounded by the King's guard and led away*

*The girl lay broken and frozen, not yet able to comprehend her fate.*

*'Are you okay?' came a gentle voice.*

*Large eyes full of shock that had not yet been expressed met deep-set, concerned ones. Lowering her welling eyes, the girl nodded. Her quivering fingers tried to locate the transparent cover to shield her from his piercing eyes. All she wanted was to be left alone to howl her grief...and her relief at being alive. She waited for the large man to trot away and leave her in her exposed misery.*

*Shaking, she closed her eyes and lay unmoving till she felt someone wrap her in warmth. She snapped her eyes open and found her eyes at level with a shiny breastplate. Strong arms wrapped around her. She wanted to flinch, to scratch at the big hands that held firm but the feeling of security far outweighed the need to retaliate.*

*He picked her up, walked to a fallen branch near the flowing water, leaving the place of her defiling behind. Leaning against it, he sat on the grass and to her utter surprise, started singing. His voice wrapped around her as she felt herself relaxing after the initial shock. Her head softly resting on his chest she listened to his deep tenor full of pain and hurt and closed her eyes.*

*Whom does he sing for and why? She wondered.*

*The song ended and yet they sat silent near the softly flowing river, both looking at the water.*

*'It's over. Clean yourself, go home and forget it. It wasn't your fault and it doesn't make you any less. If nothing else believe that and never forget it.'*

*Mute at his cryptic words she just stared at him as he disengaged from her.*

*She watched the gentle man with the golden voice turn into the hard mansabdar again, someone who had sworn to protect her tormenter with his life.*

*'Go home,' he said, before riding away.*

*She didn't know how long she sat there, clutching at the warm velvet cape he had wrapped around her. With her nose pressed to it, she wondered what she imagined...her violation or these moments of gentleness with a stern solider, the man she knew was her soul mate.*

Bhavya dreamed in colour, always had. The lucid dream left her feeling violated, her heart racing in her chest. Pulling the red shawl closer, as she had seen the young girl do, she tried escaping the remnants of the dream that still clung to her taking deep conscious breaths as Tenzin had taught her to do.

*Who am I dreaming about?*

*Noorie...I am dreaming about a young Noorie. Is my mind conjuring what would have happened to her? More importantly, why am I dreaming about her?*

After a troubled night her irritable mood was evident to everyone the next morning. Some years back Bhavya would have barked at anyone who tried to ask her about her foul mood, but not anymore.

Reflecting on her changing self she sat on her swing, letting the rays of the sun fall on her upturned face, as she again thought back on her father's words. The inner battle raged on without a flicker of the war evident on her seemingly peaceful face.

*Bhavya refuses to grow up despite her twenty-seven years. Always emotionally surcharged she keeps leaping into situations without a thought to the consequences. She would have gravitated towards her family even if she had her own house in this time of confusion and catharsis. The physical reality of being homeless troubles her perhaps.*

*Always impatient.*

*She remembered the day Arun had informed the family that he had won the case his half-brother had filed to render him homeless and I was finally theirs. Arun's stepbrother had fought over me. Had it not been for Suresh's legal expertise and help the family would have been out on the streets.*

*I shudder thinking of anyone else living in my interiors.*

*Shukrana be given to Allah and Suresh, who was able to find a way out. As a child, Bhavya has spent many nights worried over her family's fate, waking up in cold sweat while everyone slept comfortable.*

*Aruna's metamorphosis, from a young fragile girl who married the wrong man only to have her wings broken, into the beautiful strong woman of today fills me with awe. With Bhuvan, her second husband she not only found love but herself as well.*

*The three angels have grown into three distinct personalities, Etti the soundless rebel, Fanny the argumentative animal lover and Gina the gentle artist.*

*It is difficult on parents when children flutter their wings and fly away, leaving everything and everyone behind. I stand stagnant, ever watchful while my Uma smiles thinking of Tenzin as he had stood then, a handsome, tall man with salt-and-pepper hair and sombre eyes, assessing a way out of the uncomfortable situation Bee had thrust him into. Aruna had once exclaimed that he looked like that Bollywood actor, Danny Denzongpa, when they had met him for the first time at the airport.*

*My Uma had, later that night, shared her concerns with Suresh, her voice lower than usual. That Tenzin was so much older than she would have liked Bee to be with.*

*I am sure Tenzin too expected stiffness from Bhavya's family, with him being older and an orphan and maybe also because he was Tibetan. What he found, instead, was a simple family that accepted his presence and watched the effect he was having on the one they loved.*

# 13

## *Aspectabund*

## Letting or being able to let expressive emotions show easily through one's face and eyes

(Language: Rare English)

'Bhavya *di,* may I request you to avoid taking my car without first asking me?' Bhavya heard Dheeraj say the words as she entered the foyer, emotionally exhausted and mentally drained.

She could feel her insides twist, ready to spit fury. She tried to control it…but the constant shelving of her disillusionment with Tenzin and the recent realisation that Kabir was not the man she had thought him to be added to the already brimming cauldron of frustration that her out-of-control life had become. She breathed deep, trying to push her anger down and shove it under the carpet as always.

'Why don't you ever consider that others may have…?'

The storm found its eye.

She turned around and threw the keys at the hapless Dheeraj and missed scratching his face with the heavy bunch by a whisker.

'What the hell!' Dheeraj exclaimed, taken aback.

'Here, take them. Is this what you want? Take this and everything else.' She yelled at him.

'Bee *di…*' Dheeraj said, looking aghast. He ducked out of the way when Bhavya threw the crystal vase at him.

'What is wrong with you?' he shouted, jumping out of the way.

The crash of the vase brought Uma out into the foyer. She stood frozen watching the storm that had finally been unleashed as hurtful words tumbled out of Bhavya's mouth.

'Since when do I need to ask for your permission, you good-for-nothing halfwit? You were unable to do the one thing you were supposed to do—study and clear your entrance exam and you have the audacity to ask me...me... What gives you the right?' Bhavya shouted clenching her fists so hard that her arms shook.

'That car belongs to all of us. Are you not even ashamed to say it is yours? What have you done till now...huh... what do you have to show for yourself in the twenty-six years?' She shirked her eyes streaming, gasping for breath as she threw a picture frame at him that clattered to the ground beside him.

Bhavya felt her breath become ragged, her chest constricted with a scream that she wanted to let loose and never stop. She knew she had crossed a line.

'Bee, stop this right now, he is your brother,' Uma said sternly, worry marring her eyes.

'Everyone can say whatever they feel like and I can't?' She cried looking at her mother's tense face. Feeling like she was in a rabbit hole she looked away, ashamed yet unable to stop.

'What did I say? I had to go and pick up Sona from the airport and...I had to cancel.' He shouted throwing the table clock that he had caught a moment ago back at her.

'Bhuvan's sister...does he know?'

'Don't go there, Bee *di*!'

'Why not?' She threatened, walking towards him.

'You need to calm down. You are soundi....'

'What...crazy...crazy because I came back?' She said, her head ready to burst with a pain so colossal that she was unable to control herself.

'Stop it, Bhavya,' Uma said, her voice trembling with dread.

'Argghh!' She launched herself at him till both of them were in a serious tussle.

Dheeraj tried his best to catch her slippery hands that found ways to slap at him.

'Stop it... Stop it...you two!' Uma shouted feeling ill-equipped to handle her children's hurt.

Dheeraj pushed her away and took three steps back, breathing heavily.

'Ma, she is crazy, absolutely crazy. She needs a doctor.' He said, taking off his bent spectacles.

'Why can't you just talk about your issues like a sane person and not punch everyone? Ma, I am telling you she needs help.'

'You want to go get Bhuvan's sister but not me...you haven't even asked me how I am. Have you even bothered to ask me why I came back? You are more concerned with Sona and her whereabouts.' Bhavya screamed at her brother.

'Don't bring her into this. Sona is not like you.' Dheeraj said, his eyes showing the first signs of antagonism.

'She's not like...what the hell do you mean?' Bhavya found herself screaming again. The surge of her battered emotions, the confusion and murkiness of her decision drowned the voice of reason.

'I mean....'

'Are you saying I roam around at night so that makes me invincible, that I don't need someone...anyone, that I'm...inviting trouble?' She didn't know why she was still shouting.

'What...when did I say that? Ma, what is she...?' Dheeraj could not understand why his mother stood crying silently. 'What did I say?' He asked loudly to the women.

'Let me get this,' Gaurav said from behind him. Dheeraj turned and watched him talk softly to his sister.

*With pleasure, usurp me here too, why don't you?* Dheeraj thought, then slipped away, leaving Gaurav to deal with his crazy sister.

Gaurav had come to understand Dheeraj, the heir and only son of the Sharma family in the years he had spent in the *Haveli*. He knew Dheeraj did not wear the mantle of responsibility of six sisters lightly. He knew how uncomfortable he was with the expectations that came along with that title. Without a family to call his own Gaurav had adopted the one which had accepted him when he arrived at their doorstep four years ago. A vagabond, living at the mercy of the goodwill of this family since then, he had become adept at peace mongering. With Bhavya it was easier since he understood her better than her own family, or so he thought.

Gaurav wondered how best to get through to Bhavya. His friend, with the wild hair, loud mouth and sorrowful eyes was winding down. Taking a chance, he stepped closer, keeping an eye out for any flying objects. He knew of her penchant for throwing things.

'Bee, calm down.'

'I won't. What did he mean, Gaurav?'

'He certainly didn't mean what you are taking this as.'

'Oh ho, men uniting, the brotherhood withstands the ranting of a crazy woman!'

'Bee, come on, enough.'

'Who are you to tell me to stop? Who…my boyfriend, my father, my brother…no, you are nothing to me,' her voice hitched, 'nothing. And, don't think it will take a second for me to tell my parents that you invite some floozy up to your room at night. I am just waiting for the right time.'

'Okay, you can rat me out. I am your friend, Bee, you can do whatever you like but I am here, know that much at least. Also, stop calling your sister a floozy, she won't like that,' he said, then just hugged her, letting her tears soak his shirt as she let loose her anguish while Gaurav held firm, letting the maelstrom of emotion roll over him.

He spotted Etti from the corner of his eye. She seemed to just stand there at the door, a mute spectator to the unfolding drama. Doing nothing, just observing them as they stood holding on to each other.

He sighed, heartfelt, accepting that there was a lot of explaining he would have to do in the near future.

An hour later, Gaurav stood at the open window watching Etti run to the mango tree and sit facing the expanse of the backyard, her back to him, effectively shutting him out. He sighed and leaned against the window frame looking at the waving leaves. He had gotten into the habit of leaving the window open to let in the soft breeze. He enjoyed listening to the sound of the rustling leaves; they had a language of their own. He treasured lying on the bed, eavesdropping on their conversations as moonbeams made patterns on her dewy skin.

Etti, his torment and his only love.

While his guilt-ridden mind was busy berating his actions, he spotted Bhavya, sneaking up on Etti.

*Wrong move, Bee,* he thought. *In the mood she is in, she will cut like a knife and not spill a drop of blood.*

He leaned forward, wanting to warn his friend to stay away. Etti was like a dormant volcano. Right now, the vibrations were earthquake-like and he wondered what this eruption would entail.

More importantly, would the two sisters manage to sidestep the oncoming blows for they were an equal match?

*Is that what had attracted me to Etti? Could she be right about Bee and me?* He questioned himself.

*No, I don't feel for Bee as I do for her sister and therein lies the more pertinent problem,* pat came the reply.

Having an affair with Bhavya would have been easier. She was more like him, able to segregate and box emotions, while Etti was a minefield of hints and expectations, soundless. It was bliss to see her sparkling smile when her expectation was fulfilled and as much hell to see her sad eyes when not.

Right now, her eyes were anguished and so was he.

A cloud of anger hovered over Etti as she sat under the mango tree, the one that she had claimed as her own. Planted by her mother after their birth, it was as old as she and her sisters. Young and teeming with life, it was the spot she had attached herself to. Just like Aruna had her window and Bhavya had her swing, she had this tree. It was privy to many secrets whispered in delight or with sorrow.

Today, she just sat morose underneath its widespread branches. The rustling of the leaves and the soft zephyr calmed her distraught nerves as she laid her forehead on her bent knees. She knew Gaurav watched her from the window of his room.

*And, yet he chooses to close his eyes to our connection.*

She wanted him to acknowledge her, accept and proclaim his feelings for her and he wanted time.

She kept her face hidden from him, unwilling to give him the satisfaction of knowing that he could move her to tears.

*This psychology course is not helping at all, instead of finding calm, these days I feel more volatile. Fanny has JD; Gina has her paintings, Aruna didi her family, Charu didi her skill. And, I... what do I have? Whom do I have?*

*An illusion that went up in smoke as soon as it was put to test.*

'What am I doing? What is the use?' she murmured.

'Of what?'

Her head jerking up, she looked with guilty eyes at her elder sister Bhavya. She stood leaning against the tree, a hand on her bare waist where the crop top she wore had ridden up. This whole picture of false coolness irritated her. She hastily lowered her eyes.

'So, will you tell me why you are sitting here, hyper-ventilating?' Bhavya asked.

'Will *you*?'

'What?' Bhavya asked, perplexed at Etti's curt tone.

'You know what? Why did you come back? Why has Tenzin not called even once when it is going to be four weeks since you came? Why do you put up this false act of bravado, when we all know that you are decimating inside?'

'What are you...?'

'And, why have you not told Ma that you are pregnant?'

# 14

## *Efflorescence*

### A time for flowering or blooming

(Language: English, Origin: French and Latin)

'Etti...' Bhavya whispered.

She stood facing her sister, now gone pale when the questions that she couldn't answer were put bluntly to her face.

'Not so witty anymore, are we?' Etti's voice ended on a hiccup.

'Etti, why...what makes you think...I....'

'Save it, don't lie to me; I am not a child anymore.'

'Yes, I can see that. I am just going to sit down for a second here,' Bhavya said as she lowered herself to sit beside Etti.

*Was it that obvious? If Etti knew, did everyone else realise too. Did Dad know? No, he would have said something,* qualms rushed at her at a speed she couldn't withstand.

Etti, watching her proud sister crumble before her eyes, was shaken with the guilt that welled up.

'Well.'

'Well what, Etti?'

'Answer the damn questions, Bee *di,* or is it easier to just dish it out....'

'I am sorry if you felt I was intruding but what are sisters for after all if they can't put their fingers in places which ache?'

'Or show you the mirror once in a while...' Etti countered.

'*Touché*. Etti, who else knows?'

'No one, I thought y…you would want to tell them in your own time.'

Bhavya nodded her head.

'Well, at least you aren't walking on eggshells around me like everyone else.' Bhavya retorted.

'Do you blame them after your last meltdown?'

'You saw that?'

Etti nodded.

'Okay, okay, I get it; everyone knows what a crazy person I can be,' Bhavya said, the red of embarrassment staining her cheeks.

'What are you waiting for, Bee *di*?' Etti asked.

'What do you mean?'

'Are you waiting for someone to save you, because you always said you didn't need saving, that women were strong enough to save themselves. Why are you so lost then?'

Bhavya had no answers for Etti.

She would have to own up to her life choices soon.

The sisters sat under the tree talking about their lives, the wind carrying the echo of their voices to the man who stood alone and forgotten a hand span away, watching them with an aching and wanting heart.

# 15

## *Monachopsis*

## The subtle but persistent feeling of being out of place

(Language: English, Origin: Sanskrit)

Bhavya knew she had tainted the happiness for everyone in Aruna's impending delivery by her mere presence. He parents were looking at her in a constant state of anxiety. She knew they were unhappy with her decision to stay away from Tenzin. She let their disapproval wash over her as she had her breakfast, head bowed.

'Bee,' her father said, 'why don't you come with us to the shop?'

Bee looked up at him. 'I will come tomorrow, Dad.'

'Why, what are you doing today that is so important?'

'Let her have breakfast,' Uma said, always the peace-keeper.

Arun's fist banged on the table, rattling the dishes and making everyone start.

'I will talk to her today; enough of this doing what she pleases.'

Bee placed her spoon on the table and leaned back looking at her father, waiting for the anger to erupt. She was strangely relieved.

'Arun, don't let your worry come out in words that may cause hurt,' Suresh advised.

'No, I have had it up to here with her antics. What is your problem, Bee? Does he beat you like Aruna's ex-husband did, does he not provide for you, is he a philanderer, is he cruel? Answer me!'

'No, he is none of those things, Dad.' Bhavya answered, folding her arms to control the tremors that had started.

'Then, why do you not go to him, what has he done? How is being adamant going to help? Do you see the sisters before you? They have to marry. What kind of example are you setting for them?' Arun bellowed at her.

'My sisters do not need me to set an example for them. They have a working mind to tell them right from wrong. They will make their own choices.'

'Oh, like the choice you made to live with that man? I thought you had changed, matured. That Ten-sing's temperament would have rubbed off on you but no, you are still the same. Even after being with a man as stable as Ten-sing you are as fickle as before. Always running to hide from reality. Always bringing troubl….'

'Arun, no…' said Suresh, watching Bhavya's face pale, all colour leeching out at Arun's words.

'Baba, stop it,' said Dheeraj, pushing back his chair at his father's unfair words.

'…e whenever you come home.'

'Bee, he does not mean that, his worry makes him harsh.' Uma said, tears streaming down her cheeks at the chasm that yawned between a father and his daughter.

*Here it is, how he really feels about me,* Bee thought.

'I think he does, Ma. Thank you for your honesty, Dad. I expect nothing less from you.' She said her head held high and proud.

'Don't wait for lunch, Ma, I don't know when I will be back,' she said, her voice tight as she stormed out.

The office seemed forlorn. A few weeks since she had walked out and Paris felt washed pale as if it was her verve, adding the gold to the sunshine.

*Her mere presence always brought on a feeling of rightness within. I didn't need to see her or hear her voice, her scent or her laughter, just a knowing that she is near…around. How doleful…but that is my reality. I cannot share her. A glutton for punishment, that's what I am.*

*Her unrepentant ability to forgo rules…chaffed my very ordered existence from the very first day. I looked at her and my back stiffened, her need to rile me, just to see how I will react was what got us into this mess in the first place and now, she wants nothing to do with me.*

*Why? Because I want her to let bygones be bygones? We had a good time in Bali with Kabir; why did she have to meet him here? You don't keep in touch with a one-night stand.*

*But no, she wanted to be friends. Friends with a man who I let touch my…what…what right do I have on her? Who am I to ask her to do anything?*

'Oh God, it's all my fault!' He whispered rubbing his face with his hands, his thoughts leading him to examine his own hypocrisy and mind set.

'I should have just loved her silently and from afar, never should have let her convince me that we could be together. I should have known better than to let myself be swayed.' Feeling his heartbeat quicken, he remembered the day they had taken the first step towards the inevitable.

It had been a month of travelling back and forth from office together, a month of living across from her in the hotel. A month of thawing and feverishly working on the pitch for the new account while simultaneously setting up the new office.

The stretch between them was bound to culminate in an impulsive consequence.

He remembered the window being open that night letting in the cool breeze from the Seine that flowed close to the office building.

Looking like a long, cool glass of wine that goes straight to your head, she had suggested that they call it a day.

He knew she was planning to go for a classical concert at the Notre Dame Cathedral with Raul, the accountant. Like a jealous teenager, he had been wilfully trying to delay their date.

He had said something to that effect and watched her eyes ignite with irritation. Then, out of nowhere, grabbing his shirt, she had planted her half-open mouth on his. His hands grabbed her painfully hard, holding on for an instant, and then letting go immediately realising his mistake.

He looked down at his empty hands now, still able to feel the scratch of her blouse.

Reprimanding her, calling her impulsive even telling her that he was not looking for a side fling had not helped cool her interest.

She had been relentless in her pursuit of him. The more he had pulled away the more she had reeled him in. He had been wet clay in her hands from the first and she had always known it.

*We would have been better as friends,* he thought now. *No expectations, no complications, just too different to be married.*

He was alerted to someone entering his office at the sound of a throat being cleared. He swirled his chair around to face them, hardening his face to its usual impregnable mask.

'Sir, what should I do with Ms Sharma's salary?' Raul, the accountant asked.

'What do you mean?' Tenzin asked the man brusquely.

'She has been on leave for....'

'I know how long she has been on leave.'

Raul shuffled his feet wishing he was anywhere but here.

'I was wondering if there is an application...or...it is okay if...I will remit the salary in her account,' he stammered at Tenzin's piercing gaze before leaving quickly.

*Now I am supposed to call her and request for…God she makes me crazy,* he thought gleefully, dialling the Delhi number.

He had an excuse now.

*May Allah give me strength!*

*Bhavya's thoughts are dark. They come to me in waves of censure.*

*It has become disconcertingly quiet after Arun and Bhavya's anger obliterated the ease within me.*

*What has made her so cynical…so jaded?*

*I know Arun has no control over his words when raised in anger but I also know that she does not either. Their tongues as sharp as freshly sharpened knives they do not hesitate to use them on each other.*

*The sad part is that they are similar in their love and their inability to express it to the other. Arun, always hyper-vigilant of his beliefs, is unable to comprehend an opinion not his own; while Bhavya in a bid to get over the sadness that has enveloped her forgets that there is much to be grateful for.*

*Fear has made them blind to the power that all humans have to alter their circumstances. Failure seems achievable and success impossible.*

*She feels cursed and on some days…I am forced to agree with her.*

# 16

## *Minutiae*

## The small, precise details that make one unique

(Language: English, Origin: Latin)

The phone rang jarringly, the tranquil night registering its shrill intrusion. Arun picked up the receiver after it had rung a few times.

'Hel…' he stopped when he realised that Tenzin was asking for Bhavya on the other end. He wanted to keep the receiver down, give them privacy, as he would expect… but then did not.

A worried parent guiltily listened in on the conversation between his daughter and her…he did not know what to call him. For him, a man had a clear role as a husband to provide for his family but this…living together; he felt had many loopholes that one could slip through to avoid the responsibility that came along with the distinction of being a husband.

'What do you mean there is a problem with remitting my salary? Do you think I am a fool? You are doing this to pressurise me to give in. Let me clarify…I will not. You want to deduct my salary, do that, do your worst. Tenzin, you have fallen from the pedestal I put you on, don't do things like this and fall from grace as well.'

'Bee…can you calm down for a second? I am not even going to warrant your accusations with an answer. I am only asking because there are going to be unnecessary questions at the office and I don't want people talking about us. So just send an application via e-mail. Look, had you been there at the office I would have figured something out but I had to call you for this....'

'No one asked it of you, don't put that on me...and you know why I left.'

'Bee, look....'

*Why is everything about one-upmanship with today's kids? They barely listen to the other person and interrupt without giving any thought to what they want to say. No filters.* Arun thought.

'Bee, let's resolve this, one way or another. This limbo is tiresome. You cannot be obstinate about this. You are behaving like a damn victim, which you are not. Stop whining like a child and face the consequences of your behaviour. Grow up!'

Arun disliked the tone Tenzin was using with his daughter but held his silence...for now.

'And, we are back to that, are we?' Bhavya too pushed back.

'Bee, come on...can we talk for a moment? I am not asking for myself. This is work...I cannot keep covering for you indefinitely.' He said, irritation coming through the telephone wires.

'I have nothing more to say to you....'

A silence followed, screaming of hurt, labile emotions, as there was a gentle click of the phone disconnecting, far away.

'Hello...hello...Tenzin,' Bhavya said, her voice breaking.

Arun stood next to his desk unmoving, the phone still in his hand.

Bhavya replaced the receiver on its cradle as softly as she could while her mind was careening out of control.

All she could see were snippets of their life as it had begun, with charm and laughter. It had quickly given way to naughtiness, lust and then love that she had thought was the ever after kind.

*What will I tell everyone when they ask why I am leaving him, my life in Paris, my job?* She kept wondering.

*I could blame Tenzin…but of what? There is nothing concrete that stands out. He was never abusive as Rafi had been. He is not a leech or a creep. He is caring and kind, hardworking and loyal. Then why do I seek something more….*

Unknown to her she stood with a hand on her fast-swelling belly, with a frown marring her broad brow.

That was how Dheeraj found her, standing in the corridor. His eyes immediately registered her stance and the secret but he refrained from asking. After the last fiasco, he kept to himself and avoided his sister and her mood swings. He left her standing in the hallway and entered his room, closing the door behind him.

She too went into Arun's study and taking out her frustration at the keyboard, she sent the e-mail requesting for medical leave.

She got up and started poking about the books in her father's book shelf knowing she would not be able to sleep. She would need something to occupy herself and she was done with shadowing the halls of the *Haveli* late in the night.

The other night she had scared herself out of her skin when she had banged into Dheeraj who was slyly slinking back home through Charu's room. They had both gasped loudly holding on to their drumming hearts before she swatted him a couple of times for scaring her and he reciprocated. The knot their words had created in the fragile thread of their relationship smoothened out and shone with strength and love again.

Everyone had their lives to live and she felt as if she had landed out of nowhere shaking up their steady routine. They were trying their best to make space for her but she felt useless. Every time she went looking for something to do she was told to rest, to relax, take a break, which was the one thing she wanted to avoid at all costs. But here she was...again sifting through the old books in her father's shelves.

She returned to the desk to switch off the ancient PC. Bending down to stretch across the maze of wires, her eyes registered a knob on the inside of the table. Unless one was at the right angle or knew where it was, it would be practically impossible to spot. Unable to help herself and without a second's hesitation, she pulled at it. A small door swung open revealing a dusty, green velvet cloth. Carefully she removed the delicate and shredded cloth that at one time would have shone with wealth and grandeur. The intricate embroidery that had become dull with time still told her the tale of wrinkled hands and squinting eyes meticulously sewing the tiny pearls and coloured stones under a flickering light.

What she found inside had her gasping in surprise. Beaten leather-covered ivory sheets of heavy handmade pages filled with childlike formation of the Devanagari alphabets. She flipped through the pages to find words that were woven together to tell a story.

She couldn't resist, her eyes scanned the pages, and she read....

*...his hands were rough with scars....*

*Ammi came in the night to talk,* in another page.

*Why did I not listen to my head...*in yet another yellowed page.

'It's Noorie's journal...' came a low voice low as if even a soft sound would disturb the dust motes that were silent with anticipation.

'Dad?'

'I heard you moving about, thought I would come and check on you. So, you found it,' he said, looking at the journal.

'Why do you have this and how?'

'I found it in the ante chamber of the mausoleum... when we first came here. I had taken to walking there to escape the warzone that was the *Haveli* with both your grandmothers trying their best to create havoc... Found it stuck under the fireplace.'

'What were you doing searching the fireplace?'

'Where do you think you get your inquisitiveness from? I just got it home. Spent hours reading about her life, still do sometimes. The words have such a lyrical quality about them that it is impossible not to go back to them. Take it, read about her life, maybe you will find your answers in this.'

She looked at her father, the man who had a big role in shaping her personality.

'Did the stories you used to tell us originate from here?'

'Some of them,' Arun answered. 'Are you still angry?' he asked softly.

'No...no, the forgiving I take from you...and also the inability to forget.'

'You have taken a lot from me, Bee. More than you know,' said Arun, looking at his daughter with something akin to distress. 'Read her story...' he said pointing to the aged leather.

Bee nodded, then tucking the journal in the shawl, her woollen talisman, she walked back to her room, armed with something to do.

# 17

## *Apricity*

### The warmth of the sun in winter

(Language: English derived from Latin)

Tenzin was reading the crisp words on his screen that Bhavya had sent the night before when his phone rang. He picked it up quickly hoping that she had finally come to her senses.

Finding a work-related issue that sought his attention on the other side of the phone line had his spirit deflating. Panic averted, he leaned back in his chair. A chair they had christened in their own special way as they had done the mahogany desk and each piece of furniture at home.

*Crazy, we were crazy in lust with each other. What changed? Was time the culprit?*

He wished he could talk to her.

*Why does she do this, flay me with her silence. My life was perfectly fine before her, calm, flowing peacefully. After getting me hooked on to her noise, she is punishing me by keeping herself away. She is angry I get it, but I cannot live with this insecurity. I will not give in*; he told his wavering heart that missed the sun that was Bhavya with a vengeance. Aching every time he entered the office or their home, it gave him nary a moment of peace.

He remembered the day he had introduced her to his family; a family that comprised of several kids of assorted ages and an old monk, who looked after them. Everyone addressed him as *'Pah la'* or father.

He had taken her to Leh after they had agreed to marry. A fumbling proposal that she had accepted stunned before shrieking and jumping around making him laugh at her silliness.

He had suggested that they go and seek the blessings of their parents before getting married in a discreet ceremony. She knew he was an orphan, left at the steps of a monastery. With no lingering grudge against his parents, he was happy with the way his life had turned out.

He smiled now, thinking about the day that they had reached Leh. She had insisted that the taxi take them directly to the monastery, brushing aside his need for caution and acclimatisation she had wanted to hurry... always impatient. Her excitement to get to his home had been infectious.

The serpentine path had taken them towards the mountain on which it stood, playing hide and seek with its magnificence. They had gotten off at the base of the hill and she had slowly walked towards the steps leading up the ramp taking in the majestic barrenness of the landscape, unbelieving of the beauty that surrounded her.

He knew she had anticipated a small strong-hold, bare and raw. What she realised was that the monastery was actually a multi-layered modern building carved into a mountain.

Awed by its massive, raw impact unlike anything she had ever laid eyes upon; she stood rooted, gazing up at the gaily waving prayer flags adorning the few hundred steps that led to the front landing.

'How in the name of god will I ever reach that?' She had mumbled looking at the ivory-coloured, freshly painted walls carved out of the rock mountain it stood upon.

'With me,' he said, his voice sounding strained to his own ears. The committed status was just sinking in.

'Are you alright, Tenzin?' She asked, sensing his discomfort before meshing her fingers with his.

'Come on,' he said, pulling her towards the zillion steps.

She huffed and puffed up the steps slowly making her way to the top, cursing him, her lack of physical strength, the thinning air, her impatience every step of the way.

He thoughtfully refrained from reminding her of his suggestion to stay a while in the flatlands. It would have been more sensible, but Bhavya was anything but.

'Maybe it would have been better to let you take the lead here,' she conceded, as she slowed her breath and began systematically counting down the stairs, envying his calm face as he climbed the steps with an easy nonchalance, not a hitch in his breath.

He smiled encouragingly and slowed his pace, refusing to leave her side despite her frantic waving him along as she bent trying to find the air to fill her lungs. He just smiled and leaned on the rock face, saying, 'Take your time.'

And so, she put one foot in front of the other as he had told her to do. The sloping steps led to a wooden atrium where they were greeted by Tenzin's father and brothers.

'Tenzin, *Ngay bu,*' he was engulfed in the fragile arms of *Pah la,* the man who had picked him up from where he had been thrown like garbage and made him part of his family.

She had gotten along like a house on fire with his father and the children whom he now supported. The school and boarding house was where he had spent a major part of his life. His childhood and youth, though marred with doubts and struggle, remained constant and smooth, with no bumps or dramatic episodes. He was lucky to have an above-average grade throughout his years in school and college. Finding a job and working his way up to the top position had been tough and full of backbreaking work but there had been nothing else to do, no family to cloud his one-point agenda to succeed.

That is till he met Bhavya, in the fortieth year of his life.

# 18

## *Aonaran*

## A person who lives in self-imposed isolation, a recluse

(Language: Scottish Gaelic)

He sighed and shook his head as he tried to clear his muddled brain, unable for the life of him to figure a way out of this conundrum he had managed to create. He shuffled the papers, dumping them into a briefcase, knowing he would not be able to get anything done today again. He closed his eyes as he sat in the car that took him to their home.

The perfume she had loved still echoed in the interior of the car, wrapping around him, invitingly. She had been gone for weeks and still it refused to dissipate. It distracted him making him remember the car rides they had taken to and from the office when they had first arrived in Paris.

How she used to take up the space in the sedan, not with her body but with her spirit, chatter non-stop with Robin, their driver. And, when she used to sit hunched miserably in the corner because he would not give her what she wanted…himself.

*This is becoming excruciating, a daily exercise in self-control. I should ask Robin to get another car from tomorrow,* he thought.

He knew he would not, he would suffer through these fifteen minutes of self-doubt rather than let go of this connection to her.

Even the streetlights as they passed overhead, made him think of her, the night they had gone to the party, their first night. She had looked unimaginably beautiful and his heart had beaten to a rhythm that had spelled trouble.

Robin peeked at his usually unaffected Boss in the backseat looking out at the row of buildings without really seeing them. He worried that the frown lines that had taken up residence on his forehead since Bhavya had gone home would become permanent. He prayed that she came back soon; the rides were so much fun with her. She brightened the day with her infectious laughter, even the Boss had loosened up. With her gone he had again retreated, speaking to no one, just working crazy hours.

Tenzin entered the apartment trying to dodge the memories but he could not run fast enough to escape the uncertainty that crept into his thoughts.

*Is it my fault; what does she find so appealing in Kabir? Besides the fact that she finds parallels with Kabir's thoughts and dreams, he is only an out-of-work artist who will never be able to afford the lifestyle she aspires to have.*

*No...no, what am I even thinking; she is too self-confident a woman to be enticed by money. She can and will earn her own. She resists letting him go, fearing the loss of a kindred spirit. Are dissimilar expectations at fault here? How could our relationship disintegrate so fast and for no logical reason? Where have I gone wrong...well besides the obvious?*

He heated a frozen dinner while trying not to let the silence of her absence affect him then switched on the TV switching channels incessantly. And because he could hear her funny sarcastic words in his mind, he finally shut it off in frustration.

The phone rang making him hope that she missed him too as he hurried to answer it.

'Hello,' he said.

'How are you, *Ngay bu*?'

'*Pah la*...I was thinking about you today.'

'What has happened, Tenzin?'

'Why do you say that?'

'One, because you are avoiding answering my question and two because you are sounding troubled.'

'Oh nothing, *Pah la*...nothing...just tired.'

After a moment of silence, his father, asked, 'Where is Bee?'

'She is...in Delhi, wanted to meet her family.'

'Alone?'

'Yes, *Pah la*, it is not possible for me to take leave for a vacation because I feel like it...' Tenzin said.

'Ah!' He heard his father's voice and then there was silence.

Tenzin knew this tactic; he had been privy to this particular form of questioning all his life.

'It is nothing to worry about,' he said, realising he was falling for the trick again.

'I am not worried, son. You are a big man; you can take care of your house. You remember the apricot tree that you remarked upon last year?'

'Yes, the one that I had planted in my teens.'

'That has given us so much sweet fruit this year too.'

'That's good, right?' *What is he getting at,* thought Tenzin. His *Pah la* was a firm believer in subtle hints.

'Oh yes, very good. It always remains bent just as a tree that is content and abundant is going to be. Not like a tree that remains rigid and obdurate. That tree can give no life, no shade to anyone.'

'*Pah la*....'

'Tenzin, you know what you need to do. Now go do it.'

'Yes, *Gen la*. How is my *nâng-miy*, my family?'

'Everyone is fine, my son. Call me once you are there or better yet come and visit, it has been too long. I miss you and so does everyone else.'

'Yes, I will. Bye. Take care.'

Tenzin sat on the red sofa, Bhavya's favourite. It made him feel close to her. More often than not, he would find her curled on it. It had made him feel good to see her claim a part of the house as hers, as she had the wooden swing in Delhi.

All his life this was what he had wanted; to make a home where everything had a back story. He wondered if it was his lack of belonging that made him fanatical about having a history with things.

He had learnt about self-reliance and sharing from the beginning, the Buddhist teaching forming the backbone of their education. He knew *Pah la* had been disappointed when he had chosen the world over monkhood but he never wanted another child at the orphanage to go hungry or without warm clothes in the future. That he knew could only be achieved with money. As soon as he was able, he had started repaying his debt to *Pah la* by caring for the school and upbringing of the 100 children in the Leh orphanage that he called home.

No one can fathom living in lack, unless they have done so themselves. Killing one's needs slowly; strangling wants with one's own hands was not for the faint-hearted. He had seen boys emerge as men, stronger than the strongest that the world could prepare them to be.

The brittle harshness of the landscape, the biting winters, the soft summers became a part of the people who lived in the land of the mountains and fluttering prayer flags.

He was now the sole provider for the school and orphanage and he was proud of achieving that more than any other awards that he had amassed over the years.

It was on this sofa that he had told her of his loneliness, the feeling of disquiet and not belonging to anyone that dodged his steps wherever he went and despite whatever he achieved. It was here that he had told her how important loyalty was to him, how if she said yes to him, she would do so to the exclusion of everyone else. They would be one unit, different bodies but the same heart.

She had agreed readily to the words saying that she too had always wanted to belong to someone. She had wanted to explore her life not encumbered with the adjustments and compromises that came with being in multiple relationships. She too had wanted to be exclusive and separate.

*Was that all a lie, then? And my fault…in falling for her words, believing that what she said was what she meant, or would stand by those same words forever.*

Tenzin held his throbbing head and wondered what he should do. He could not talk to the one man who he least wanted to disappoint and would inevitably hurt if the reason of the conflict with Bhavya became public. He felt desolate, unable to decide if he was in the right.

His head said he was; his heart was another matter.

# 19

## *Kalopsia*

## The delusion of things being more beautiful than they really are

(Language: English derived from Ancient Greek)

*I should stop thinking altogether; it does not help in any way except give me a headache. This baby is making me insane. God! What must Etti be thinking of me, what a mess! And Dheeraj, why did I shout at him the other day? It isn't his fault that I have messed up my life without any help,* thought Bhavya, as she trudged out of the *Haveli* after getting into another tiff with Etti on how long to leave the rice to cook.

'Have you ever cooked in your life, Bee *di*? How would you know?' Etti had said in jest. Such a silly thing but every word that she uttered seemed to scrap against her pride.

'Stop poking your nose into other's business,' she had shouted at her shocked sister, immediately regretting her outburst. Bhavya knew she was overreacting but was unable to help herself from losing control. She could feel herself sliding back into her old self—the aggressive, slightly obnoxious and always ready to throw the first punch person.

'Etti...Et...' Having said the words Bhavya could not take them back, she had to stand by them, whether she wanted to or not. She watched Etti leave the kitchen, her chin trembling and she had felt like the worst kind of person.

She had rushed behind her, apologising, making amends but she knew her words had led to a rift between them. After much grovelling, Etti nodded forgiveness, but the feeling of guilt and remorse remained every time Etti avoided crossing her path.

In leaving Tenzin she had been following a familiar pattern. She had expected that she would be able to deal with the surging emotions once she had put some distance between them. Find firm ground under her feet and then decide what she wanted to do about the baby.

His words of distrust regarding her friendship with Kabir and finding out that he was still in touch with his ex-girlfriend had acted as an impetus. The final break had been his insistence that she break all contact with Kabir.

What she had not expected was how deeply Tenzin had made his way into her....

*Can I compromise? Should I? Would it not be setting precedence for future compromises once we are married?*

*Not once did he talk about marriage after that day in the house. Maybe, he realised that he was not sure about committing to me. This entire commitment phobia was an excuse, who would know this better than me?* Her throat clogged with unshed tears, as she sniffed past the hurt and confusion that had gripped her.

*What if the tables were turned, would you let him feel complete with another woman?* Her mind questioned. There was no answer forthcoming.

Her thoughts dark, she realised she had walked up to Noorie's mausoleum. She thought of retracing her steps to the *Haveli,* then realised she had made a colossal fool of herself in full view of her family and was not ready to apologise just yet.

Even though there was still some light left, the small bulbs lining the path flickered on. Walking slowly, she took in the dilapidated structure. The fading light lent it an ethereal halo.

Bhavya stopped, gazing at the onyx stone structure. Her eyes became unfocused. She knew she stood in the present, but heard the *tanpura* and saw the glory it had once claimed when it had been a melting pot of musicians and artists from all walks of life. Shaking her head at her flight of fancy, she wondered why it looked like a small outhouse rather than the mausoleums built all around Delhi.

She walked around the perimeter of the mausoleum picturing how it would have looked back then. Her mind conjured pictures of hundreds of lit lamps, the oil burning, stinging the nostrils, trailing black soot with the warm flame.

*What happened to Noorie, how did she come to live here? There is obviously a connection with the Haveli. But what?*

Realising that it was getting darker she turned towards the *Haveli*. In the dark, she saw what once Noorie would have been able to see. The ivory of the *Haveli* shone like the solitary moon against the purple sky. A strong majestic symbol of power and opulence stood a little apart and yet as if only a grasp away. The lights shone, twinkling, as the millions of lamps would have done in the past. It was the yin to the yang of the shimmering ebony of the black stone behind her, a perfect compliment. The fragrant gardens with the *Raat ki Rani* flower drenching the air with perfume that intoxicated and seduced, enveloping her in its sensual embrace.

'This was their love nest,' she whispered.

She walked inside the towering double-domed arch guided by the last few rays of the sun, and looked up at the protruding window, the *jharokha*. Bee gasped when she saw the girl who frequented her dreams, standing there looking towards the *Haveli*.

A velvet, ruby-coloured shawl covered her hair. She stood poised at the window waiting, expectant eyes gazing outwards, the last ray of the sun illuminating her breathtaking beauty.

A royally dressed man suddenly surprised her from behind and she turned laughing in his arms; a picture so perfect it made Bhavya want to smile through her tears.

The next instant the happy couple vanished and left Bhavya wondering about the illusion. She entered the room closest to the courtyard forming the centre, thinking about these strange visions, hoping she was not losing her mind.

The bare room she entered swam before her eyes. She somehow knew the room was at the end of a long passage that circled the perimeter of the tomb. She walked to the fireplace on the side.

A large gilded mirror had hung there, its surface shiny, reflecting the girl of her dreams as she adjusted the beautiful green dupatta on her head, as she fussed with her earring, looked at the door, sighed, then giggled at her silliness, a young girl waiting for her lover.

How she knew this she wasn't sure but she knew this room held memories, moments of love forever captured within its walls. An empty echoing room, it had patiently waited. There was some light filtering in from an overhead *roshandan,* allowing her the luxury of sight. It was a room that was most likely used by Noorie herself.

The tomb was a mix of Mughal and Rajasthani architecture. Bhavya took in all the small details that amalgamated the two varied styles, the arches and beams effortlessly merging with the decorative corbel brackets, the *chataris* and the *jaalis* or lattice screens reminiscent of the palaces of Rajasthan.

She walked ahead, the filtered light illuminating the stone path under her feet from the overhead prism-like glass squares. Small pools of rainbow hues danced at her feet forming a patterned pathway of light.

*I have crossed Noorie's tomb so many times and yet never saw the splendour that lay before me under the dust and neglect. Someone really put a lot of thought to make this house exquisite,* she thought.

Bhavya walked along the path created out of reflected light, her thoughts on the journal that she had neglected till now.

Her fingers trailed on the grey-chipped walls as she moved from room to room, empty but full of memories and music. As she looked at her trailing fingers, she saw another hand superimposed on hers, a thinner, younger hand.

Vermillion glass bangles tinkled at the fragile wrists. Laughter rang out as a lithe, young woman ran down this curving, tunnel-like passage. Her light hair the colour of sunbeams curled at her temples and shone in the lamp light as did her eyes that sparkled with joy…the kind Bhavya recognised comes from the knowledge that one is loved.

A subjective emotion but it brought Bhavya to her knees.

*Why am I dizzy? I shouldn't have come on my own,* she thought. *Is it the baby?* She sat down on the dusty floor of the courtyard, her back to the rough wall, knees bent.

She closed her eyes and leaned her head on the wall behind, deciding to rest a while. She knew something was pulling her, helping her along as Charu would say and she wanted to go wherever she was being led. It would give her something to ponder on instead of her own problems for a while.

*Running away again, Bee?* She heard Tenzin's voice in her head. She closed her eyes tight, not wanting to remember.

Her mind scrambled to gain purchase in the vision of the young girl of her dreams, writing intently in the light of the lamp. The ease and confidence indicated that it was a nightly ritual.

Blinking, she dusted the visions away from her eyes.

Aimed with a purpose she strode towards her home, her heart pounding. Her mind latched onto something else besides her own worries after a long time. Buzzing with possibilities, she did not see the glimmer that leaned on the wall. Nor did she hear the tinkle of soft bells as if loving hands were caressing an anklet.

After fielding a slew of preachy sermons on safety from her mother…she hurried through her dinner and then excusing herself on the pretext of tiredness, quickly locked herself in her room. Nestled in the bed she opened the thick handmade pages and began reading the words slowly, carefully.

*I am Noorie, a poor outcaste. I begin my life today. A new life. I wish to erase all traces of what was done to me before this point in time. Though that means that I shall have to forgo the telling of how I first met the man I shall love…forever, the one I know is my other half, my soul mate.*

*So be it. The blot on my soul at the hands of the prince demands that sacrifice. So, all I shall say is that I met him the day the old Noorie died. He is the one who was meant for me.*

*My life, as the daughter of a small Hindu military analyser in the Mughal court of Baz Bahadur, at Malwa, was filled with restrictions and lines that could not be crossed. As the sister of a boy who desperately wanted to be included in the circles of the most powerful in the realm, I was forever on the lookout for being offered as bait. My innocence ended after I had lived for sixteen years on this earth. The week of the annual bazaar is the one I hate with a searing intensity since that day, the day that marked the death of Noorie, as I had been for all those years.*

*It was something that happened often and many times but I blame myself equally, even though Hamad says I shouldn't. I can't help it though. I wish I had been sensible enough to go to the bazaar with my mother and aunts as we normally did. But, I wanted freedom, the price of which I paid with my life. To cut a long story short, I was used, as were many others in those days, by the prince and his entourage of bad-tempered, unruly, drunk-on-power boys. I don't know whether to be happy or sad about that humiliation that has blotted my soul since that shadowed afternoon that turned my life on its head….*

*Why happy you ask?*

*It is because I met the one who is my soul mate, on that day. Hamad Bahadur.*

*He sang to me that day, holding me close till it was time for him to go back to being the Mansabdar, a soldier, protecting the boy who took away the precious gift that I wanted to give to the one I married and loved.*

*Asking me to go back home, he left me on the banks of the Narmada but couldn't take away the fragrance of his gentleness that clung to my heart, reviving it, making it whole.*

*So, I did what he had asked. Draping his cape on the branch that was the only witness to what had transpired, I limped back to my family, determined to forget that horrible afternoon.*

*A month passed without any incident or consequence and I thought I could breathe again. Since that day I had stopped stepping out of the house in fear of coming face to face with my tormentors.*

*Fate decided to decree further punishment. My brother Prithvi stormed into my room one evening and proceeded to reward me with slaps and blows for spoiling his friendship with the young prince. When Maa tried to intervene, he described my fallen status at the hands of the prince and his coterie to my gathered family, thus making my disgrace complete.*

*All the various aunts and uncles and cousins who lived in the house were now privy to my humiliation and rape by the prince and his friends. Baba frowned at me, shaming me further, cursing me for even being born. Maa cried and asked someone to call the vaid, our family healer. Further humiliation of the doctor's questions and a confirmed pregnancy later, I was locked in my room.*

*Whispers reached my isolated incarceration.*

*Whose baby was it? With so many boys involved, it was hard to say.*

*Is there any way we can turn it in our favour, better our lives? I heard my brother ask my father as I pressed my ear to the wooden door.*

*As the days merged one into the other, I heard that now the whole court was aware of my status as the despoiled daughter of a lowly analyst. The Emperor pardoned everyone but only after a deal was struck. My brother was placed at an important position and my father celebrated his steadily growing coffers at the expense of his daughter's ripped innocence.*

*In the process, I felt myself sliding into an abyss of grief and disillusionment. Once the conditions were met, I was once again left to my own devices. No one bothered to ask me about my walks that sometimes lasted a whole day. I was soiled goods, no one cared, not even Maa. My cousins looked at me with pity sometimes but they had been asked to stay clear of me as if even my shadow would bring the same fate upon them.*

*I certainly didn't want to create any further tension so stayed as far away from any human contact as I possibly could. If it wasn't pity, hate and guilt took their place in the eyes that blamed me for what had befallen me. I took to going back to the fallen branch and staring at the waters of the Narmada that flowed nearby.*

*On one such day, as my spirits were ready to give up, I stood close to the edge, contemplating my dilemma.*

*'It would be so easy...I know...all your troubles recede, and the water is cool and will wrap itself around you, welcoming you. It will just be a couple of minutes of pain and then you shall be free of this body.'*

*I didn't turn; I knew who stood behind me. I hid my face, as I did not want him to see my dripping eyes. I had only his gentleness and his song to anchor me in a world filled with disillusionment.*

*And, even he wants me to end my life...I remember thinking.*

*Why can no one love me?*

*Maybe, I should jump. It will be the answer to everyone's pain, I thought then....*

Bhavya jumped as the lights went out. Cursing, she closed the journal, careful of the yellowing pages and the delicate leather. Keeping it safely in a lined box she lay thinking about the young girl from her dreams.

This story seems similar to the ones that Dad told us, minus the reference of the rape of course.

Is that why I had the dream and what I thought was a vision? Because the stories are familiar and I remember Dad describing them in detail. But she has not written the detail, how did he know what colour bangles she wore? Bhavya questioned.

Her thoughts then turned to the words she had read....

*There has never been such hopelessness in my life to warrant even the thought of suicide. What heartbreak Noorie must have had to go through for her to think that drowning herself was the only way out?*

*Was there no one she could go to?* Bhavya pondered.

*Isn't the fear of prejudice keeping you silent? What if today everyone came to know about your peccadilloes? At least Noorie did whatever she had to do to survive. What about you?* Her inner voice questioned.

*I didn't do anything wrong.*

*How many people do you think will agree with you?*

*Society can take a plunge for all I care....*

*And, does this uncaring attitude include your family as well? Do you think your father would approve? Would you be able to meet his eyes? How long can you hide the truth from everyone?*

*I am not duty-bound to tell them anything.*

*Agreed, but similarly neither do you have the right to judge. People in glass house and all that....*

*Stop with the lecture.*

*And I rest my case.*

Losing the battle with her own inner voice did not improve her mood.

*What in the name of God was wrong with us? Why did we think that such decisions could be brushed away with a flick of our wrist? How could we have been unaware of the long-standing consequences of such choices?* The battle in her mind raged on.

She wanted to call Tenzin and speak with him about the journal and her dreams. Talk to him about his childhood and his life as an orphan but even as her eyes sought out the phone, her hands remained unmoving, caught in the trap of her ego.

Restless, she walked out to the porch to watch the sky change colour. As she observed the iridescent blues bleeding away into nothingness she acknowledged that she had several unanswered questions. Questions she should have had the maturity to ask Tenzin at the time she had walked out.

She slapped her forehead, wondering if she had ever really gauged his depth or the struggle that he went through as a child. She knew some bits of his childhood but she had been so focused on living in the moment, on moving ahead that she had missed finding out what had made Tenzin the man he is today.

'Now, I don't know what to feel, shit...' she muttered, angry with herself.

*Where do I go from here?*

*Bhavya sleeps the troubled sleep of humans who have much to hide.*

*She worries too much. Uma used to call her 'my troublemaker' and the moniker stuck. She would attract stray souls to her from the beginning. She would bring them home and then expect her family to find the solutions to their problems, the most recent example being Gaurav or maybe, Tenzin.*

*She is the warrior, winning the war and leaving others to deal with the routine issues and problems that are resultant of any action.*

*Tenzin too is a lost soul whom she found and wanted to put back together. An orphan with no background or family and yet she chose him to stay with. What a dramatic eruption it was when she informed her family.*

*The straight talking Bhavya would not let the news that she was living with a man without marrying him reach her family from some other source. Therefore, she sent Tenzin on an errand and broke the news. She knew her family was already taken with him and his elegant, reserved charm. And so, before her family, she confessed of her living arrangements.*

*She withstood Arun's harsh words that do not bear repeating but almost folded at her mother's disappointed gaze.*

*'Why?' My Uma asked heartbroken.*

*'Because he matters.'*

*'Then marry him,' shouted Arun.*

*'I am not ready for that.' She had not bothered to glance at her seething father.*

*'Why not, you are doing everything else,' he said, drawing first blood. I cringed at his words.*

*He has not developed a sieve to his tongue even now, after he was left apologetic and beset with guilt the last time. His similarly crude words at Bhavya's role in Aruna's first marriage ending in a disaster had taught him nothing, it seemed.*

*'That is not your concern, Dad. And, I don't want to marry him because I have grown up with your example before me. I don't want to repeat the same mistake that you both made.'*

*She met his eyes, head on, not a flicker of fear or shame in them.*

*Two tall warriors facing each other ready to battle, only the swords were missing.*

*'Bhavya, that's enough.' Uma warned.*

*'I am not asking for your permission, I am affording you the respect of letting you know. Please don't mistake my courtesy for weakness.' She said before sailing out, her head held high.*

*An exceptionally uncomfortable dinner later, it was Tenzin who went up to Arun and reassured him that he was not taking advantage of his daughter and he would do everything in his power to ease her life there. Arun knew that once his daughter dug in her heels he had no influence on her. So, he nodded and remained sour-faced for the rest of the days that Tenzin and Bhavya were here.*

*Uma took one look at the sincerity and determination in Tenzin's eyes and gave in. She worried but not so much now. Good at reading people, she knew Tenzin was overly protective and her daughter would find the stability she needed with this man. Diametrically opposite in nature as Tenzin and Bhavya were, these two strong individuals were bound to create friction, she knew. That night, her mind had worked double time trying to come up with what she would tell the relatives if they came to know.*

*Now Bhavya is trying to outrun her thoughts, her problems. That feat can be achieved in many ways. Some immerse themselves in their work; try to find the way out of their problems and others read long-lost journals.*

*Bhavya finds solace within the fragile pages of the journal written with henna-dyed hands, centuries before her.*

*What remains to be seen is where it will all end.*

*How I wish I could narrate this story....*

# 20

## *Hiraeth*

## A homesickness for a home that you can't return to or that never was

(Language: Welsh)

The next day passed in much the same way as the day before that and the day before that...Bhavya slipped into Charu's room needing to be close to her younger sister.

*It is like I never left?*

*How do they love so deeply, so unconditionally? I always knew I could return home anytime. In this same house are people who do not have that option. Gaurav can never go back to his family and Suresh Uncle does not have anyone but us. When and why do we start taking families for granted?* She thought tracing the mural with her eyes.

Most days she felt part of the fabric of her family who had found ways to include her in their daily routine.

From discussing the latest case laws with Fanny who had joined Law College to gardening with Ma and laughing over the silliness everyone got into, she was accepted into the fold.

And yet the feeling of being alien prevailed....

She opened the crumbly journal, and gave herself up to the events that unfolded before her.

*As I swayed forward, a large hand wrapped around my fragile elbow and pulled me back. He shook me hard once, his face red with anger, his eyes filled with worry.*

*'Really, is that the answer? What about your baby, this innocent being that is part of you?' He shouted at me.*

*'I don't want it, it is evil,' I said.*

*'Is it…why?'*

*'I…I…every time it moves I remember everything; it has tainted me. Everything was fine…' I said, crying at the unfairness of the times.*

*'The baby that is not even born yet has spoiled your life, not the bastards who raped you, not the brother and parents who betrayed you but this…this little baby is the cause of all your problems?' he said, his voice deceptively measured.*

*'What do you want from me? I am doing what I can to survive.' I said his words making me rethink my own feelings.*

*'It does not matter what anyone else wants; what do you want to do?'*

*'To kill myself.'*

*'You are so…foolish, do what you want.' He said and turned around to leave.*

*'Wait,' I said, grasping at his arm. He shoved me away but as I stumbled, he righted me gently, and then silently walked away leaving me standing there, as if all the words he wanted to use on me had dried up, as if he couldn't bear to look at me anymore.*

*'What do you want from me?' I screamed at his retreating back, not wanting to lose the one person who stood beside me.*

*'I want you to fight…fight for yourself, for this baby, for everything that has been taken away.'*

*'How? Why?' I said confused, unable to fathom how I could possibly fight the forces that stood against me…status, money and gender.*

*'Because you are alive, don't throw that away, Noorie.'*

*'Why do you care?' I asked, wanting to hear just one kind word from his lips, a hope that I knew I would cling to for the rest of my days.*

*That made him turn around.*

*'I…I…don't care.'*

*'Are you telling me you follow all the young girls the prince rapes, that you check after their health...that you sing to them?'*

*Where was I getting the courage to talk to him like that even I didn't know, but the words just kept flowing out of my mouth?*

*He looked at me with panicked eyes and then shook his head as if to clear it before walking away.*

*I stood at the edge of the churning water and smiled for the first time in months; my eyes saw hope and a clear path before me. I would not give in to the despair that wanted to drown me. I would survive because that was the choice I made that day.*

*My days took on a different hue since that evening. I spoke to Maa asking her what my future held.*

*A corner in the house, forever dependent on my brothers for everything, I would essentially be a bonded slave, who would not even be paid.*

*The alternative was equally horrible, a marriage to a widowed old man who would overlook my tainted status. Maa warned me that since the word had spread that I was pregnant, even that would be unlikely.*

*Hurt beyond words at her pragmatic answer, I asked her the fate of my child, my own I could still handle. Her answer chilled me to the bones. She told me to pray that it was not a girl; otherwise a pot of milk to drown her awaited her arrival into this world.*

*Her words ringing in my ears, I took matters into my own hands.*

*And so, on a full moon night, I, a girl not yet 17, tied a few clothes together, took the coins that I had saved and slipped out of my place of confinement.*

*It had stopped being my home a long time back. Lighter after having shed the weight of honour, I walked to the area not frequented by decent women. Our weekly jaunts to the market had meant that we had to hurriedly cross the road in front of Panna Mandi. None of those furtive, wide-eyed looks had prepared me for the glittering and striking place that sheltered the most cultured and refined ladies of the night. I had never imagined that I would take the turn into the packed road that led to the houses run by the women who lived there.*

*Walking up to a man who stood before the biggest and cleanest house I asked to meet the madam. He took a minute to assess the raggedy clothes and the rounded stomach and took me to rooms that were palatial in their decorations.*

*'What have you brought me, Shafquat Mian?' said a bold voice from behind a heavy curtain of beads.*

*'I am Noorie and I chose to leave my house. Will you train me, Madame? I can sing,' I said, my voice trembling, my eyes fixed on the coloured beads.*

*I have to confess that if she would have asked me to sing I would have simply fainted, for I had never sung a note in my life.*

*'You look like you belong to a good house,' the voice remarked.*

*'Can you see this baby I carry?' I asked, pressing the loose kurta snug over my just-starting-to-show belly. 'It has no father; or rather there are too many fathers out of whom I don't know which one is responsible for this.'*

*There was a hearty laugh and then silence. After a couple of minutes, which had me sweating and wondering if I could retrace my steps, for if I was refused, there was no other way forward for me, the curtain of beads parted.*

*A big, bejewelled woman came out from within its interiors looking at me with kohl-lined, opal-coloured eyes that seemed to pierce my soul.*

*'You girl are a tigress, and don't ever forget it. Now tell me your story. Come.' She said gazing at the softly changing sky in the distance.*

*We sat together as I recounted the past months to Ammi, as everyone called her, till the moon crawled across the sky and gave way to the sun. The other girls came and went, listening and sympathising with my predicament. I cried and was held against the soft bosom of a woman who, for the first time since that fateful afternoon, had not shunned me...besides, of course, the man who I had no way of ever meeting again.*

*'You are brave and did well to come here. Allah knows what your family would have done to this child if it is a girl.' She said, sadness surrounding her like a shroud.*

*I knew but didn't want to dwell on it so just sniffled and snuggled deeper in her perfumed softness.*

*'Come now before you fall asleep on me, I will take you to your room,' she said after a while, shaking the pity away.*

*'I can stay here you mean?'*

*'Silly girl, of course, but you will have to pull your weight. Remember, nothing is ever free; there is always a price to pay.'*

*I followed Ammi into the interiors of my new home, ready to do what was necessary to survive on my own terms.*

*As the days passed, I heard my parents had declared me and my unborn child dead. I had apparently taken my life by drowning myself in the river in the forest. Shafquat Mian said they found my dupatta on the banks of the calmly flowing river.*

*When Ammi came to know of this she asked me to start writing down what I had gone through.*

*I think she worries for my mental health. She says it will be like a marham, a balm on my wounds, whatever that means, but since I have decided to start this new life it is only right that I begin from here again. The old one does not matter anymore.*

*She thinks I am troubled about what has happened to me, what my parents did. But, I am not concerned with them. They did what they thought necessary, what they had been taught to do. I have to move forward for this child that grows inside me at whatever cost to myself.*

Bhavya shut the sewn pages closed, the words blurred because of the tear film that covered them. The words strung together by the young Noorie ricocheting in her head, seeming too close to her own feelings.

'I have to move forward for this child that grows inside me at whatever cost to myself.' She said aloud to the empty room.

*When does our innocence get corrupted? Is it when our bodies are raided or our minds or is it when our heart is shattered,* she wondered,

*Why does he not understand?* She asked herself for the umpteenth time missing Tenzin with an ache that permeated her bones. 'Bee.'

'BEE,' her mother said again rattling the handle of the locked door. She quickly shut the book and wrapping it in its cloth placed it gently in Charu's foot trunk. Rubbing her eyes, she yanked the door open.

'Why have you locked this door?' Uma asked walking in, looking about her to see what her daughter had been up to.

Bhavya yawned, faking sleepy eyes. 'Oh! I just went to sleep, Ma,' she said lying down on the bed.

Uma sat next to her, rubbing Bhavya's forehead with her soft fingers.

'Bee, you were never able to lie to me. You don't have to, you know right?'

'I am not....'

'Anyway, I wanted to tell you to be ready tomorrow afternoon.'

'Why, where are we going?' Bhavya asked, skipping over the part about lying to her mother.

'To Darshana Aunty, the gynaecologist, you need to meet her now.' She said, getting up to tidy the *dohar* that lay at the foot of the bed.

'Ma...' Bhavya whispered, her eyes tearing up. 'I wanted to tell you....'

'It's okay. Sometimes we need some time to let it sink in. Is this why you came back? Don't you want the baby, Bee?'

When Bhavya just kept silent, Uma tried again.

'You know you can tell me, I won't make the same mistake as I did with Aruna. I will try and understand, Bee...your reasons...I...just...kept waiting for you to tell me...but not anymore. You are coming with me, okay?'

'Yes, of course, Ma...I am sorry,' said Bhavya, wrapping her arms around her mother's ample waist and holding on tight. Uma clucked her tongue at her daughter's silliness but held her tight against her.

Bhavya reckoned that Noorie was talking about 'this' feeling of comfort that spreads all over when we know that we are accepted, unconditionally.

'You don't ever have to be sorry, *meri jaan.* You know we are always with you. But don't hide anymore. Deal with your life, Bee; it is not going away just because you choose not to see it.' Uma said, stroking the flyaway curls on her daughter's head that were so like her in their adamant unruliness.

'Oh Ma! I messed up. Really badly and I don't know what to do now, I feel lost and alone.'

'Is Tenzin involved in this mess that you have created?'

'I…Ma, I ca….'

'Hmmm…first things first,' said Uma, 'come and have dinner now, the rest can wait.'

She slowly limped out of the room, her deformed leg aching from standing too long on it.

Bhavya sat on the side of the bed, her head bent, wanting to cry.

*I am such a failure, always a disappointment. I should have told them, all of them. Why do I keep thinking only of myself? Is he right…am I selfish?*

Maybe it was the words Noorie had written so many centuries ago, the young girl who lost her childhood and her family's love in a flicker an eyelid…or was it the uncertain future of her unborn child that was bringing on this feeling of vulnerability? It could have been the look of disappointment in her mother's eyes or the realisation of her own over-entitlement….

Whatever the reason, Bhavya admitted to herself that her family had always stood by her. Whatever happened she had been able to count on them and now she was holding them to ransom, expecting them to understand without asking questions.

*If only Noorie could have had a family like mine she would surely have had a different life. Why does it take someone's misfortune to show us our own good luck?* She wondered.

With her mind made up, she walked out to the dining room and looked at the family gathered there. There was noise and commotion with Dad and Suresh Uncle discussing the ins and outs of the oncoming expansion with Gaurav. There was love evidently displayed as Bhuvan snuggled his sleepy daughter on his shoulder and Aruna looked at them indulgently, stroking her rounded belly. There was bickering between the triplets and Dheeraj, something to do with what was on the menu tomorrow. And, then there was Ma, her eyes calm and supportive in the midst of the storm she was going to unleash today.

She took strength from that and squaring her shoulders raised her voice over the din.

'Everyone, listen, I have some news to share. I am no longer with Tenzin...I mean for...I am still deciding what I will do in the future but that much is certain and...' she gulped the fear in her throat, '...I am pregnant.'

Of all the reactions she may have expected what she got was the last she could have fathomed. Everyone gasped, then looked over her shoulder. Her eyes moved from one family member to the other, her brow knitting in confusion.

'Really, this is news for certain. Whose is it and when were you planning to share this news with me?' She heard Tenzin say from behind her.

# 21

## *Soliloquy*

## An act of speaking one's thoughts aloud when by oneself or regardless of any hearers, especially by a character in a play

(Language: English with Latin roots)

Bhavya shrieked and whirled around.

'Ten...Tenzin... What are you doing here?'

'I came to meet my fiancée,' who it seems has many things she would like to explain. When were you going to tell me, Bee?'

'I...I...' she knew there was no backtracking.

*Your penchant for grand declarations has to end.*

'Lost for words, are we?' He said softly. She could see the hurt in his eyes.

'Ten-sing *beta,* come in and have some dinner, Bee was just...' Uma tried intervening, trying to diffuse the volatile situation.

'Ma, I heard every word. There is no mistaking what she said. Though Bee, I wish you could have told me first before you declared it to your family. After all, I am the one being left...' he said, taking in her wide eyes and still form.

'I apologise for the disturbance, I will wait for you to call me. We need to talk.' He said to the silent audience before quietly walking out of the door.

In the pin-drop silence of the room Arun's controlled voice rang out like glass crashing.

'What did he mean by whose is it, Bee?'

Tenzin heard her father ask the question in the otherwise quiet house as he was about to close the door behind his back. Wincing he considered going back and clarifying, obviously she had not told them everything. Then decided against it, he just did not have the strength right now.

*She could handle the backlash of the decision now that she had clearly decided on leaving him…and for what?*

A smarting conscience made him slow his steps. He knew her too well not to be able to predict her next move. The sound of her approaching footsteps had him sagging with gratitude. He was about to get into the car and would not have been able to delay driving away any further. It also told him she had not answered her father's question.

'Wait,' she shouted from some distance away. 'Why did you say that?' Irate when he sat behind the wheel, she got in the other side. 'And whose car is this?'

'What did I say? And I hired it when I landed.' He answered.

'Whose is it…the baby…whose is it? Really, did you really have to ask that?' she said, annoyed.

'Did you know about the baby when you left Paris?'

Silence.

'You knew this when you left and you chose to keep it from me. It makes me wonder about your intentions with the baby. That is one reason. Second, you were willing to tell your family before you told me.'

'Tenzin, most of them figured it out, the rest would have in a while.' She said, not meeting his eyes knowing she had been unfair to him.

Tenzin was silent; she knew he was hurt and angry at her misstep. And it was a huge misstep, she would have been livid. But the fact that she admitted it to herself did not mean she would admit it to him.

'Well, are we going to tell them the complete truth or only what suits you?' He asked finally.

'Why do you keep making me the culprit? We went into it together and obviously I cannot tell them that I am unsure of the father of this baby because I had sex with my fiancé and another guy.'

'Kabir, your friend, you mean,' he spat out. 'I hope you can see how complicated this makes the whole situation. We could have just done what was necessary without involving....'

He took a deep breath, and then started the engine to drive to the empty lanes of the India Gate quadrangle. They sat in silence as the intermittent street lights bathed them in shadows and muted light.

'Why are you here?'

'To see you, why else would I come here, I don't have any family here. First you leave me and run to your family refusing to cut the umbilical cord. Then I hear that you have left me for good and then you break the news that you are pregnant to them before you tell me. What do you expect me to think?'

'That's unfair and what is all this about umbilical cords...you want me to cut ties with my family too?'

'No...no that's not what I...I want us to be a family, Bhavya, but you are too dependent on yours to make one for yourself. You run to them when you face problems outside and away from them when you face issues within. Instead of coming here could you not have spoken to me, been patient, worked though our issues together?' He tried to explain.

'This is getting us nowhere...the point is that you know about the baby now and...you too could have trusted me to know what is good for me. You too could have told me the truth.'

'What truth?' Tenzin asked confounded at her inability to see that keeping the news of the baby from him had hurt him terribly. 'What could be bigger than what you have just disclosed? You are pregnant...PREGNANT!'

'I know what I am, I have known for a while....'

'How far along are you?' Tenzin asked softly looking at her, his eyes still shocked.

'In my second trimester....'

'Secon...that means 4–6 months right, but you were not showing...When did you know...for how long?' Tenzin asked his voice tormented.

'I had just come to know a couple of weeks back that I had been three months pregna...I...I didn't realise...I...I'm sorry Ten....'

'You knew about the baby when you left Paris...didn't you?'

Bhavya wanted to lie, say no to his question, knowing she had hurt him immeasurably by only thinking of herself at the time.

'Yes,' she said instead, knowing she had to stop running, face whatever came next.

'You were three months pregnant when you left m... And you chose to hide this from me...why Bee...why would you do that to me...do you really hate me that much?' Tenzin said devastated at the unrelenting hurt that had lodged itself between them, opening a chasm so wide that he felt unable to cross over to her side.

'You never wanted...kids,' she said after a while.

'Neither did you and yet here we are...facing the reality of our choices.'

'What...what reality? Have you ever considered that what you claim to be unimportant may be important to me? I don't want to be controlled.'

Tenzin looked at Bee who sat with her arms crossed, chin jutting out, her face set, looking out of the window, shutting him out.

*This woman is still a mystery to me.*

He knew she carried baggage from her life before him but then so did he. He had figured that she would begin to trust him with time but all time had done was highlight their differences.

*And, she was spooked... Spooked at the possibility of spending her life with him or because of the baby?* He wondered.

He had tried to prove his commitment to her again and again and yet she denied its depth. *What more can I do*? He questioned looking at her profile.

*Baby, a baby, mine...and Bee's,* he felt a rush of such gratitude, his heart trembled.

He knew whatever happened in the future he would do everything in his power to keep the baby she carried safe and loved.

*My baby will not be without his father as I was,* he resolved in that moment.

Taking a deep breath he tried again.

'So your fear is that if we get married or you have this baby I will make you give up your job and your freedom, dictate who you will talk to, who you will meet and essentially control you and all your decisions. Is this really how you see me, Bee? How may I ask did you come by this consensus?'

Silence.

'Ah! Let me guess, because I am not agreeable to your continued association with Kabir, because I asked you to stop meeting him?' Tenzin said his words ice cold.

'I thought you were different. You kept in touch with her, behind my back. How are you not a hypocrite?'

'I fought the system for you, didn't I?'

'Are we again on the rant about that? Let me tell you, you did it for yourself. You wanted to be with me, you did not do me any favours, Tenzin. How can you put this all on me? If you defied the company and started a relationship with me, it was not as if I twisted your arm, so stop lording it over me. It was your choice. I did not coerce you in any way. The proposal was again yours. Yes, I accepted but I did so in good faith. How am I to know that you did not do that to solidify your position with the company's big honchos?

'And what of your ex-girlfriend? You are still in touch with her, aren't you, sending her messages and such. Have I ever asked you to break it off with her? How can the rules be different for us?' She accused.

The silence that followed her monologue was deafening.

'The rules are not different. You know about my childhood and reality of it in Leh and it was to escape it, make something of myself, that I left. I can admit I should have told you before we went there but I did not think it mattered. I was nineteen, Bhavya, a child and you are an adult. There is nothing going on, we did not sleep together.' He said.

'She remained unmarried; you are sending money to her since forever.' Bhavya retaliated.

'It was her choice to remain unmarried and not because of me. Everyone's goal in life is not to marry, Bee, you know that. Some people would just like to....'

'Oh come on! You keep fooling yourself, buddy. That lady is carrying a torch for you and you know it.'

'Our situations are different, Bee. You cannot compare the two. I transfer the funds to her because she manages the accounts for the school and the NGO. I send the books and gifts to her for the children at the orphanage. I have no say in her life or the decisions she makes. That is all and you know it.'

'And, I don't think this is necessary or should be the topic of discussion right now instead of the baby but I want to put your mind to rest once and for all.

'About the company, you know me better than that...I would not propose marriage to save my job. Kabir, on the other hand, depends on you to guide him, discusses everything with you, and I am pretty sure you do too. I am sure you can see a difference...' he said, his tone stiff and exasperated that he was being forced to explain himself.

'It matters to me. You talk about trust, how will I ever trust you knowing that you purposefully hid this aspect of your life from me? What makes you think that I will not wonder what else you are hiding?' She said frustrated at his inability to accept his need to keep in touch with his first love.

'Are you telling me that...forget it... Where is all this coming from and since when have you been carrying this spite inside? Look, this isn't the time, why can we not talk sensibly even for five minutes?'

'I don't know. You should never have proposed marriage; we anyway never got around to talking about it after the initial euphoria died down.' Bhavya said, frustrated.

'Look, I am tired and need to sleep. I came straight from the airport wanting to see you. Let's talk tomorrow.'

'Where will you stay?'

'I will get a room.' He just wanted silence.

'Come to the *Haveli*, stay there.' *Why did I say that?*

'I don't think that will be wise.' *I cannot deal with this right now.*

'Why? Can you not be civil until I decide how to proceed?'

'We...you mean....'

'No...I...or do I need permission for that as well?' Bhavya said, unable to help the barb she threw his way.

'That's not the case and why are you hell bent to construe every word that I utter in the worst possible way?' He said, exasperated.

'Then come, I will not be...able to explain your leaving to my family.'

'Ah...the truth...finally. What do you want, Bhavya?' He said and turned the car towards the *Haveli*.

'I...I don't know.'

He got out of the car and walked back to the *Haveli*. It felt peculiarly angry with him.

Shaking his head at his fanciful thoughts, he entered the threshold only to bang his forehead against the overhead hanging light that illuminated the main door. Once a welcoming pool of light, it seemed to have turned against him.

Rubbing his hand on the bump he could feel forming on his forehead, he walked down the corridor to reach the dining area, wondering what he would see in her family's eyes.

*Defensive anger, what else? You are responsible for their daughter's pain. What did you expect?* He thought as he walked in to be judged and found wanting.

*That girl, she didn't even tell Ten-sing...why? What is she hiding and why?* Uma thought worrying the edge of her saree. She looked at Suresh who was talking to Gaurav. As if sensing her eyes on him he turned his head to look at her, communicating the need to be patient to her. Her fingers relaxed and her shoulders that had drooped a minute ago, straightened.

*They would find a way,* thought Uma.

Some movement outside alerted her to further revelations. Bhavya and Tenzin walked in together, much to her relief. Their body language was a different matter altogether; both seemed at odds with each other holding themselves apart.

*Well, at least they are trying to sort out whatever is ailing their relationship,* she thought.

Tenzin, the confident man who had swept her daughter away to distant shores, stood radiating uncertainty before her family now.

'Come in Tenzin, have a bite,' Bhuvan broke the tense silence. 'You must have come here straight as soon as you landed.'

'Yes, thanks.'

He looked at Uma, for her approval to enter her domain, her house.

'Ten-sing *beta*, come, there is *bhindi*...what do you call it...lady's finger and lentils, simple food, but we will eat it together. Let me make fresh rotis for you, these have grown cold,' Uma said, flustered at her inability to work out the etiquette following the revelations just made by her daughter.

'No, no, Ma...' he looked at her guiltily, not sure he had the right to call her Ma anymore in the wake of Bhavya's announcement.

Uma walked up to Tenzin, taking his forearms in her small hands she looked up at his tired face.

'Whatever happens in the future, Ten-sing, you are my son, and you can call me anything you like. Always remember that. Now sit,' she said giving instructions for another place to be set at the table.

Tenzin bent his head and smiled at her, this small lady with a spine of steel. His admiration for her equalled the love he felt for her. He remembered laughing with Bhavya over his child-like infatuation with her mother.

'You are marrying me for my family,' she had pouted.

That had set them laughing till their insides ached.

'It's true...seriously. Since I never knew mine there has been a vacuum that I didn't even realise existed in my life.

Being with her and surrounded by her care and her compassion I realise what I had been missing. You are a lucky girl, Bee, to have this in your life.'

'I am, and you too now. Just remember you said this when she starts running your life for you.' She had said before pouncing on him, smothering him with kisses.

Tenzin was brought to the present when Uma moved away to get the food patting his shoulder as she left.

And so, the tall man, with the head of salt-and-pepper hair accepted that some things will never change and some things never stay the same. He then turned to face the rest of the family to see if he would have to deal with change there or he could rest easy in their familiarity.

*Tenzin is back.*

*Now my Bhavya can smile...or fret, for that is more likely.*

*Sometimes I feel no one has really understood that girl. Everyone sees her the way they see themselves. Arun looks at her and sees trouble and Uma finds the wilful stubborn reflection of her own youth. Aruna and the three angels see her as this strong virago who does as she pleases while Gaurav sees her as a saviour. Dheeraj...well...Dheeraj sees her as a puzzle that he is unable to solve.*

*Everyone loves her as she loves them but no one is able to join all the pieces of her to complete the jigsaw that is Bhavya. Her soft heart under the prickly exterior that she cultivates has been wounded many times.*

*It began with the fear of being left homeless when her parents fought over the way to proceed with the case they were fighting over Me.*

*Then came the crushing guilt she felt at Charu's kidnapping.*

*Arun did not help matters with blaming her for not taking better care of her sister.*

*Ah! Parents, the words they utter in desperation or fleeting helplessness, wound the soft hearts of their children so deeply that it changes them forever.*

*Why do parents forget to think before they speak?*

*But, what do I know; I am stone-hearted...they say.*

*My Bhavya suffered too that day. Watching her sister being sent away left a mark so deep that it took away her ability to enjoy her childhood. And so, a carefree, isolated woman with a bruised sense of self had evolved from the scared, confused and insecure child.*

*Can they not see that she is drowning?*

*They either do not want to hear her cry for help in her bursts of temper or choose to look another way.*

*Only Suresh senses the fractured image of self-worth that she carries within. He was the one to convince Uma to let Bhavya leave for the job in Chandigarh.*

*After having to separate herself from Charu, Uma was not willing to let her go, she saw it as abandoning the family. It was Suresh who helped her understand the difference in Bhavya's personality from her own.*

*My Uma thrives with people around her while Bhavya gets crushed under the weight of expectations. Left to her own devices she will bend backwards for her family but she withers when choice is taken away.*

*Convinced, Uma supported Bhavya, I think she realised that a happy child far away is better than a sad one, close. By letting Bhavya spread her wings and explore open skies she gave her the gift of striving for what she most wanted... freedom.*

*Her prayers to bring her back were heard but my Uma is now worried for the reason her daughter has come home.*

*This night is not easy for me. The stones try hard to cover their ears but so much conjecture is difficult to suppress.*

*Arun is sequestered in his study which has become his safe haven. He fears the words Tenzin had used.*

*Has Bhavya done something to shame him in society? What if it got out? He thinks, worries, always more concerned for his name, his standing in society.*

*Do souls ever change, I wonder. Lifetimes can pass and yet the insecurities remain the same, as does his struggles it seems.*

*Uma and Suresh whisper worried at the crisis brewing. The topic remains the same but the direction of thought is disparate compared to Arun. What should they do to mend the gap between Bhavya and Tenzin that was evident to them?*

*As Uma grows impatient, Suresh calms her telling her to give the two space to sort out the details in their own time. He is a sensible man, our Suresh. Having known him for decades, I can safely say that he thinks like me.*

*All the inhabitants that rest within me are thinking about the same thing tonight. Each one in this family would stand before Bhavya to protect and help, their love strong enough to make them overlook their own judgements about her actions.*

*Now that is what I long for....*

# 22

## *Kairos*

## The perfect, delicate, crucial moment; the fleeting rightness of time and place that creates the opportune atmosphere for action, words or movement

(Language: Ancient Greek)

The discomfort of sharing space with someone who has hurt us is a difficult proposition. Add to that simmering tensions and it makes for a toxic mix.

When Bhavya took Tenzin to her room, he just stood at the door and could not seem to take the step forward to enter. He looked at the bed that held memories of dark, velvety nights and bright, sunny days.

The sun had dripped on her uncovered body, filtered through the unrealistic gauzy curtains with holes in them.

*What had she called them…chikankari work,* he remembered, *from Jaipur.*

He remembered kissing the spots of sunlight that formed perfect circles on her skin. The giggling, the muted laughter and the joyful abandon that sharing more than just your bodies brings.

*Where had all that fun gone? Was he irresponsible, too old, too simple in his demands, too vanilla as she had accused him of being?*

He looked at Bhavya, who stood lost in thought her back to him.

She had not been able to tell Tenzin but she had in a moment of weakness considered aborting the life that was now growing strong within her, then had thought of giving up the baby, just leaving and never coming back. She had immediately felt repentant, apologising to the baby for her thoughts that whispered doubts.

She could barely take care of herself, what gave her the idea that she could take care of a fragile baby?

*Could she even love it as a mother was supposed to?*

She was not sure.

She loved Tara she knew but she also knew that she could be the good aunt that spoiled her rotten, not the disciplinarian mother. 'Oh God, I am so fucked up! What gave me the idea that I could have this baby?' Bhavya said under her breath.

'Bee?'

Bhavya spun around. She was trying to compose her expression...to hide...though there was nothing left to hide from him.

Noting her troubled eyes Tenzin said, 'I think I will take one of the rooms upstairs.'

'Why?' She asked, taking a step forward, standing too close.

Her smell wrapped its feathery arms around his head swaying his resolve. He had come to talk, find a solution and work at the problem. The fact that she was pregnant was a concern that he had not foreseen but he realised there was no way he could leave now without resolving their issues.

He took a step back. The dance ensued.

They looked at each other, silent, locked in their minds in a battle of wills. Who would admit that they needed the other first?

Placid eyes turned smouldering in a second. The elegant and debonair man before her turned into an Adonis. It was a subtle change that would be easily missed if one was not paying attention. His breathing became deeper, his face intense, focused on her. With his angular jaw rigid, and his mouth a thin line, he watched her with a piercing gaze that arrowed down her body, igniting an analogous flame within her.

His body strained and held itself in check, barely, as his muscles rippled under his white shirt. His hands at his side clenched and unclenched as if he could not wait for her invite to put them on her. She could sense the need rising within him though he would never advertise it till she gave him a hint that she was willing.

Instinct and need took over, panting she nodded, then waited for him to pounce.

The weeks without her had resulted in dominance over himself, hard won but existent nonetheless. Tenzin shivered, straining against the control he stood exerting over his will to devour her.

Their eyes on each other, both did not know the exact moment when their lips met. When did his hands grip her hair, arch her neck to bite and lick at the pulse that throbbed. When did she push him against the wall to rub against him, an invitation or a pleading?

Her fingers pulled at his nape, trying to bring him closer even as she latched on to his lean, hard body. Curling her leg around his thigh she tried to appease the ache that thrummed within, against his straining need.

When even this became unbearable, they moved towards the bed. All finesse and softness lost, he grabbed skin that needed rough hands to rub and mould and squeeze. Their lovemaking had never been undemanding. Both sought reaffirmation of their desires and needs that exploded inside them with a mere caress.

All they wanted was touch, the rougher the better. Biting, licking, sucking down the expanse of her body, Tenzin reached the nub he sought. As his lips surrounded the throb there, Bee flew. A burst of colour…a rainbow exploded in her mind as he used his hands and lips to torment and to lap at and sooth the ache he created. She lay panting at this assault and he still wasn't done. Grabbing her by her bare thighs, he plunged deep, eliciting a guttural cry from her parched throat. A punishing pace, eyes that scorched skin, fingers just a tad less than cruel and she was flying again.

'Te…Tenzin…let me up,' she muttered after a restful minute.

'No, I am not done.'

'Wha…' was all she got out before he flipped her, over sheets that smelled of them. His lips ran a line down her spine and kisses turned to nips.

Bhavya rejoiced, finding the freedom to become her true self. The one that could equal each bite with one that was harder, more painful, and equally erotic. As she turned her head to tell him that she wanted her turn, he pushed her head down on the pillow.

'Shhhh, today it's my turn, you get yours next time.' He whispered and proceeded to destroy all defences she had erected.

Raising her knees his hands found and exploited hidden treasures. All Bhavya could do under his never-ending assault was relax her mind and her body to follow him down the path he was leading them. Her mind scrambled as she received the gifts he bestowed on her.

However, a small part of her brain, that stood slightly apart observing his onslaught, wondered cynically:

*What was the urgency? What was he after? Was this some kind of a test?*

'Where do we go from here?' Tenzin asked, passing the bottle of water to her.

Bhavya understood exactly what he was talking about.

'I don't know, Tenzin. I don't know how to begin mending what I don't consider broken.'

'Why did you hide it from me for so long...four months?'

'Does he know?' he asked as an afterthought.

'Yes,' she said.

Both kept silent after that, their thoughts taking them to their own realities that their mind had conjured about their marriage. She turned her back to him, staring at the wall and thought of all the times she had disregarded his need for reassurance.

*But did a grown man need so much reassurance?*

She opened the journal to read the next few pages, Tenzin's presence next to her filling the space that had needed a familiar comfort. Sighing, she opened the page she had bookmarked and lost herself in Noorie's life.

*One chapter closes and another begins.*

*My training is well underway, the days are filled with riyaaz and learning to play the tanpura. My only anchor in this unpredictable abyss called life is the baby I have come to love as my own and no one else's. Ammi oversees my daily schedule and I share my thoughts with her fearlessly. The only secret I guard is the memory of a man who was as rigid as he was gentle. I keep it alive like a flame that dispels the gloom and gives the illusion of warmth that one can see but cannot touch.*

*I keep his memory alive, despite knowing that I will never see him again, reliving in my mind the moments we had spent together. Every night at dusk I cloister myself in my quarters and for ten minutes, not more nor less, I think of him, weave impossible dreams, hum the song I had heard him sing, hope against hope that he would find me, then smile and berate myself for this foolhardiness.*

*One day, while preparing the hookah for Ammi, lulled by exhaustion I hummed the notes of that song, wishing for the impossible.*

*'Where did you hear that song?' Ammi asked suddenly.*

*Looking up I saw that Ammi was sitting, her hand holding the paan frozen midway to her mouth, her expression aghast.*

*'Nowhere...just something I heard a man sing, once...in another lifetime.'*

*'A man? Which man? The one who...' She asked, her face ashen.*

*'No, no Ammi, he was the one who saved me, even from myself.' I said, trying to reassure her.*

*'Have you met him again?'*

*'No.'*

*'Why?'*

*'He is....' I stopped, not wanting to share any more about him. He was a spot of sunshine in my otherwise dark life, the only thing that brought some light and colour to it. I selfishly wanted to keep him all to myself.*

*'It doesn't matter, I am sure he doesn't remember me.' I said instead.*

*'You talk in riddles, girl,' said Ammi but I could see that her mind was churning behind her composed eyes.*

Bhavya wiped a tear that had slipped out of the corner of her eye and swallowed a sob that rose unbidden from her throat.

*What strength it must have taken for her to be able to hold on to this perception of hope without even the possibility of it ever coming to pass,* she thought, before marking the page.

# 23
## *Alexithymia*
### The inability to describe emotions verbally

(Language: English, Origin: Greek)

Tenzin looked at Bhavya at the breakfast table, as she cut open the fruit precisely into squares. Remembering her need to gobble it whole versus his need for correct presentation, he could not help but ponder on the effects of time and conditioning.

*Did I do this to her? Can someone influence another life to such an extent that it changes their personality? Does she resent me for this change?*

Bhavya's face mirrored the emotional roller coaster she was on. She sat looking down at the neat squares, her brow furrowed as if she had not realised what she had been doing.

She looked up meeting his eyes, a similar realisation welling in hers. Tenzin saw her expression go from confusion to accusation to anger. She got up and walked away, bristling. Sighing with regret, Tenzin looked at everything but at the innocently sacrificed fruit. He felt responsible for causing her pain and he did not know what he could do to get things back on track. It was not easy living with her either.

*Could they have made a mistake? Was marrying her akin to caging her as she had accused him of doing?*

His mind posed so many questions to which he had not even one answer at his disposal.

Gaurav looked at the man before him, not sure if he wanted to punch him or sympathise with him. He looked so forlorn sitting at the table, shoulders drooping, completely out of his element.

He knew how difficult Bhavya and her mercurial mood swings could be and by his assessment Tenzin was essentially a straightforward guy who expected everyone else also to behave similarly.

In business, that translated to astuteness but in the matters of the heart the poor man was at sea. Bhavya could be hot one minute and cool as ice the next, adamant or laidback, all with a monstrous ego. As a friend, he too had been hard-pressed not to throttle her a few times, more than a few, truth be told.

All he wanted to do now was to keep his promise that he had made to himself. He remembered feeling immensely grateful that first night he had bunked at the *Haveli,* at the mercy of this large boisterous family.

He would keep his head down and do his work, not ruffle any feathers, never break the unspoken trust this family had placed in him. He would never lead but neither would he get plastered.

He pitied these two strong people and their need to assert themselves. He was more of a compromise seeker.

*You do realise that you have already broken two of these three promises.*

Shying away from his own glaring shortcomings, he went back to eating his breakfast of *aalu* parathas.

*Life was so much better without drama...I had enough of it in my house, if I can even call it that. I am going to stay away from difficult, emotional people.* He thought, chewing slowly and then his eyes met Etti's and all these sensible thoughts scattered like dust.

She smiled, with just her eyes and he would swear he heard his heart laughing...and insultingly rolling on the floor while doing so.

Aruna also saw Bhavya get up and leave, full of hostility.

*Something has to be done,* she thought.

Tenzin's crestfallen expression, his confused eyes, was the same look that men have when they don't know which way to go. She had seen it on her husband Bhuvan's face enough times to recognise it for what it was.

*Why is my family so melodramatic?* Dheeraj thought, as he looked at them, their thoughts written clearly on their faces. The morning table hummed with anxiety.

*Baba refuses to bend; he should talk to Tenzin, man-to-man, ask him to solve his issues, instead of hiding from the responsibility in his study. I wonder how I would react if my daughter came home pregnant and announced that she was leaving her partner.*

Dheeraj felt unable to voice his thoughts, still unsure if he would be heard over the female voices. He was merely the son that they had wanted and once they achieved that goal, he was left to spring up on his own, like a plant.

With so much happening around him, he sometimes felt invisible, a failure. His sisters were achieving their dreams and he sat in his father's house, eating his food, thinking how weak he was. No wonder no one took him seriously.

# 24

## *Kadota*

## To disappear, vanish, to fade

(Language: Finnish)

Bee barricaded herself in Charu's room and left her family to deal with the precariousness of having an uncertain houseguest. Tenzin had never really spent much time with her family.

She knew Bhuvan would ease him into the family; Aruna's gentle giant was a man who knew how to salvage a situation. Their mother had summoned Aruna...*and like a good daughter; she had arrived as requested, to contain the storm that was named Bee.* They didn't know what to do with her.

She wished she could discuss her problem and the solution thereof with her family, with Ma especially. But, she knew the subject was too volatile for her family to deal with, where would she even begin explaining? Tenzin and she would have to find their way on their own.

With her mind tangled with doubts and hurt, Bhavya could not seem to get her bearings. The harder she tried to find reason, to find the strength to look forward, the more she felt pulled into the past. Like quicksand.

*I could call Charu, ask her to look,* she thought, *I could tell her everything. She would understand.*

*You just want to ask her to tell you the way forward.*

*Well that too,* Bhavya clarified to her inner voice.

*Do you really think anyone can tell you what to do in such a situation?*

Knowing that her inner voice was making sense, she could not refute the logic to keep this to themselves. She lay on her younger sister's bed looking up at the wings of the fan, barely making a sound. She could lie like this for hours, just letting her mind flit about like a cloud.

While the rest of the sisters shared rooms, Charu had her own, owing to her sightlessness. It had been a bizarre decision to her mind to leave Charu all alone and Ma had been so heartbroken when she had sent Charu to their grandmother that no one had the heart to ask for the extra space vacated at her departure.

Charu had never really wanted to step out of the room anyway so Dad had converted the small store at the back of the *Haveli* into a room for her. Facing the mausoleum, it had an unobstructed view of the backyard to the dome of Noorie's resting place, not that Charu had ever beheld the beauty but it was the thought that counted.

Bhavya looked out now, remembering the many times she had stood at the window, murmuring to Charu. Her preoccupation with colours had allowed her to paint pictures of the riot outside the window for her sister.

The tranquil emerald greens of their backyard dotted with flowers in jewel tones that Ma planted every season, merged into the busy grey and brown of the intersection. Contained by the low dusty edges of the park that surrounded the ebony-coloured tomb of Noorie, she had a clear view of the path Dad took for his morning walk.

*I miss you Charu,* she sent the thought out into the universe. She tucked the naughty lock of hair that tickled the corner of her nose behind her soft ear telling herself she would make more of an effort to get her sister to open up…the next time they were together.

With only Noorie's journal to keep her company, Bee spent the day in Charu's room, reading about another woman's tumble into love.

*Today, as I sat in the empty hall, singing about lost love, Ammi walked in. She sat on the velvety cushion and gurgled on her hookah. Since it was a common occurrence, I did not think much of it and just closed my eyes and continued my riyaaz. It was the change in the very air that I was breathing that had me opening them, perplexed at the cause. Before me stood the one man I had been longing to see again. So surreal was this culmination of my dream that I kept on singing while looking at him leaning against the pillar, thinking he was an apparition, my mind playing tricks. The song over, I laid the tanpura down, not wanting to blink for I might miss that moment he vanished from my conjured dream.*

*'I didn't know you sang so well,' his voice woke me to the reality of his presence.*

*'You are really here?' I asked.*

*'Yes, and so are you. I thought...' He looked down at his boots caked in mud from his panicked ride to Ammi's house.*

*'What?' I asked, 'What did you think?'*

*'That you were lost to me...I mean to us...I heard that you had...drowned.'*

*'No, I...' I stood up then, my heart beating as if it would jump out of my chest wanting to reassure, to soothe.*

*He was looking at me with pain, hurt, and a hunger. I recognised the denial in his eyes but didn't understand it. It made me full of want, as if I was immersed in a hot water spring.*

*The baby kicked in that moment and reflexively my hand shot up to soothe the impatience that only a mother's touch can settle. Our moment of intimacy fractured, I could see he was retreating and felt adrift for his eyes no more anchored my own.*

*'So, you two know each other?' Ammi's voice came to me as if from afar.*

*I realised that in the excitement of seeing him, I had forgotten that we were in the presence of Ammi. Flustered, I backed away, rushing out of the room, chased by a hundred thoughts and questions.*

*Why was he here? What did he mean when he said that he thought that I was dead? Did I mean anything to him? How did he know I was here?*

*The last question gave my flight pause. I slowed my hurried steps, retracing them to stand behind the gilded door left ajar by my own hands, eavesdropping.*

*'...no Ammi, there is no need to assume anything,' he was saying.*

*'Don't get in the middle of this, Hamad. The prince is a spoilt brat and Noorie is carrying his sin.' Ammi used a tone that was both reprimanding and filled with worry.*

*'Ammi, I am not in the middle of anything,' he said.*

*'Is that why you came rushing here straight from the practice pit?'*

*'I came...because....'*

*'Yes...Hamad, I am waiting for that answer you are finding so difficult to give.'*

*'Ammi, I...I don't know what happened. She was so broken, like a little bird, an easy prey, for these young, rich louts to target. I...I couldn't let her....'*

*'What?'*

*'She reminded me of you. I saw the anguish in her eyes that I have witnessed in yours, the pain of rejection, of being used, even by your own family. Her brother struts around town and the family lives in splendour because of her and she...she lives a life of a...pro....'*

*'Hamad Bahadur,' Ammi said, her voice heavy but stern. 'There is a difference between Noorie and me. I was born to this life; I just had the inanity to fall for a coward. Actually, I can't blame him; the crown is a heavy burden. Love can barely survive in thriving conducive conditions. With everything going against us, it was puerile of us to think it could survive our difference of birth.' Ammi said her voice sad.*

*'But Hamad, Noorie is different. She chose to better her circumstances. Her way may not be conventional but she got out from under her oppressive upbringing and family. Maybe it was the fear for her life and that of her child; still, she took the right step.'*

*'Very few people would agree, Ammi.' He said, his voice carrying a hint of laughter.*

*'Well, they don't know how it is to be a woman blamed for a man's wrong. Who decided women were less than men? Men...that's who.'*

*'Okay, okay let's not rile ourselves up.' He laughed.*

*'Yes, you are right; I will just get my blood up. Anyway, before I went on a tangent I was saying, she is a courageous girl and I just wanted to see if you felt anything for her. I have, in the minutes you could barely blink when you looked at her as if you had found lost treasure.' Ammi said, laughing at him.*

*'I wasn't…I was just surprised and your message was vague and….'*

*'My sweet boy, what will they do to you if they know of your kind heart?' Ammi said with a heavy sigh.*

*'Why do you think I keep it well hidden?' He laughed. 'Don't cry, Ammi, I am alright.'*

*'Sometimes I wish I had taken you away from here but your father wanted you around him. He depends on you, you know that…right?'*

*'He is not my father, Ammi, he is the King, so stop weaving dreams,' he said, his voice irritated now.*

*Before I realised what was happening he had already opened the door and stood facing me. Anger and hurt were coming off him in waves.*

*'Listening at doors, why am I not surprised?' he said.*

*'Why did you rush to come here? Because you pity me or because you wanted to see me?' The words rushed out before I could stop them.*

*He wrapped his scraped fingers around my upper arm (I swear I felt each finger for days) and dragged me into a shadowed corner. There we stood silent, looking defiantly at each other.*

*'I did not rush and I was just checking,' he said, his big bushy eyebrows in a ferocious frown on his large, sweaty forehead.*

*'Just like you check on all the other castaway girls that have served their purpose. Don't intimidate me with your glower. I don't get scared easily anymore.'*

*'Noorie shut up and go to your room.'*

*'Or what? I am not scared of you.'*

*'You should be.'*

*'Why, what can you do that has not already been done?' I asked, daring him though I was trembling inside.*

*He looked at me with both surprise and hurt, then slowly lowered his head as if asking permission…waited a whisper away from my lips. I wanted to scream at him, to close the distance, but my throat was parched. I licked my dry lips unsure of what to do and then I saw it, the flame that leapt in his eyes as he saw the tip of my tongue.*

*A corresponding flame ignited within me and I…I…was the one who closed the distance that separated us. I grabbed his leather armour and pulled him closer to mesh my lips with his in a bruising kiss that I had been the recipient of, it seemed in another lifetime. Instead of crushing me to him as I had expected, he pushed me away with his hands on my shoulders to look me in the eyes.*

*'Feel it first, close your eyes, Noorie,' he said against my lips before possessing them in a softer kiss than the one I had initiated.*

*He peppered my face with gentle kisses, too many to count. His soft lips, not leaving any part untouched or unloved. From the arching winged eyebrows, to the pointy chin, every inch of my face was admired and then sealed with a wet kiss. Taking my lips between his, he suckled on them starting a similar tug lower down in my body. I tried to get closer, wanting to rub the throb away but he held my hips away from himself.*

*'Please,' I said, not sure of what I was asking.*

*'Noorie, you slay me.' He whispered as he gulped in air, with his eyes closed and his face a mask of pain.*

*'What did I do wrong?' I asked.*

*'You can never do any wrong. I am in the wrong here. No better than that prince...I can't explain. I have to go now.' He said and then looked at me.*

*'Noorie, why do you cry?' he asked.*

*'You are nothing like the Shehzada, nothing like him, do you hear, he...he....'*

*'Yes, I know, but I shouldn't have....'*

*'Why not? Did you not want to?'*

*'Oh my dear, you don't know the half of it...but I'm married.'*

*'What? I...I don't mind. Don't leave.'*

*'I...there is no excuse. Forgive me.' He said then bowed before me and he left without a backward glance.*

*I stood at the door looking at him riding away, the sweet smile of hope lighting my face. Ammi who had heard every word of our exchange also smiled.*

Bee sighed. She wondered if maybe Noorie had it better in the cloistered, ostracised life than she herself did with her freedom to think and do as she pleased.

# 25

## *Aeipathy*

## An enduring and consuming passion

(Language: English, Origin: Latin)

Since he had arrived, Tenzin had been unable to talk to Bhavya about what was uppermost in their minds—the baby and their relationship. In addition, it felt like her family was zealously guarding her. Every time they would begin talking, someone would walk in, then look at them with guilty eyes and walk away, apologising.

Tenzin felt constrained, cornered, wanting space to talk to her. He wondered why he had agreed to stay in the *Haveli* but the peace that had descended upon him when he had walked into its gates was unparalleled. He only had ever felt this degree of contentment when he caught the first sight of the fluttering prayer flags waving gaily at him, asking him to hurry back home.

On his way from the airport, he had worried, unsure of how much and what Bhavya had disclosed about their situation to her family. He was least prepared for the announcement that he heard on entering the dining area. His heart felt frozen, with delight or shock, he was not sure yet.

Realising that she had not told them everything, he had taken a deep sigh of relief. He loved her family as if they were his own, but...he was a man first. To admit to sharing his fiancée with another man would be too big a step for him.

*What made me do it, suggest that we add another man to our bed? It is entirely my fault. Had I just kept my mouth shut all this could have been avoided*, he asked himself again as he strolled across the grounds the next morning.

*Instead of talking about why she hid the news of the baby for four months, why did I give in to my need to make love to her? Why am I unable to control myself around her?*

His thoughts pulled him back in time to the first time they had been intimate. He had not been able to walk away, he knew he should have but he hadn't.

A clichéd scenario, if there was ever one invented, had finally broken his reserve. An office party, a new low-cut dress and the knowledge that she looked exquisite and he had a difficult time erasing the fire from his eyes when he saw her saunter out of her room.

Sensing her intent and realising that he was likely to capitulate, he had left the party early after the perfunctory meet and greet.

All that was achieved was a series of jealous images of who was getting to hold her for the dance, who was hearing her robust laughter, who was losing themselves, spellbound by her charms. An excruciating two hours later, he heard her footsteps.

Before he could stop himself, he had opened the door to Bhavya. She walked with drooping shoulders and embarrassed woozy eyes, crossing the corridor as silently as possible.

'You are late.'

'Yes...Sir,' she said, not bothering to veil her sarcasm.

He had not expected her to shut down his triad on 'safety at night in a new place' with an agreement after having worked himself up for a sermon. After a moment, she walked to her door and carefully tried to fit in her key in the lock.

'Murphy's law,' she groaned, resting her head against the cool door when she couldn't find the keyhole.

What had made him put his hands on her shoulders, rest his forehead on the nape of her neck, before taking the key from her hand to open the door?

'I don't know why I like men in white shirts.'

When he turned her around to face him at the murmured words, she asked, 'Did I just say that out aloud?'

'Yes.'

'Oh shit!'

'Come on, you are wasted.' He said smiling.

He held her arm as if to pull her inside the room. She stumbled, falling into his arms.

'Don't do this to me, Bee. Please. I am human, I cannot take anymore. I am going mad.' He said his eyes tortured.

'Why do you resist?'

'I don't want to be that boss that takes advantage,' he said, not letting go of her arms.

'Advantage? Of all the lame excuses!' She said her jaw rigid storming into the room.

He had not known what to do, that was the last reaction he had expected and therein lay his fault. He had since then become wiser; he knew he should expect the unexpected from her on most days.

'You, you have kept me at a distance for so long just for some archaic work ethic...whatever? I happen to be an adult and I know what I want. Please, if I didn't want your attention I would make sure you know it. No one takes these things lying down now; women have evolved, if you didn't notice.' She said, blazing with irritation.

'Think logically,' he said.

'Here, do you think I am weak?' She pushed at him with anger, leading her to rashly poke at the smouldered fire within him.

He just stood looking at her, his head cocked slightly, sliding his hands in his pockets.

'What is your deal?' She rounded on him, all ire and hurt vanity. But nothing worked neither restrained platitudes nor the in-your-face drama. She had tried both.

'Are you gay?' She asked nastily, wanting to see how far she could go.

'Are you easy?' He taunted back, unexpectedly.

Inevitably her hand shot out, caught in his before it could connect with his cheek.

She struggled to free her hand, indignant at his words, the hurt making her blind to the cracks in his defences that were crumbling like dominos. She somehow knew that she would not be able to hold back or keep a part of herself separate from him, as she had with all the others.

One minute they were engaged in a battle of smarting wills and the next she realised that he had pulled her hands above her head. Her back was flush against the wall near the door that stood ajar; a doorway to liberation should either of them want it.

He stood panting, as did she, unsure for just a moment before lowering his head, when he hesitated…testing her patience. He tempted, coaxing her to give in, and then lowered his lips barely touching hers. It made her heart stutter, her breath uneven. His lips skimmed hers, just a lick here and a bit of tongue there and the breath that she was holding shuddered out. His lips moved to her neck, biting, sucking…leaving behind a trail of searing warmth.

She growled at the time he was taking to claim what she so desperately wanted to give. Heeding her command, he brought his lips back to her mouth and this time she was ready, willing, eager. She tasted unrelieved passion, frustrated desire, simmering anger as his mouth crushed hers. He demanded…and then demanded more…and despite having promised herself to keep it light, she gave… and then gave some more.

The contact did nothing to soothe and everything to arouse, taking them further…further down the spiral of oblivious desire.

He still had not touched her and her body was on fire.

She felt his fingers at the zipper of her dress and opened her eyes to look into his possessive eyes.

'Our first time has to be on my terms,' she said when his gaze sought permission.

A slight nod and her dress fell to the floor. Bared to his gaze she stood tall, watching him rake his eyes on her stocking covered legs that reached mid-thigh. He drew his hands down her hips, running gentle fingers where silk met soft skin.

'Let go of my hands, Tenzin,' she said, her voice strong, her eyes firm, brooking no argument.

He lifted his brow and took a step back, releasing her hands and her pleasure grew ripe, became bolder. She yanked off his shirt, tugged at his slacks with growing impatience, and then took a step back to let her eyes feast on his uncovered skin.

Taking her fill, stroking the skin over his taut, muscular chest she could not help but run her hands over the expanse of bare skin, from neck to waist, cupping his fluid lines, taking this liberty of exploring…of discovering.

He stood, cheeks flushed, taut…tense…his arms to his sides, unmoving, letting her have her way with his body. His eyes closed on a sigh as she skimmed his jaw line with fairy kisses and felt his gradually accelerating pulse. Her hands roamed of their own free will to explore, as did her mouth.

She tasted his skin as he had tasted hers but a moment ago, revelling…delighting in the deeper, darker flavour that was his and his alone.

They strained, pushed at each other; he had pulled at her clothes then kissed her with a vengeance, a storm breaking free. His mouth wasn't tender as it left hers in the quest for other delights and found them. He zeroed in on the bare, vulnerable skin of her neck and shoulder… lingered. The cool collected exterior forever shattered as he ravaged her body with his hands, his teeth nipping, tormenting. He alternated between pain and pleasure, keeping her unsure. And she, like a slave to this exquisite torture, begged for more.

'If there is someone else I don't give a damn.' He had whispered close to her ear.

'No…there is no one else,' she whispered back on a moan.

The feral beast roared at her words, snapping its sharp jaws at the freedom it could taste, feeling the cracks in the impervious tower that caged it within, arousing her further.

His impatient hands made a mockery of the slips of silk that still covered her skin from his gaze. Tearing, ripping anything that blocked the path his lips, trailed fire down her heated skin.

Without finesse, his relentless fingers found her wet core. Gasping for air, her fingers dug into his back as his fingers took quick and complete possession of her body. From her bared shoulders to the stiffened pebbled peaks that were calling out for his attention, he made sure that no inch of her body remained neglected for long. His hands arrowed down, to where she was parched, melting, throbbing, aching for his velvety encroachment.

Strumming her quivering nub, plunging within her moist centre, his fingers first conspired to make her lose her mind. Unaware of her surrounding, she realised that he was kneeling down before her, whispering words that echoed in a language she did not understand, on her skin.

His mouth on her, he did not allow a moment of respite, a moment to breathe. Her fingers gripped his hair as she, with a moan of acceptance, let herself fly.

Her legs buckled and she went limp against him.

Unwilling to relent, he held her close as his lips and teeth played hers in a tune that she did not know existed.

Then, as she opened her heavy eyes, the sparkles within her unwilling to subside, she waited for him to take a bigger sip from this brimming pool of ambrosia called pleasure, she waited for him....

Tenzin's erotic musings were interrupted when he heard the car outside. He let out the breath he had not realised he had been holding. Bee's father was off to work and he was just standing here, doing nothing substantial to put his life back on track. Instead of reliving their earth-shattering sexual escapades, he should be convincing his headstrong fiancée, who wanted nothing to do with him, to move ahead...but with him.

*And the baby? What about the baby? Whose is it? Mine or Kabir's?*

# 26

## *Tacenda*

## Things better left unsaid

(Language: English borrowed from Latin)

Tenzin's predicament came to an early resolution. The whole family was going for a wedding nearby. Bhavya knew it was her mother's ploy to make sure that she and Tenzin could have some time to themselves to talk things out.

Tenzin looked especially guilty at the forced outing.

'They are going because of us.' He said.

'Yes,' she said, waving at her sisters' sullen faces. They hated being paraded. Despite wanting this space to talk, now that Tenzin had it he did not know where to start the conversation that would make things easier to process. He could not remember a time when he felt so out at sea on how to proceed.

'What is it you want, Bee?' Tenzin asked as they sat at the table.

'What I want has not changed in the time I have stayed here, Tenzin. I still want to live my life on my terms.'

'What you mean is you want to keep meeting Kabir and have a side fling.'

'Tenzin, we have discussed it before....'

'He knows, you said?' Tenzin asked tersely.

'Yes.'

'How?'

'I...met him to let him know.'

'Where?'

'His flat.' Bhavya said, her eyes sliding away from his.

'Did anything happen?' astute to Bhavya's expressions he dreaded her answer. 'I...we...' Bee could find no words to justify herself. She could only look at him with utter remorse.

'Are you kidding me, Bee? You are saying you went to meet him after harping about just being friends. You chose him over our relationship because I warned you that this will happen, eventually. And, now you are telling me it did, why...because you wanted it to or because one man is not enough?'

'That is cruel, even for you.'

'And what are you? I am not Bhuvan who will forgive lies or suffer in silence. I concede he is a better man than me but by God you are stretching it.'

'I am not lying and don't get my sister into this.'

'Aren't you? Obviously you fucked him before I came and then you fucked me, what does that make you Bee... ever thought of that?'

'You bastard!' She screamed. 'I hate you!' She pushed at him, then immediately put her hand on her stomach feeling a pull. She gripped his arm as she felt a spasm, her focus on her unborn child.

'Yes, I am realising how much.' He said softly, watching her face for any shadow of pain. 'Calm down now,' he said to her, taking a deep breath to release the frustration that had built inside him. 'Are you alright?'

Bhavya nodded as he guided her to the sofa.

'Why did you hide the fact that you met him from me?' He asked, unable to let the betrayal go unexplained.

'Because I knew this is how you would react. It was just...Tenzin...I did not go with the intent to...I just went to tell him...it was just a kiss and nothing else...' Bee tried again, fearing there was no way she could explain her actions.

'And, the next time you meet him...what will it be then...just a fuck?' He said quietly, his lack of anger worse, somehow, than the outrage. At least that told her that he felt something for her. This icy calm scared her more.

'Look, I like the idea that you think like a man when it comes to sex but I am through dealing with your need to always have a plan B. I understand that it stems from your insecurity of abandonment but...Bee, I can't do this anymore.'

She swallowed the tears that threatened to make their presence felt.

'I love you but I will be damned if I am forever made to feel like I need to prove that I love you. I have my flaws, I have never hidden that. I will need you to accept that before we move further.'

'What?'

'That I will disappoint you, again and again, as you do repeatedly and that does not mean you run and hide, every time life gets messy.'

'I do not run.'

'Really?' He turned to her now, his eyebrow raised at an ironic tilt.

'Then what is this that you are doing? Coming so far away to your family because you don't want to face the consequences of your actions? That is the definition of running, Bee, and you are getting better at it. Grow up and then find me!' He said and started towards the door needing to put distance between them.

'Grow up—hasn't that been the problem? That I am not mature enough because I don't have a frown on my face at all times?' She shouted.

'What?'

'You find me silly and immature and unable to handle tough situations. You don't answer questions about your childhood; you barely talk...what kind of life is that?'

'One second, so you are saying that your friendship with Kabir is a rebellion against my so-called autocratic attitude? Because our relationship is not ideal, you think this…will help. You think Kabir can give you the love and the understanding that you desire?' He said his voice filled with mockery. 'You know what, Bee, I say go for it, no one can love you the way I do. And, I am willing to bet my life on it. No one is perfect, everyone will disappoint you and you will always look for something more.' He finished.

'Kabir is not the issue…*you* are!'

'No, my dear…the issue is you, actually. It is neither Kabir nor me. We are just collateral damage in the war that you are waging against yourself.' He said with what she saw as a sneer.

'You are grasping at straws, Tenzin, to put the blame on my shoulders. You said that I have shattered you, destroyed you, how do you think you have influenced my life? You too have taken away my ability to be myself. The anticipation of your disapproval keeps me from being able to do what I want to. Instead, I have to do what you may think is right. I am not saying that you have ever asked me to change who I am but…the way you sermonise it seems you are forever wondering why you are even with me.'

'That is not true, Bee and being considerate of others' reactions, in this case your love, supposedly, is called growing up. That is what I am asking you to do, for God's sake!'

'That is so unfair, consideration goes both ways. You can't be the one to always take…you too will have to give.'

'Is that what Kabir did? Make you feel loved?' He said with a quiet regret.

'Yes, as a matter of fact he did! We share something that I never had with you, an equality, where both of us were important in the relationship. Not this skewed one… the way ours is. You don't respect me and never will,

I get that now. Had I not been pregnant do you think we would even be having this discussion? We want different things from life. You want to stay at home and I want to explore the world. You want stability and I want freedom to discover, the world, myself… How could I have ever thought that we could make it work? I convinced myself that our differences could be celebrated with both of us making adjustments.

You cannot fall in love with my free spirit and then want to smother it only because you have a ring on my finger. I knew if we ever get married, it would fail.' Bhavya's impassioned words crashed on Tenzin with the force of storming waves that have the ferocity to shatter rocks.

Belatedly she saw his colour blanch at her words and realised most of them were not even true, well…at least not the cruel ones. Anger had again made her tongue razor sharp and she could see that she had with her own hands ripped the fabric of their love.

'Tenz….'

'Got it. Whose is it?' He asked, his eyes lowering to the soft swell of her belly.

'I…I don't know.'

'We…both…God this is sick. How did this even happen? We both used protection.' His mind was ready to splinter into a million pieces at the curve ball that life had thrown his way…their way.

'Nothing is a 100 percent sure. I didn't do this alone. We were in it together and if there is a baby we are equally responsible.'

'Yes, I know that logically but….'

'But what?' She asked, raising her terror-filled eyes to meet his.

'God, Bee, it was meant for fun. I am sorry…I…' he said, feeling like a pendulum.

'Well, the experiment proved too costly, more so for me.' She said bitterly.

'Are we really going to worry on who will pay the heavier price?' He asked. 'What should we do?'

'I don't know.' She said, turning her face away.

'What did he say when you told him about the baby?'

'Nothing.'

'What if it is his?'

'So, what if it is? Are you saying you will not bring up a baby that does not have your blood?'

'Blood! Bee, you know about my lack of knowledge of my own background. It has nothing to do with blood. His is probably better than mine. What I don't want is Kabir hanging over my head for the rest of my life.'

'What is your problem with him?'

'Besides the fact that he fucked my wife, you mean?' Tenzin shot back. He then took a deep breath knowing that he had spoken from an angry place, a place where the anger was directed at him and he was unfairly projecting it on her.

'Don't be crude and I am not your wife, yet.'

'Yes, you are right...I apologise.'

'I am not having this conversation again. The gynaecologist said the time to abort is over as I am already nearing the end of my fifth month.' Bhavya said, rubbing her slightly rounded belly tenderly.

'Four months, you hid this from me for four months... it begs the question what else can you hide. I am sorry, Bee but I am hurt and you may have had time to process this but it will take me time to understand all that this entails.'

'No, Tenzin, that is not...I was still coming to grips with it myself. It was not to...I am just as puzzled as to how I should process this change, Tenzin. Please try to understand, the news caught me unaware. I didn't know what to do. I did what came naturally. I came home.'

'I have no problem with your coming home, Bee, the problem I have is with your need to hide it from me,' said Tenzin.

Bhavya fell silent again.

'I cannot look at this child and wonder, Bee,' he said, sharing his worst fears.

'Fine, then we move to the next step.'

'What next step?' He asked.

'A paternity test,' she said, looking straight into his perplexed eyes.

# 27

## *Sillage*

## The scent that lingers in the air after something or someone has been and gone

(Language: French)

'No, NO...you cannot be serious!' said Tenzin Bhavya looked at the man before her, the familiar and the altered. The thick grey hair; the shiny, broad forehead; the amber, almond-shaped eyes under heavy brows that were at the moment hooded.

*The frown lines near his eyes have deepened; did I cause the fatigue that I see in them? What will the baby inherit, his strong nose, the angular, clenched jaw, the stubborn chin or the height?* She wondered, then shook off her thoughts coming back to the present.

'Why, don't you want to know whose baby I am carrying?' She asked

'Why do you want the test?' he asked instead his hands again going into his pockets.

'Tenzin, I am not going down this route with you. I want to get the test because it's best to know, you can make the decision when we know.'

'Decision about what?' He asked, calmer now.

'Whether you want to still stay with me or...if the results are not to your liking, I mean. I will call Kabir tomorrow to tell him, then let us take a call one way or the other,' she said into the stunned silence.

'I liked the old Bee better,' he said after a while.

'What...what do you mean?' She asked, surprised at his gentle tone.

'The one who threw things, shouted, got angry, even your anger had a truth about it. The old Bee did not indulge in these games of wrapping what she really wants to say. Where did she go?' Tenzin said looking sorrowful.

'Well, you made me what I am.'

He only nodded eyes downcast.

'Is it so easy for you, to think about moving on, Bee?' He asked, her blasé tone leaving a red welt on his heart.

'Well, if we don't match…the temperaments don't, what is the fucking point? There is nothing in common, we don't see eye to eye on anything…I….'

'So calling it quits is easier?'

'No, but I don't see the need to stretch a relationship when it has run its course.'

'Bee….'

'Look Tenzin, as partners, we meshed our different… almost opposite temperaments igniting sparks. I will admit that you know me better than anyone else but this knowledge cannot be used to pull me down, to hurt me, to break my spirit.'

'Bhavya, you are being unfair and unreasonable now. I love your spontaneity, your ability to embrace newness and that was why I suggested the threesome because I knew I could discuss anything with you. That is what I find the most attractive in you. I know you, yes…and yet I find you a mystery….'

'Bee, it is not for the lack of trust. Do you really need Kabir to complete your life…that is like saying that I am not enough? Continuing to spend time with him is inviting trouble. A man and a woman can never be friends, especially if they have already done the deed. What is stopping you from doing it again?' Tenzin said, running his hands through his hair, trying once more to explain his side.

'Bee, being independent does not mean you have to rebel even when there is no cause and things can be worked out.' He said his hands outstretched.

*You only have to meet me half-way Bee, please.*

'How convenient! And I am not without cause? Truthfully, did you not want to put me in the wife mould once we decided to marry?' Bhavya countered, eyes narrowed.

'I did no such thing, Bee, don't exaggerate.'

*Did I do that?*

'Okay, tell me, why were you attracted to me?'

'Your vivacious spirit attracted me, your zest for life.'

'And, did that same spontaneity not bother you after we started living together? That I asked you to pick up after yourself, behave like a big boy. That hurt your ego that I was unwilling to mother....'

'Don't go there, Bee.' He said, his voice dead.

'Okay, but why, why this wall? I know you are an orphan. Why do you refuse to talk about that? You know everything about me.'

'Yes, sadly I do.'

'There it is, that long-drawn sigh of oh my god you've been a naughty girl. Yes, I had affairs before I met you. Some good, some not so good and yes, I had sex before I met you. Who gave you the right to judge me for my choices?' Bhavya asked, hurting.

'You decided to marry me knowing about my past, now you throw it at my face as if it is a dirty bit of my life that you would rather not know about? Why this hypocritical attitude? If you did not have a relationship before me is that my fault? I told you the truth because you asked for it. If you were unable to deal with it you should have told me.'

'Yes, I know about your past, Bee. It has not mattered because it was your past...but this our future...ours. Are you saying that only you will get to decide the direction we take? I am equally affected by the choices you make now. This has been the apex of our disagreements, hasn't it?' Tenzin said.

'What?'

'Your need to stay separate and my need to form a team...become a...we.'

Bhavya looked at him quizzically, wondering what she could say to him since he spoke the truth. She saw her individuality as sacrosanct and was unwilling to trade it for a ring.

She did not yet realise that she did not have to sacrifice one for the other. That she could have both.

'Look, there is no point of going back and forth, again and again, down this spiral. I will talk to Kabir tomorrow and we will do what is required. You can be a part of it if you wish. I asked Ma to get a room ready for you upstairs. Take that tonight.'

He nodded, feeling excluded, though it did not show on his calm face. The conversation was obviously over.

'It's best this way.'

'Suit yourself!'

'Let's deal with this tomorrow, finish this!'

'Okay. Fine.'

'Tomorrow then.'

'Meet me at the clinic.'

'Okay,' he said and walked away.

Bhavya stood numb, eyes brimming suddenly, watching him leave, wanting to call out but refusing to do so; she didn't know what she would say to him.

Feeling much older than her twenty-eight years, she slowly walked back to her room and closed the door.

That night, she quietly retired knowing that she would be taking the first step to ending her affair with Tenzin.

Sleep eluded her as she lay shaken by her own inability to decide what she wanted more.

Love or individual choice.

# 28

## *Depaysement*

## When someone is taken out of their own familiar world into a new one

(Language: French)

Full of soundless regrets, Tenzin stood smoking in the backyard thinking back to the times that she had referred to, the day he had proposed, the day she said she regretted.

He remembered it like yesterday.

He had been tapping away at his desk and she sat working on the unkempt bed. Her mobile had vibrated on the white sheets, heralding an assault of family. She grabbed it and walked out of the room. This was their way, after all. They kept a house together and shared their bodies but the matters of the heart they kept to themselves.

'Hello.'

'Bee.'

'Aruna, what happened?' she asked, 'Why are you crying?' He had eavesdropped as he usually did, his eyes still on the papers before him, but his mind wondering if today she would share what was happening with her family. The last few days had been difficult with something going on with her elder sister. She had been constantly on the phone with one member of her family or another.

He never asked and she never shared. He was there to rub her back, or make her a cup of tea when she finished her call; her eyes worried, her face strained as she sat looking out of the window. He knew she wished she could go to them. He wondered several times if he should ask but was unsure if she wanted to make him part of her family's problems.

He knew her sister's first marriage had ended badly and it seemed the second was also not faring too well by the looks of it. Keeping a distance was not as easy as they had assumed when they had set the ground rules for their relationship.

'What do you mean?' He heard her say then. 'You are telling me the short version, Aruna, and you know I like the long one. Tell me everything.'

She had listened quietly as Aruna retold the events of the past couple of days, and then sat silently letting the tears come washing away the worry from her bruised heart.

Days later, she had told him that Aruna was finally free of her first husband who had been the cause of so much pain in her life. Reunited with her current husband, Bhuvan, who had stood by her as she took the difficult and long journey of self-discovery, she was now at the cusp of fulfilling her dream, one of partnership and shared respect and trust.

At the time, he had taken Bee in his arms, where she, much to his surprise and for the very first time since he had known her, proceeded to let her concern and heartache flow out on his white shirt. He only rubbed her back for he wanted to savour this feeling of being needed.

They were in a strange place. He too had not wanted the emotional entanglement of love and she ran the other way every time he showed any signs of wanting to deepen the relationship. Therefore, they had cruised along, work colleagues who lived together, enjoying the benefits of sharing their bodies without the hassle of sharing their heart. It had suited them just fine.

When she woke up sometime later, she had crossed the room to land a kiss at the crown of his head. He caught her hand and pulled her into his lap.

'What was that for?' He asked.

'Just because...' she stopped, the line that they had drawn burned.

'What?'

'Thanks for being there.' She said simply.

'Okay, but you don't need to thank me. I just held on.'

'Yes, you did.'

'Where should we go for dinner?' He said turning to look out of the window.

'Can we stay in tonight? Moreover, I have too much work to do in any case. You see I have this strict boss, who will drag me over the coals if I don't have this presentation line-up ready,' she said.

'Does he now?' He asked.

A tickle and tumble followed where they both tried to sweep the unsaid fears and disappointments under the carpet. What remained was an uneasy silence they tried their best to underplay.

While having dinner and watching the sunset, he could not help asking, 'Bee, what are we doing?'

'As in?'

'Where are we going with this relationship?'

'I want everything, Tenzin, the works. Don't get me wrong. I understand that this is a passing fling for you. Slumming it with an underling is fine for a couple of months but... So while it's okay to be fucking me, I get that it's not okay to be involved in my life and vice versa.' She finished with a flourish.

'And, you are okay with that?' He had asked, motionless.

'No...yes...well, there is nothing else to do here. Is there?'

'I am serious, Bhavya.'

'Using my full name, am I in trouble...Sir? Should I be punished?' She said, batting her eyelids at him.

'So, if I asked to marry you, what would be your answer?' The words had leapt out of his mouth.

'If you…' Her smile vanished.

'Hypothetically?' He stood up, as did she, mirroring his nervousness.

She gulped the wine that went down the wrong pipe making her sputter, which made him thump her on her back in turn.

'Bee, only you can fuck up a proposal.' He said with a smile in his voice.

'Tenzin, what are you saying?' She asked.

'Answer the question.' He said, piercing her with his eyes.

'Hypothetically, I would say….'

'Yes?' He asked

'What?' Bhavya squawked.

'What would you say?' She asked him instead.

'I would say yes.' He countered.

'Why?' Bhavya asked dumbfounded.

'Why, what?' He questioned.

'Stop being dense. Why would you say yes, you barely know me?' She asked clenching her fingers.

'But, I do know you, I know your smile…and what makes you roll your eyes, what makes you angry. What makes you cry. I know the dimples that peek out and the come hither eyes, I know the….'

Had it been a beginning or an end was a question he had asked a hundred times to himself since Kabir had entered their life.

# 29

## *Inconnu*

### A person who is unknown; a stranger

(Language: French)

The meticulously researched clinic gave them an appointment with the doctor in a week's time. Hence Bhavya did everything possible to keep busy and out of Tenzin's way. She went to the saree shop with her father, helped her mother. She gossiped and bantered with Aruna over the phone. She fought with her brother and sat silently with Suresh Uncle and yet she could not find the courage to talk to her family about the thing that was on everyone's mind.

Tenzin would come and watch her, silently waiting for her to show an interest in speaking to him. They were at a crossroad and both needed to take the path of their choice.

Tenzin did not want to influence her decision in any way. He wanted her to come with him of her own accord, not because she had no other choice or that he coerced her into going back with him. It had to be her decision.

Bhavya took to going to the park, spending afternoons at the mausoleum, with the red shawl and the journal her only companions.

'Ma, I am leaving.' She said as she picked up the orange from the pyramid that Dheeraj loved constructing, tucking her hair behind her ear.

'Bee, why have you started going there so regularly?' Arun asked, making her stop in her tracks. 'I mean, why don't you come with me in the morning, we could go together.' He added, feeling all the eyes in the room on him.

*Did Dad actually just ask me to join him in his morning walks?*

'Okay Dad, but I like the sun. It warms me to my bones and I can soak in it the whole afternoon. So…' Looking at her father she quickly added, '…but let's do that soon, what you suggested. Go for an early walk together. You could tell me her story.'

'Yes, I…let's do that soon.'

'Okay…right…bye.'

As she quickened her pace to walk out of the room, she knew that everyone was wondering what was happening. Days were turning into weeks…four…six and still she kept silent on the cause of her pain that was obvious to the people who loved her. Tenzin's arrival and subsequent silence was a warning bell that rang every time he came by, watching her with loving eyes.

Yet, no one wanted to push, to ask, it was driving her up the wall.

She walked into the mausoleum and skirting the front, where a few people milled around, went to the back where the sun shone brightest and no one disturbed her. She took the journal out of the bag she carried and settled on the packed mud, her back to the wall, legs crossed and stretched before her.

Bhavya could not concentrate on the words today, Tenzin kept interrupting her thoughts. She knew that the office in Paris would be suffering.

*Why won't he leave? He just wants me to admit that I am wrong, which I shall never do,* she thought.

Her only solace was Noorie's words that called out to her. She immersed herself in Noorie's life for she had lost all control of her own. Bhavya felt her life...her image...juxtaposing with Noorie's. She felt compelled to read Noorie's story, finding strange similarities with her life.

The dilemma that Noorie faced when she found herself pregnant, the strength she had to find within herself to leave her family and forge her own path, the love that was incapacitating even as it was fulfilling.

Bhavya felt both Noorie and she were prisoners to circumstances beyond their control. Their situations were different but the result was the same. Both of them had to take matters into their own hands, unable to depend on their elders to support and protect them. Her childhood under the cloud of insecurity of a stable home had changed something within her, broken her, she knew just as Noorie was changed by her situation.

Some would call the resultant devil-may-care attitude strength, she knew it was self-preservation.

Noorie too was stuck between her past and her present, wanting a better future for herself. If Noorie had found a solution, would that solution not be applicable to her too?

She was coming to depend on Noorie's life to figure out her own.

*In the days that followed, I alternated between praying to God for good sense even as I cursed Him for afflicting me with this disease called love, for that is how I felt. I was feverishly hot one minute and frozen cold the next. My soul became a battleground between my heart and mind, the right thing to do and that which my heart desired.*

*The angel and devil both are inside us; my mother had once told me when she had finished thrashing the devil out of me for some mistake I had committed. Maybe she was right; the devil was the one that I wanted to listen to.*

*I spent long nights wanting, my mind conjuring things that I could hear through the paper-thin walls. His scarred face, the one that I wanted to see above me, thrusting in me, lying beside me. Since the stolen kiss...something, a languorous, sinuous ennui, seemed to have overtaken my moral line that became blurred beyond recognition. I could not find it. I wanted him and I knew I would find a way to get him.*

*Unknown to me, Ammi was keeping a hawk-eye gaze on my preoccupation. She let me fret until I finally mustered the courage to approach her, after I had made my decision.*

*'Ammi, may I come in?'*

*'What do you want to know?' She asked, letting me know that my confusion was not as well-hidden as I had thought.*

*'About him...Hamad, I can't stop thinking about him.' I said, savouring his name on my tongue.*

*'He is my bastard son, conceived in an illusionary and weak love. Tormented, he is a sentinel, cursed to stand at the window, guarding, gazing at the happiness inside the palace but not allowed to enter. He is married in the eyes of the world but not in his heart.'*

*'Is he...the King's?'*

*'Yes, my situation is different from yours only to this extent. I was born into this world of naach-gaana. It was not as degrading as it is now but yes, the dancing girls were always living on the fringes of society. Needed...but not wanted.*

*The prince used to visit the kotha with his father for the mehfils. That is where I met him. We fell in love, or at least I did. He... he went on to fall for Roopmati, you know of her don't you?*

*The rest is history, as they say. When Hamad was born, I told the King. He took it upon himself to keep him close. Guilt, I suppose. Even gave him his name, Hamad Bahadur. He is not an acknowledged son of the King, but a son nonetheless.'*

*'Am I being foolish? This is wrong I know, but Ammi, I don't think this will go away.'*

*'Yes, well, it seems like that now. I will ask you again in a couple of years. Noorie, you may be confusing gratefulness with love.'*

*I too had asked myself this question in the sleepless nights.*

*'I don't think so, Ammi. I just know. I have searched my depths for the reason for this fixation or fascination, whatever one might call the feelings that I have for him. I have come to accept, to forgive that what was done to me by the Shehzada and his cohorts, only because it brought me to Hamad. I love him, Ammi. I know it is wrong to love a married man but....'*

*'Noorie, child, what is right and what do you call wrong? What may be right for you may be wrong for someone else. We make our own rights and wrongs...there is no line, no dayra. Draw these lines only for yourself, giving anyone else the power to do that for your life will only lead to disaster. But, remember that every choice has consequences.'*

*I contemplated her words, realising that though she was not supporting me, she was also not going to stand in the way of my love.*

Bhavya closed the heavy pages. Her thoughts in turmoil she could not help but draw parallels between Ammi's talk of moral lines, of every choice having a consequence and her own circumstances.

*I too made a choice when I agreed to Tenzin's idea, blaming him entirely for that is wrong on my part. The consequence of that choice is why there is a minefield instead of...togetherness, between us.*

*Is Kabir the thorn in our relationship?*

*On the other hand, could it be Tenzin's lack of faith in me the reason for this turmoil, or is it my restless need for newness?* She pondered.

That there were no answers to her questions was more worrying. The white and black of her assured stand was bleeding into greys as she introspected on her situation.

## 30

## *Cordolium*

## Heartache, heartfelt sorrow

(Language: Latin)

*Waiting…for him to come to me again despite his better judgement makes me identify with an alpviram…à comma…a pause in time or more appropriately with a slowly melting candle. I diminish, one breath at a time as the days passed, hoping against hope that he too would be going through the same painful, searing process of separation, as I seemed to be enduring.*

*The fear of being the only one drowning in these burning waters was too heart breaking a possibility, so I kept my mind away from the chance of his disinterest.*

*Then one day, he stood before me as the moon became visible. He came like he always did, without warning. The pleasure of his sight fell on me like moonbeams, making me forget the weeks of agony that I had endured.*

*If you looked at him you would see a man as sturdy and tall as a Baobab tree. With hair that curled at the nape of his neck, his square face scarred by enemy hands that he tries to hide behind a neatly trimmed beard. His chiselled body is of a soldier, always covered in armour, his onyx-coloured eyes never still, as if always looking for danger lurking in shadowed corners.*

*I did not see all this; I only saw the gentleness and the battle in his eyes, his clenched hands, as I leaned closer and his need to devour me.*

*This ability of reading his starvation was the result of my education in Panna Mandi. Here, men and their needs were discussed and laughed about as if they were no more important than women were outside the towering gates of this oasis.*

*'Ammi is not here, she has gone to the Bazaar' I said, my eyes on the lamps that were blinking on all around bathing him in the colours of fire.*

*'Why didn't you go along?'*

*'I...I don't like to go there anymore.'*

*'Why?'*

*I did not know how to tell him that the joy of the glittering market place had all but been reduced to ashes for me. It reminded me of my foolishness and my fear.*

*'It's done, Noorie, no one can touch you now. It's been months,' he said, taking my hands in his.*

*'Yes, but I can't seem to....'*

*'It's okay let it....'*

*'Ahhh...' I cried in pain.*

*'What happened?' he asked worriedly*

*All I could do was close my eyes and breath deep, he was holding me right next to his chest with his large arms around me, can you blame me?*

*'Are you hurt, tell me Noorie, where does it hurt?'*

*'No, no, the baby kicks and sometimes it aches.' I said.*

*When his arms dropped away taking their warmth with them, I regretted not lying and saying anything else rather than mentioning the baby.*

*'Oh okay then, take care. Tell Ammi to call the vaid so that he can check if everything is fine,' he said and then turned to leave.*

*'Wait.' I yelled, not ready to let him go, yet unable to stop the questions that had been swirling inside me for so many days.*

*'Don't go...I...can you stay? Have a glass of sherbet; Ammi should be back in sometime.'*

*He looked at me, his eyes burning with unmet desires. I knew he was going to refuse and then suddenly he nodded his head, his eyes confused at his own actions.*

*We walked up to the covered veranda where the air was sweet smelling, the softly swaying wet strings of jasmine that Ammi hung there every morning serving a double purpose.*

*Two glasses of sherbet in silver filigree glasses were placed before us. We sat in silence, both unsure, the evening breeze the only thing that was between us.*

*'Why did you come today, is everything alright?' I asked, unable to keep silent any longer and not sure of how long he would stay.*

*'Yes...well as right as it can be. I wanted to ask you... No, I wanted to say goodbye to Ammi, I leave for a battle tomorrow morning.'*

*How did the glass slip from my fingers, the red sherbet staining my white kurta like blood? Dizzy, I looked at him, shocked at the news.*

*He looked at me, his eyes amplifying my fears.*

*'Don't go, you....'*

*'Don't say things you have no idea about.'*

*'I...love.'*

*'No, you don't. Tell Ammi I came to say goodbye.'*

*'Come back to me,' I whispered tears rolling down my cheeks as I watched him gallop away as if the hounds of hell were at his back.*

*Was I destined to lose everything? My dignity, my self-respect, my love...well then there was nothing left. I vowed that day to never let myself depend on anyone, ever again. This dependence only led to disappointment and heartache.*

*A change came over me as I sat on the floor, my heart broken, rejected by the first man whom I had ever loved. I vowed I would become the best tawaif Panna Mandi had ever seen.*

*Kings would come from faraway lands after hearing about my skills.*

*And then he would know whom he had rejected.*

*What, how could he leave her?* Bhavya thought skimming through the next few pages only finding accounts of days in which was concealed a drive, an obsession to achieve the goal Noorie had set for herself.

Noorie practised her singing and witnessed the baby growing within her, promising to love the child come what may. It was them, against this heartless world.

She mentioned her worry for Hamad occasionally and sarcastically, making Bhavya smile at her futile attempt at anger. Bhavya could read the despair and sorrow of a young girl who was trying desperately to deny her own pain, spread clearly on the pages.

She read the path of Noorie's life wondering if people were just fools to think that they had any control over their lives.

The day began like any other day, with the sun rays tiptoeing into the room as Bhavya watched; heralding the day she would go for the appointment at the clinic.

She got ready and left the *Haveli* without confiding in anyone. Last night had been especially difficult, with everyone asking about Tenzin's absence. She had made hurried excuses about some friends from his college getting together.

Not wanting to repeat the conversation about what to make for Tenzin's dinner today, she escaped. She knew her mother would scrape out the truth if she lingered.

She met Tenzin at the hospital for the initial consultation. The test was non-invasive yet exorbitantly priced.

'This looks more like a five-star hotel rather than a hospital,' she said when they were greeted with folded hands by the uniformed front-office girls.

Tenzin remained mute.

His phone rang and he excused himself as Bhavya picked up the pamphlets that would tell her more about the procedure as she waited for the doctor to see them.

Tenzin observed her from the other side of the glass. She looked radiant.

*Maybe what they say about pregnant women glowing is true.*

She read the pamphlet that she had picked up with a single-minded focus. He had seen the same vertical line on her father's forehead as was now etched on hers. The only change in her was the curve of her lips.

*Did my presence in her life invert the smile? Is she so miserable with me?* He could not help thinking.

The voice in his ear buzzed away into nothingness as he remembered when that smile had made his heart flutter. Their friendship proved that sometimes the most unlikely things could lead to big breakthroughs.

After the kiss in the office he had stonewalled her bold pursuit that led to an uncomfortable expectant stillness that had him more aware of her than ever before. She had obviously resisted pushing back, using all the wiles she could employ but when he had been unrelenting she too gave up and kept her distance. Working together became uncomfortable and fraught with nervous silence.

He had heard the door of her room open. In the stillness of the late night, he had felt duty-bound to ask her what the matter was. In reality, he had been on the same page of the book since she had started moving around after shutting the TV off. The quiet night allowed the sounds to reverberate and their adjacent rooms at the end of the passage added to the visual pictures that he conjured about her.

'What happened?'

'Nothing. I need to get a few things from the chemist.'

'What, I have some medicines if you...?'

'Personal stuff,' she said, looking everywhere but at him.

'Oh...okay.'

She moved to get away but he had been unable to let her go just yet. Constantly maintaining a distance after their kiss had taken a toll on him.

'Wait,' he said. 'Let me come with you. I don't want you walking around at night,' he said, turning to close his door.

She looked at him, trying to gauge if his concern was genuine or...then just shrugged her shoulders.

They walked three blocks without sharing a word. At the pharmacy, she went in search of what she needed and he felt odd trailing behind her. Realising what she was looking for, he picked up the packets of sanitary pads and took it to her.

He casually strolled over to her to ask if they would do, then felt weird, like a married couple, buying sanitary napkins together.

'Thanks, this is what I needed, darling,' she said; the impish smile stealing his breath, calming his mind.

On that day, he realised that as long as she smiled all would be right in his world.

'Really...okay,' he said, taking out his wallet as she placed her items at the check-out counter.

'Please don't, there is no need to do that, I can pay my way.' She objected.

'I know, Bee.'

She looked up at him and recognised that she was not alone in this bubble of self-deprivation.

'What is the problem if we both feel the same way?' She had asked on the way back. He knew he had been giving her mixed signals and so he had to come clean.

'My age, my background, that I am your boss and the fact that I will never marry or have children...ever.'

'The way I feel I wouldn't care if you were younger than me so neither should you. Backgrounds are just soils that are responsible for our germination. What we eventually become is usually on us, as humans. Is there a clause in the contract that does not permit us to be friends? In addition, I do not remember ever implying that I wanted to marry you, just looking for a good time. I am all for staying away from commitment myself.'

He bent his head and slowed. 'No, there is no clause like that.'

They walked on silently, the pace now a crawl. It was a beautiful night after all.

He took her hand meshing his fingers with hers, his shoulders relaxed. She turned her face up towards him, the smile blooming in her eyes. The streetlights bathed her upturned face in a golden glow and he knew. He knew that this was the moment, he had dreaded all his life, when he lost all control over his senses.

Before him was a woman with hair the colour of liquid firewood, shining eyes under winged dark brown brows, no perfect arches for his Bee.

She was not a traditional fragile beauty but had the look of a tall warrior, a centurion. Someone who would laugh aloud head thrown back or pull out her pistol to fight rather than twist her hands waiting for her knight. Instead, she would steal a horse and save the man for good measure.

'Sir, Sir…are you there?' The voice in his ear demanded his attention and he was brought back to the ground with a thud.

She was checking the time now, irritation at being made to wait coming off her in waves. He had to go to her before she picked a fight with the receptionist who was giving her wary looks.

It felt strange to have gone from one extreme to the other in a couple of years. Now she had nothing left to say to him, or cautiously filtered whatever she did.

He would have felt sad at the demise of their friendship if he could stop feeling so hurt.

# 31

## *Virago*

### A strong, brave or warlike woman

(Language: English, Origin: Latin)

'Bee...Bee...hold on.' Tenzin pulled at her arm.

'Why did you come with me if you did not want to stay for the test?'

'Bee, I have to get back, I cannot stay here for two more weeks.'

'Fine.' She shot back at him.

'Why are you angry with me?'

She stopped and turned to say, 'I don't know I barely know what I am feeling these days.'

'Okay, okay,' he said.

'You don't have to sound fed up.'

'I am not.'

'Come on.'

'Look Bee, let's not do this. I will keep in touch over the phone but I need to...the office...I haven't said anything to them...we will have to figure out if you want to come back or do we fill your position.' He said.

'Are you seriously thinking about the office right now? How insensitive are you?' She shrieked.

'I think it is called being practical. We can think of hiring someone for the time being and then when you come back....'

'Yeah, don't be too sure.'

'Exactly.'

'Tenzin you...you can't be thinking like this.'

'Why? The work does not stop just because someone is going through a rough patch.'

'I am leaving!'

'Bee calm....'

'Don't even say it...I don't want to calm down.' She screamed and walked straight to the car, her breath choppy.

'I will let you know whatever the result is,' she said and got into the car to drive away without a backward glance.

Tenzin stood watching the car speed away, his thoughts bleak; she would cut him out of her life without spilling a drop of blood. He had seen her do it to other people and now she would do it to him.

He felt eclipsed.

Bee wiped the tears from the corner of her eyes before she went into the *Haveli.* She was bound to run into someone or the other before she reached her room. She saw her mother in the kitchen and walked stealthily past her. She lay on the bed, not understanding why she was doing this to herself.

She picked up the leather-bound pages and began reading.

*I can only write this now, after my strength had returned. Giving birth is not an easy feat. But, it makes me feel powerful as if I can do anything now; move mountains, build kingdoms, destroy them if need be, for this gift from the heavens.*

*Rumi, I have named her Rumi, for she is other-worldly to me.*

*My life seems to be a series of missed chances, it seems. When Hamad left, I tried my hardest to harden my heart towards him, but that day after around five months of his last visit, the sun shone the brightest. When it was at a right angle to my head, at noon, Shafquat Mian interrupted my riyaaz and told me that Hamad was visiting.*

*(Shafquat Mian had been teaching me to tell time with the movement of the sun across the sky, I was silly enough to ask him what I will do if it was cloudy one day, only to earn his swats.)*

*'What does that have to do with me?' I asked, my heart ready to jump out of my chest. His pitying eyes lowered, he said nothing.*

*I continued my riyaaz, my ears trained to hear his heavy footsteps. My concentration lost, I grew silent, the sound of my anticipation echoing in the silent room. The musicians looked at my crestfallen face and left.*

*Was there anyone who did not know about my feelings for him?*

*I strummed the tanpura's strings absentmindedly and then suddenly Ammi called.*

*'Noorie. NOORIE.' I heard her shout.*

*It took me considerable effort to rise from the floor even with Shafquat Mian helping me heave my body, heavy with the baby, off the floor.*

*I rushed to Ammi, as fast as I could, where they sat in the baithak. I entered, eyes lowered, knowing that one look at his face and I would come undone.*

*When no one spoke, I looked up and saw the stark white bandage covering his forehead and arm. How could I stay unaffected? I walked slowly to him and touched his face, caressing the small scars that had been absent the last time he stood before me.*

*Leave this fighting to others, I wanted to say, the words leapt to the tip of my tongue but I swallowed them back for he was as stuck in his life as I was in mine. Both of us could not leave… there was nowhere else to go.*

*The rustle and tinkle of a heavily embellished body leaving the room entered my subconscious mind but not enough for me to be diverted from my focus. I leaned down to kiss him softly on his chapped lips.*

*He had most likely come here before going home to his family, straight from the outpost. Feeling special and needed, I held him close. He nestled his forehead between my full breasts, and an exhausted sigh escaped him.*

*I do not know how long I stood just holding him to me, a minute, an hour but in that moment, I wanted time to stand still.*

*But, when has time been kind to me? Some movement outside burst our cocoon of heaven. He got up and just as I thought he would ask me to come away with him…it was in his eyes, water gushed from between my legs and a pain like I have never known gripped my insides in angry claws.*

*I froze, gasping loudly.*

*Hamad immediately gauged the reason for my pain and called out to Ammi. Fatima and Ammi rushed into the room, moving her heavy girth with lightning speed.*

*She shoved Hamad out and I spent the most excruciating ten hours of my life. They were made bearable with the knowledge that he waited outside, concerned for my well-being and the child's.*

*The first cry and I was relieved and utterly exhausted.*

*'Call him in, Fatima,' I said, desperate for him to see this little part of me that he had helped bring into the world.*

*Fatima exchanged a look with Ammi that I found strange. Hamad walked in and looked at the baby, then at me and my heart stopped at the expression in his eagle-like eyes.*

*They were blank, with no anger or happiness. His eyes were dead. Then he said the words that broke my heart into two. He said, 'She does not look like the Shehzada, plus a daughter will never be a threat.'*

*My smile slipped away.*

*He was, after all, like everyone else and I had been a fool to play with fire. Men would always find ways into a woman's heart through any path they could and women, despite their better judgement, continued to be taken in by their false promises.*

*He left and I refused to see him when he returned after a week. Ammi tried explaining that he did not mean it in the way I was taking it but his words had pierced my pride and I would not forgive easily. I came to know today that he had come to visit Ammi before leaving again for another battlefield, this time following the river Luni to invade more lands for the Great King Baz Bahadur.*

*Since Rumi's birth, I have been thinking about the Shehzada. Why is he so heartless and cruel when his own father, the King, wants progress of his people? He is so conscious of the rights of women. A few days ago Shafquat Mian told me that the King had given a farman that a library shall be built for women!*

*Can you imagine, for women?*

*Is it a sort of atonement for his son's sins...maybe, but it gives me hope for Rumi.*

*With a good education, she could rise above this life. Become a respectable woman. Have a house of her own.*

*Empty dreams perhaps, but such pretty ones! Rumi is fretful, the little angel.*

*She seems to sense when I am thinking troubled thoughts.*

Bhavya kept the delicate pages aside, her mind playing havoc.

*What if the baby was Kabir's? Would Tenzin also feel nothing just as Hamad had felt with Rumi?* She knew how he felt about children. She had even understood it, shared it.

Knowing that one had been left on the steps of a monastery in the hands of fate had to have left a lasting impression in his mind. It was easier to provide financial assistance from a distance than to take on the responsibility of loving a child.

*He loves the kids in the monastery,* she justified.

*If the baby is Kabir's, he will forever be entrenched in our lives. Will this relationship survive that?*

# 32

## *Nyctophilia*

## Love for darkness or night

(Language: English borrowed from Greek)

She knew she was sleeping.

She felt it, the awareness of her hand under the pillow, the other on her softly swelling belly, her legs straight. She could hear the whirring sound of the fan as it circled overhead even as she heard the music. A young voice was singing sweetly...a lullaby, to soothe, an eternal expression of love.

*Who is singing at this hour*? She wondered.

Her lips formed the words: '...Rumi...Rumi...sleep now, my love, *meri jaan*.'

She could make out a slender hand caressing a small head, the henna on her fingers contrasting beautifully with the golden brown, soft curls on the child's head. The dancing yellow and orange bangles on her wrists creating their own music adding to the sweet sound of the *tanpura* that someone was tuning nearby.

Bhavya's lips curled as she turned to her side holding the pillow as one would a small child. She opened her eyes slowly as if expecting to see the little girl nestled close to her heart. She gripped the pillow closer, an acute longing overwhelming her at the realisation that she was dreaming of Noorie's child.

After tossing and turning for the better part of an hour, she finally got out of the bed.

*Maybe if I eat something*...her growling stomach agreed. She sneaked out of her room to tip toe to the kitchen where she found a plate of food ready to be nuked on the granite slab…again.

'Oh Ma!' She whispered. 'I hope I am able to become even half the mother you are.'

She took the warmed plate to the porch and sitting on the swing ate the rice and *rajma,* with relish, realising her appetite had increased. With her eyes on the far horizon, crickets singing in her ears and the cold marble under her feet, she felt at peace with herself, for now.

She wondered how Tenzin had fared today. He had not called for the last two days, worrying her family.

*Did he get the air tickets, or has he left without even telling me? Maybe going back and reliving the life we had made with each other would help him come to his senses. He cannot cage me; tell me who I can be friends with.*

*Are we still fooling ourselves?* The inner voice made its presence felt.

She heard a careful stride and recognised it instantly.

'Coming home late again, my dear brother?' She whispered.

The footsteps stopped and changed their direction.

'Why are you sitting here, outside in the open?'

'Is it an issue if I am, it is also my house?'

'Why do you always assume the worst about me?' He said, taking the plate from her and gulping down the rest of the food like a starving man.

'By default I suppose. I just feel like I have to warrant my being here like this, a burden. As if every question is a finger pointing at me in judgement even when I know it isn't…sorry…and get your own food!'

'Well, I only meant that keep that red shawl you are never without around since you are preg…' he stopped unsure, uncomfortable about the topic.

'You can say it, you know, it's not like I am going to die.' Bhavya laughed.

'Okay then... Are we being candid?' He asked, turning towards her, keeping the empty plate aside.

'Yes...sure,' Bhavya said.

'There is going to be talk.'

'Why are you so sure that we won't get back together?'

'Tenzin's eyes have changed, they are sadder, disappointed.'

'As in...and mine?' She asked, knowing Dheeraj could arrow down to the moot point when everyone else was lurching around in the dark.

'You don't look at him in awe anymore.' He said softly.

'What do you think I should do?' She asked.

'Stay strong. Get a job. Do what you think is right.' He said, watching her nod a yes.

'What about you?' Bhavya asked her brother.

'What about me?' He asked.

'How is it going with Sona?'

'Good, so far, though she treats me like a child, which irritates me.'

He realised that he had stepped in it as soon as the words were out.

'You can't tell anyone, Bee *di*.'

When Bhavya smiled, he got flustered.

'Bhuvan will kill me...and Ma will....'

'Dad will kill you.' She added.

'Yes, that too!'

'Please promise, promise me...' He nagged.

'*Uff* okay, but you do know that she is Charu's age?'

'Yes, two years elder to me, I have even been made to count the minutes. What is the big deal?' He said, relaxed now that she had promised.

'The toy boy has cougar issues.' She teased.

There was nothing like teasing your siblings to get your mind off your problems. Instant fix.

'Shut up!' He swatted her playfully and for a moment they were giggling teenagers again.

Arun saw his daughter and son laugh and fight as they had done when they were young. He had watched Bhavya from his study since she had come out to eat the food he knew Uma would leave out for her.

She was collecting herself to rise again, phoenix like. So he gave her time. She was the most like him and that is what scared him. Pleased that she had Dheeraj for company, he walked to his room in the dark to his softly snoring wife and felt thankful for their times together. Uma had stuck it out with him, despite everything. These days, finding a partner who accepts you as you are, is near impossible.

His thoughts turned to Bhavya and Tenzin. What could have happened? It has just been four years since they met and this...this unresolved issue between them, it seems too deep. Fraught with disappointment and hurt that he heard in Bhavya and Tenzin's voices, the underlying distrust... the future scared him.

*What if they separate?*

*What is wrong with my daughters that they cannot sustain their marriages? First Aruna and Rafi and now Bhavya and Tensing. Where are we going wrong in the rearing of our children that they are unable to compromise and adjust?*

*Have we not been doing just that, for years now...too many to count. I have lived with a woman who I care for as a wife but she is not the love of my life or I hers, but we have been making do. Why can't my daughters?*

*The vicious doubts stemming from his worry for his daughter made him frown and that was never a good sign.*

Bee tried to will herself to sleep knowing that her need to read about Noorie and her past had blossomed to the point of obsession. She promised herself a couple of pages and that was it.

Switching on the reading light she opened the journal again.

*Today was my first mehfil. Rumi was fretful tonight until Fatima put her to sleep.*

*I was eager to put my riyaaz to use. It was a test. I would either sink…forever relegated to helping the favourites from behind the purdah or it would be my debut into this world of mausiqui, where people would come to hear my nazms from far and wide.*

*Ammi said that it went very well, with the Maharajas and Nawabs whispering that I was the new 'Noor' of Panna Mandi. They said they could not get enough of me, that they would come to hear me again tomorrow.*

*And so it began the carousel of attention, appreciation, applause, adoration… They came to meet me bearing presents of expensive silks, pearls, jewels and golden asharfis.*

*Ammi was happy and I was happy for her.*

*Shafquat Mian has told me that my commission will increase if I remain this popular.*

*'The more you get for the kotha, the more you can save for Rumi.'*

*He is advising me on money matters these days. He says I should be aware of all this if I don't want be dependent in my later years.*

*I agree with him whole-heartedly. I never want to depend on anyone else ever again.*

*Some weeks ago a boy, what am I saying…a man, came and joined the mehfil, hesitantly sitting at the back, just as I was finishing the last ghazal. One look and I knew it was his first foray into the Mandi. I do not know why my eyes met his and why the hair on my neck stood up when his eyes slid away guiltily. He would not meet my eyes, sitting in the corner until all the Maharajas,*

*Nawabs and Nizams had been satisfied with a private audience with me. You can imagine how long he waited.*

*He looked at me with an obsessed light in his eyes and then closed his eyes as if he was in pain. When everyone had left and Ammi was busy counting and laughing at the gifts, he came forward. I looked at him, expectantly, but he neither had a bag full of coins nor any gifts to show his appreciation.*

*He just looked at me and whispered, 'Noorie, I am so sorry. Please forgive me.'*

*I did not recognise the face but the voice I would recognise anywhere. The same voice had urged the Shehzada and the others to stop the 'fun'. The only one who had been heckled into doing what he had not wanted to. He had continuously repeated that he was sorry after he had finished.*

*How do I know this? His tears had mixed with mine when he had tried to wipe them with my hair so his friends would not see him cry.*

*I looked at him, waiting for the anger to overtake me... nothing...I felt nothing. No anger, no remorse, no guilt. My defiling had ceased to become the event that defined me. I was free.*

*I whispered, 'What is your name?'*

*'Chirag...' he said.*

*Just then, Rumi who had woken up while I was performing the mujra came out running.*

*'Ammi, Ammi...' she said having just learnt the word.*

*I smiled and held her close, expecting the boy to have left.*

*But he was still there, looking at me and at Rumi with a strange expression on his face, as if he had found a treasure he had been looking for. Then, he abruptly got up and walked away.*

*I watched him leave, realising that I had moved on. My past was just that...the past.*

*The future wriggled in my arms as I tickled her to fill the hall with the sound of innocent laughter and joy.*

# 33

## *Seelenverwandte*

## Two people or two souls who might not be blood related but are two of a kind

(Language: German)

Morning came and brought with it a firm resolve to let bygones be bygones.

'Think of the future, Bee. No more procrastinating, no more hiding. If Noorie could let the past go, you too can make the effort.' Bhavya looked at her reflection and tightened her resolve. Feeling stronger after weeks of lying dormant she needed to get back in the game. With a determined step, she went to have breakfast with her worried family.

'Dad, can I come along?' Bhavya asked as she gauged the mood.

'What?' asked a perturbed Arun.

'Nothing, I...I...was just getting bored so I thought I would go with all of you to the shop, get the hang of it.' Bhavya said at everyone's surprised faces.

'Oh, why so much surprise? It's not like I can't have an interest...okay a new interest.' Bhavya said, peeved at being the oddity in the room.

Arun stood up, and all pairs of eyes rose with him, the dining room hushed for his judgement.

'Go and change into something appropriate. You cannot go to the shop in these jeans. We will wait for you in the car. If you are not outside in twenty minutes, we will leave. Come Gaurav; tell me more about this website that you were discussing yesterday.'

Gaurav got up to follow Arun to the car, stuffing his mouth with the soft paratha that Uma had especially made for him. He stopped to look at Dheeraj who still sat at the table.

'You coming, Dheeraj?' He asked.

'Why? He wants to talk to you. Go ahead, I will come with Bee.' Dheeraj replied, his tone brusque enough to halt Gaurav's step.

Unsure, Gaurav looked at Suresh Uncle who was looking dapper in his white shirt and black trousers, ready for court. An imperceptible nod from him made Gaurav retreat from the vicinity. He knew Suresh Uncle would handle everything, ruffled feathers and all.

'Dheeraj?' Suresh asked the young man who sat with fists clenched on the table.

'I don't know why I am so angry with him. He has not done anything wrong to me. In fact, he has been pulling the lion's share of work while it should have been me who thought about the expansion and the internet and the website but I am just…' He bent his head, unable to put his thoughts into words.

A long-standing friend or a proxy father knows when to just listen. Suresh knew the turmoil Dheeraj went through to reach even this state of awareness of his shortcomings. He stood up, with a hand on the young man's shoulder, a son, almost his own.

'It's okay,' he said and walked out of the room.

Dheeraj kept sitting on the table, his thoughts tumbling over one another, counting every day of the three years he had spent just going from day to day. He thought of the hours he spent staring into space, wishing there was a button he could press to put a break on his thoughts.

'You coming, Dheeraj?' Bhavya asked, as she stood wrapping the cotton dupatta around her neck, looking pained.

'Forced to wear ethnic…and making even that look chic, I have to give it to you Bee, you are something else,' said Dheeraj moving his leaden body towards the waiting car.

Bhavya stood slack jawed, staring after her brother, his words of favour warming her troubled heart.

By evening, however, Bhavya realised the futility of trying to outrun her thoughts. Everything reminded her of Tenzin.

It started with a cup of coffee....

*The sun's rays had touched the couple who walked the streets of Paris, taking in the sights, unaware of what lay in store for them. The girl was brimming with possibilities and the man sure of his place and his path.*

*She saw the girl lean up to say something even as the elegant man resisted. She knew these words by heart.*

*'Let's have a cup of coffee,' she said.*

*'Okay, let's go in.'*

*'No, Tenzin, I want to sit outside. It's such a beautiful day.' She smiled, inviting. Have fun; live in the moment, it said. He resisted.*

*'Bee, I am not sitting on the roadside, it's like sitting on the damn footpath....'*

*'Snobbish much, Tenzin? We are in Paris for heaven's sake, the city of romance, why would we not do as the Parisians do?' She said, taking a turn arms outstretched, charming him at her display of joy.*

*'Okay then, outside it is.' He said after a moment, giving in with a half-smile. 'I also think it's time I educated you about the symphony of wines that this land produces.'*

*'Why does everything have to be a purpose, just enjoy the moment.'*

*'And, do what?'*

*'Sit and soak in the sun, have a croissant, feel it melt in your mouth, smile at random people and smell the coffee or wine, as you prefer.' She said.*

*He looked at her, indulgently, as she quickly pulled him towards a café that lined the street.*

*To a passer-by, they looked like any other couple, a young, vibrant girl who caught everyone's eye not because she fit into the world's idea of beauty but because she had a fire that made her unique.*

*Opposite her was a man, his hair going to salt, his bearing regal, slightly still, detached. She was gushing, her hands flying around as she articulated her words with every part of her face and body while he sat looking at her, observing everything, each flicker that crossed her mind, not moving a muscle. The half-smile on his face was the antitheses to her loud laugh. They both looked the perfect foil for each other.*

*Her fire to his ice. When did we hit the first hiccup, the speed breaker that awakened us from the rosy dream that we had seen together?* She wondered.

'Bee, BEE…Earth calling Mars.'

Twisted in her thoughts, Bhavya did not hear Gaurav, who stood at her back looking at her with concern.

*I should talk to Tenzin; this has gone on too long. She will kill me…but so be it,* he thought.

'Hey.' He said, tapping her on the shoulder and handing her a cup of tea.

She took it from him, and burnt her tongue as she took her first sip, trying to wet her dry throat.

'Be careful, Bee,' called out Arun, he too had been watching his daughter take the trek into her past.

She lowered her eyes, shaken, realising the wall that she had built around her mind and heart was cracking.

*Was it time to let everything out rather than fight against the inevitable?*

'You have such an expressive face, Bee, quit thinking about him,' he added, and then turned to answer someone's query.

After spending most of the morning re-learning the intricacies of running a retail business in Delhi, it was late afternoon when Bee found a quiet corner to rest her feet.

If she stayed in Delhi, she knew her first order of business would be to get a job. This was not her cup of tea.

She opened the journal that she had stuffed in her bag at the last minute, her constant companion.

*Every night I sing for the Nawabs and Sheikhs and the rich men who flock the kotha just to get a glimpse of me. I have become the undisputed 'Noor' of Panna Mandi.*

*Noorie Bai, they call me with respect and yet…my eyes search for the glimpse of that one face for whom, I do the solah shringar every night.*

*Only the parting in my hair remains empty. Waiting.*

*I let my voice carry my heartache as I sing for the men who shout their praises and yet the voice I want to hear remains silent. But, I won't think of him tonight. I shall strive to be happy with what I have.*

*Dreams are for fools and the insane, and I am neither.*

*I waited and prayed for his safe passage, promising never to ask for anything else if he returned safely from the battlefield. I had not realised that though my prayers were answered, Hamad would keep himself away on his return.*

*I did not believe it when Shafquat Mian told me sheepishly that he had been back for weeks. Ammi too had nodded sadly at my question.*

*But, I didn't lose hope even then; I persevered, hoping for his heart to change. I had seen the need in his eyes, felt the want in his touch.*

*Why then had he deserted me? I could not fathom. I do not ask for any promises or any commitments and still he wants to stay away. Am I wrong in my assumption that he loves me? He has never said the words.*

*Yesterday, he sent a message that he is on his way. After 12 months of being apart, I was trembling with anticipation.*

*I wore the deepest shade of vermillion and sat, the heavily embellished yellow dupatta covering my oiled, perfumed hair.*

*The kohl was thick in my anxious eyes as was the rouge on my cupid-bow lips. Fatima had made a beauty mark just above the corner. She said it enticed the men to investigate further. Today, I wanted him to find all my secrets and more.*

*I heard the scrape of his leather slippers as he walked towards my door.*

*He waited a moment after rapping his knuckles and then entered. I looked at the man who had been the reason that I was still breathing.*

*'Noorie. . .you have grown up,' he said, coming closer. He looked struck by the changes.*

*'Why are you dressed like this?' He asked, used to seeing me in a simple muslin kurta, gharara and dupatta.*

*'Like what?' I asked, taken aback at his curt tone.*

*'Like the other girls,' he said.*

*'I am one of them now.' I said, wanting him to understand my changed status.*

*'Yes, I heard,' he said, not meeting my eyes.*

*'How are you?' I asked, quietly.*

*What I wanted to do was to shout at him instead. I saw myself scream at him, hit him, demand justification for his absence from my life for 5,25,600 minutes.*

*What was my fault to be sentenced to this hell of waiting for his arrival, with every minute without him a separate lash on my soul?*

*But, all I did was lower my lashes demurely, letting him take his time to answer.*

*'I am. . .as I was. The same.' He came closer, sat on the jewel-toned, velvet bedcover that I had lovingly readied for tonight.*

*He looked at my face as if he was searching for something; I thought validation for his love. He leaned closer and whispered next to my lips as he gripped my hands.*

*'Noorie, I can't see you under all this powder, please remove it. I want to see you, my Noorie,' he whispered.*

*Then, without waiting for help, he fetched a wet cloth and rubbed the colour from my face, heaping praise on each inch of skin he uncovered. I could do nothing but sit still and let him find the Noorie he wanted.*

*He needed me, really cared, just was unable to show it, I thought. I didn't know what I was supposed to say but before I could say another word he pulled me closer. There were so many questions I....*

*'Your eyes shine like the armour under the hot sun.'*

*I could not control my giggles at his simile. He paused at my laughter looking embarrassed and said, 'Do you laugh at me; I do not have your hunr with words I admit.'*

*'So, you have been listening to my ghazals...and I laugh at your expression, my solider.'*

*'Your solider?'*

*'Yes, mine.'*

*'I am marri....'*

*'I know, just keep me with you, here.' I said, leaning my head on his shoulder, my hand warm on his heart, knowing it was a dream but oh such a pretty one.*

*'I shall marry you,' he said, his voice resolute, and I closed my eyes and nodded. My heart stopped. Were these just words or did he really mean them?*

*'You will marry me, won't you?' He asked.*

*'Ye...yes, my love, do you even need to ask?'*

*We were silent for a while and then I could not help myself. I had to know why, why now. What had changed?*

*'Is everything alright at home?'*

*'Yes,' he said after a moment and I knew something was not right. I just hoped that his words of marriage were not a reaction to whatever had triggered them.*

*'Will it not cause problems with...your wife and her family?'*

*'She is my biggest headache. We lead separate lives but she wants to interfere with mine, has the whole zanana spying on me. She does not like that I come here but because of Ammi...she cannot really say anything. She pretends to be so pious, always muttering, constantly listening to that maulvi, that religious fanatic, who interprets the holy book as is suitable to him. She does not use her brain to interpret the truth for herself.*

*She wants big things for me she says but the ambitions are hers. I just want a small place to live and earn and raise children. All this court politics, the plotting and scheming are not meant for me. I am tired of everything.' He said.*

*I kept my head over his heart giving him time, scared that he would take his words back. They were an illusion I wanted to hold on to.*

*'I am lonely, Noorie...so alone. I need someone who belongs to me. Only me. The day I saw you I felt you too were alone, as alone as I am in the midst of all these people. All I want is to be with you, hear your voice as you sing, your bangles clink as you brush your hair and your anklets tinkle as you dance for me.' He said, turning my face up to seal his words on my lips.*

*My happy ending was here, I thought. All that I had wanted was close. He could marry me and the three of us could be a happy family.*

*The rest of the evening was spent sipping khus sherbet, making plans for the big day and catching up on the political intrigue that was surrounding Malwa. He told me of his plans for asking for a jagir in Delhi and shifting there to live; he was tired of the fight that seemed to have no end.*

*He talked well into the night before I silenced him with my lips. It had been so long since we had been together last that I had been worried that he may not want me after Rumi. My body has grown more curvaceous, my breasts full and heavy with milk, my thighs and stomach fuller, rounded.*

*But, I was silly to worry, he likes my changed body, considering the time he spent worshiping it. He said my body was that of a woman now.*

*He has left for the day.*

*As I watched him wear his clothes, his eyes unable to leave the muslin barely covering my heavy breasts that he marked last night, I felt the first stirrings of guilt.*

*I had completely forgotten about Rumi.*

## 34
## *Dudgeon*
## A feeling of offence or resentment

(Language: English, Origin: Uncertain)

'Bee, where are you lost and what is this?' Gaurav asked, peering into the pages.

'Nothing,' Bee slammed the journal shut, looking up disoriented. Then realised there was nothing to hide. She had been hiding her thoughts from everyone for so long that everything she did seemed wrong somehow.

'It's Noorie's journal,' she said sheepishly the next minute.

'Oh okay. She was that courtesan right, the one who has the black tomb, sixteenth century? Any interesting content to read?'

'Nope, just a tale of love.'

'That sounds interesting...not. No intrigue?'

'Is it time to go?' She asked, smiling and answering in the negative.

'Yes, long past.'

'Okay.' Bhavya said and got up.

'Tenzin called and said that he needed to speak to you.' Gaurav added as he helped her up.

'Okay.'

'Is everything on the right track?'

'I think it will be.'

Bhavya called Tenzin from the *Haveli*. He answered before the bell could finish its first ring.

'Bee?'

'Yes.'

'I have to rush back to Paris. There is some big client... the office wants me to handle the account personally. I know it is the worst time...I wish I could have stayed, spoken about how we will proceed, what we should do... see the result with you but...Bee...say something.'

'I don't know what to say, Tenzin. You were incognito for the last two days. Where were you? I wish you...' Bhavya said, her words interrupted by the lump in her throat. 'Let us talk once I get the results.' She ended.

'Yes, alright. I...I have left the sample in the clinic. Have also transferred the money for....'

'I said I could foot the bill.'

'Look, you can pay me back okay, let's not fight. The test will take 2–3 weeks after you give...ummm...all the samples. So please hurry. Mine will be saved, frozen I suppose. I didn't ask. I have to go, we are boarding. Bye Bee.' He said then paused for a moment as if wanting to say something before disconnecting.

Bee held the phone in her hand for some time, her mind not processing what had just happened.

*He left, actually left*. She thought.

*What did you expect? He is not going to stay here while you procrastinate. He came to take you back but you were hell-bent on pushing him away. Now sit here and mope.*

*Bah! She does not care for him. Stop making her feel as if she needs him to define her...He never wanted the baby. This is a way to slither away from his responsibility.*

*That idea was ours.*

*So what, he could have said that it did not matter, that he was happy it was a part of us. But no, he readily agreed. If the DNA test reveals that the baby is not his, he can walk away. I say, we should do that before him.*

*Calm down...don't go spouting nonsense...for God's sake. Even my inner voice has split,* thought Bhavya.

But now that the possibility had entered her head, she could not shake it off. She knew herself. She would rather leave than be left. She wanted to cry and scream out her frustration. Maybe three years back she would have done just that but now she walked into her room and closed the door and started reading.

*He comes regularly now, every day. These days are like perfumed mistrals, golden in their hue. I have started understanding how the court works. Everyone is insecure of their position, everyone wants to get noticed and closer to the Bahadur's ear and no one is safe. Hamad has already spoken about the jagir in Delhi. He hopes to become a support to Mir Bakshi, the Diwan-i-Arz.*

*He is happy with that, I think. He talks for hours about his plans to solidify the military intelligence under Mir Bakshi's tutelage. With murmurings of Akbar gathering his army with Adham Khan at the helm, a great threat looms. Hamad says that the King cannot see anything beyond his nubile wife, Roopmati, unwilling to pay attention to the mutterings.*

*Being in Dilli will certainly get him out of the eye of the storm when it hits. His eyes shine and sparkle when he talks of Dilli. He says any day he will be asked to pack up and leave. I know I should be happy with the time I have with him but I fear it will be impossible for me to let him go. How will I bear the separation? Already his frequent trips to the palace take days away from us.*

*It is during those days that Chirag comes. We talk about this and that. His father's autocratic rule, his trade of cloth and monopoly over the palace supplies, his timid wife who knows nothing beyond the kitchen...everything, anything under the sun. He plays with Rumi, teaches her the alphabet, and sings songs to her. I think he feels Rumi is his or wants to believe it... maybe it feels nice to be a part-time father.*

*That sounds so cynical but I suppose life does that to a person, saps your innocence and fills the hole that is left behind with doubts and mistrust.*

*Chirag is a nice man, weak but nice. I wish I had met him before...well...no point going into the past over and over. He will make a great father one day. He spends his days with us under the garb of lies, I know. I asked him why he defies society's rules. He only shrugged his thin shoulders saying, 'No one sees me outside these walls. For them I am only the son of an influential zamindar. I have no other identity.'*

*'And here?' I asked.*

*'Here I can write my poetry in peace, be with Rumi, and I see you and you see me.' He said looking intently at me, then cupping my face he added, 'Come with me, Noorie. We can run away.'*

*When I laughed, he lowered his eyes, his hand dropping away.*

*'I thought you were joking.' I said softly, realising that I had hurt him.*

*'No, I want to take you away from this life, away from this kotha, make you my wife...I...I know you love Hamad but he will never marry you. You will always be his whor...' He stopped not wanting to offend my sensibilities maybe.*

*'Noorie let me make you a respectable woman.' He said with absolute conviction.*

*'Chirag, you are my dearest friend. But I don't need saving, I am content with my lot in life. I have for the first time friends who talk to me, people to love and care about my future. I am fine.'*

*'Noorie, I want to atone for my sin, how do I do that...how do I help you?' He asked me, gripping my hands in desperation.*

*'I will ask for help when I need it, and hold you to your word to help me then.'*

*'I shall do whatever you want of me, whenever you want.'*

*'Be careful what you say, Chirag, I just might ask you for the moon.'*

*'And, I shall endeavour to give it to you or die trying, my queen,' he said, bowing before me with a flourish imitating the cocky court guests.*

*We laughed and Rumi chortled along merrily.*
*The illusion of a happy family.*

As Bhavya read over the words written so many centuries ago she felt Noorie's struggle become her own. She felt invested in her life as if her own troubles could be solved as long as Noorie found happiness.

She turned to the next page....

*It has been six days since I last saw him. Hamad sent his man-servant to deliver a letter to me saying he had to go to the court and would be back in a few days. Chirag came every day, keeping me from falling into despair. He is a dear man.*

*I know he wants more from me than just friendship but I shall not give myself to anyone other than Hamad. Though most days I spend the nights in the arms of the memories of our nights together, there are some nights when I am unable to help wishing for his closeness, his hardness covering me.*

*I can admit here that on those black nights I want to wake up Chirag and let him take me to the wonderful places my body yearns to go. On those nights, a woman's body awakens and throbs with the need that remains unappeased.*

*Fatima finally taught me how to take care of these urges myself. This knowledge of self-pleasure has freed me, given me a strange control over myself that I lacked before.*

*Another letter came today morning. Only six words: 'I can't wait to see you.' I am walking one foot above the ground! Fatima lost her patience while getting me ready for the night as I turned at each sound that seemed to filter into the room.*

*The gods having blessed us with a slight shower in the afternoon as if to welcome my love. The long awaited relief from the oppressive heat of the summer seems to have invited the men to venture out in droves on this clear night. Every hall was packed and brimming tonight.*

*Today, men of all walks will sit through the night to listen to silken voices weave their dreams and shower asharfis at the dancers' feet in appreciation of their art. And, sometimes, their restless spirit will take them to a different establishment to slacken their other appetites.*

*I say it is better. Let them get their fill of willing bodies here than to guilt them with moral platitudes. It will, maybe, save some other innocent girl from being accosted in an alley or forest to be held accountable and forced to commit suicide under the weight of her family's honour, later.*

*I need to shake these depressing thoughts away before he comes. It is a night made for loving.*

*Tonight the moonbeams shall shadow my anklets that will create magic as I dance and sing for Hamad, only for Hamad. Each twist of my hand and thaap of my feet shall entice him and spark a fire in his heart. He will never want to be away from me again.*

*I just know it.*

Bee rested the open journal softly on her tender breasts, a testament to the changes that were taking place in her body. She rose from the bed and dialled Kabir's number.

*Why am I calling him? He has made his stand clear.*

'Hi.' the voice on the other side was happy and sure.

'It is....'

'Bee, I was just thinking of you. Can you come over tomorrow?'

'Why?'

'Please don't say no. I have started a painting and I need you. Say yes.'

'Kabir, this is not the right time. I am...not feeling up to it.'

'I can't believe you are saying no. You never used to earlier?'

Kabir's assumption irritated Bhavya but she chose to ignore his words. Then a thought struck.

*He is right. A few months back I would have jumped at the chance to get out and meet him. What has changed?*

'Come please, Bee, you will get a chance to get out and about and I will be able to finish my painting. I...um...also wanted to talk to you about the other thing.' He cajoled.

'Okay, I will come for a bit.'

She said briskly keeping the phone down.

She was not unaware that his enthusiasm had lifted her spirit as well. She remembered how he had made quick sketches of her face on napkins, in his notebook, one time even drawing on the back of a parking ticket. That had fallen in a heap of giggles when he had asked for the parking ticket back after paying the fine.

She smiled now, remembering their laughter on the streets of Paris, how it had enveloped them in that bubble of togetherness.

*He is such a happy person, always up for a good time. Quite like how I used to be...before I got....*

Then another thought struck her.

*Why did Tenzin never stop me from going out with him in Paris? Had I been in his place I would have sensed that he was growing more attached...could it be because he wanted me to have what he knew he would not or could not give me or could it be that he did not care?*

She did not think, picking up the phone she called Tenzin's cell phone. 'Hello, what has happened?'

'Why didn't you stop me from meeting him?'

'Would you have stopped, Bee?'

'No.'

'Well, you have your answer. I am in a meeting, Bee, I need to get back.'

Bhavya slowly replaced the phone on the stand, her mind churning.

# 35

## *Shoganai*

## Resigning yourself to a situation

(Language: Japanese)

'Bee, look what I found!' said Uma, walking up to her with an album under her arm. She placed the album on the dining table with a flourish.

'What is this, Ma?' Bee asked, wondering what her mother was trying to hint at now.

'Tara's baby book, *tsk*, you haven't even seen it yet and it is time for a new one,' she said and pulled her chair closer to sit with her daughter. Opening the pages the two women talked and laughed.

Bhavya turned the pages, looking at her younger self, a younger Tenzin. Someone had clicked a picture when he was looking at her as she was laughing loudly. She brought the album closer, trying to see the look in his eyes.

*Where did this man go?*

*Why can't I make out his expressions anymore? Years with another person should aid familiarity but I feel as if this Tenzin is someone I never knew. A man so far removed from the one he is today that I sometimes feel I fell in love with a completely different person.*

She shook her head, not wanting to go down that path. She turned another page and found the picture that Suresh Uncle had clicked at the airport when she had left for Paris with Tenzin.

'I can't believe I wore this old thing to Paris,' she said.

'But it was so pretty, Ten-sing could not take his eyes off you, see how he looks at you, with such passion,' said Uma.

'Passion Ma, blasphemy! You old woman...taking vicarious pleasure through your daughters, bad mother!' Bhavya joked.

'Well, what is one to do, the bones ache but I am not dead yet.'

'Ma, oh my god, that is not a picture I want in my head.'

'What...you think you people invented sex and only you can talk about it? The things we have...' Uma went on.

'No...no...noooo, this is not a conversation I am having with my mother.'

'Old fashioned!' said Uma, her hands on her hips as her lips tried and failed to hold the smile that shone through, lighting her daughter's world.

Uma laughed as she saw her daughter rush out of the door screeching and laughing. Her laughter faded away when she heard her start the car and drive away.

She wanted to shake Bhavya, and tell her to stop running. God had blessed her with a kind loving man and now she was going to be a mother, why could she not be happy with this, why did she want everything?

Bhavya drove down the road lined with the fiery vermillion of the gulmohar, her mind still tangled in the album and Tenzin's pictures.

'I thought I had found passionate love with Tenzin but even the prospect of marriage rotted that. We are like any other married couple—bitter, unfortunate in our choice and yet unable or unwilling to leave each other.' She said aloud in the empty car, lamenting their slide into the ordinary.

She told herself to stop the pity-party and enjoy the day as she got down from her rickety car. With a smile firmly pasted on her full lips, aviators shielding her eyes, she caught the frown of the lady who looked at her baby bump that was on full display in the figure-hugging lycra top. She smiled, shark like before climbing the steps to rap forcefully at the door.

'Why do women judge other women? Should we not support each other…our clan?' She said irritably when he opened the door.

'Wow, let's discuss this in detail,' he said, smiling at her thrumming energy, as she sailed in without a by your leave.

'What got stuck in your craw?' He asked, when she came to a stop before his work table.

'The aunty who frowned at my carefully cultivated casual look.'

'Judgmental much?'

'Me and judgmental, are you joking?'

'What is with the aunty business? Just because she was wearing a….'

'It is not about clothes please, I hope you know me better than this. It is about the frown that says cover up, you are pregnant or you cannot be going around wearing what you like and are comfortable in, where is your loose-fitting top, where is your…?'

'There it is, why do you assume?'

'I do not assume, it is in their eyes.'

'As it is in yours that you don't care…so don't care. Maybe she thinks this because she wants no *buri nazar* to fall on you or guys to accost you. You do realise the unsafe scenario of our country, I hope.'

'Ummm…okay sagaciousness does not suit you. Is that why you decided to leave this country?' She said pointing to his packed bag near the door.

'Oh, I was always wise; just covered it up with euphemism to dumb down for people like you.' He said teasing back.

'Ha ha ha very funny.' She laughed thinking how easy it was to banter with him.

'Now tell me, how are you, Bee?' He asked in a serious voice.

She stopped and turned to look at him, his eyes were almost sad.

'What?'

'When do you want to get the test done? It has been two weeks; Tenzin has come and gone, you have passed the point of doing anything to retain your old lifestyle. Are you aware of how big a responsibility this baby will be?' He asked.

'I thought you wanted to paint me…had I known you only wanted to talk about my scattered and shit life I would have stayed at home.'

'Bee…this affects me too.'

'How…have I asked you for anything? Have I?'

'No, you haven't but I don't know what I will do if the baby is mine. I have been thinking about it.'

'As per our last conversation, you wanted nothing to…'

'Yes, I realise that but….'

'But what?'

'Okay, I don't know how to string pretty words so I shall give it straight out. If the baby is mine, I want you to leave Tenzin and come with me.'

'What?' She barked in irritation.

'Why not? You are obviously not happy with him.' He said his ego bruised at her reaction.

'In which world are you living, Kabir? I happen to love him.' She scoffed, unable to even look at him.

'And me?'

'You…you are my friend. My…' Now she stuttered, unable to find words to explain herself.

'What am I? Your toy boy, whom you can play with for the time being and carry on with your life for the rest of the time, are you even aware of how selfish that is?' He said.

'Are you saying you have feelings for me?' Bhavya asked.

'Yes. I have feelings for you.'

'Love?'

'Well, nearly there kinds.' It was his turn to look away.

'Is that good enough to alter your life for, Kabir? Look at me, yes we did something in Bali but that was just an act. What I found with you later was a friendship I never want to give up. Something I fought to keep even at the cost of my relationship. I love you but as a friend.' She took him by the hand and sat with him, looking at his confused eyes.

'If you think about this some more and truly remove the family-man spectacles that you are wearing, you too will see that you balked at the idea of throwing everything away that you have worked so hard for, as a first instinct. And, you know what I always say about the first reaction.'

'That it is usually what you really want to say and do.' They both said in unison.

'Maybe you are right and people like us should not have children. But, I will have this baby, with or without any help. I may curse my situation but I love the little bump and I don't want anyone to feel tied down because of the baby or me. It is my choice and mine alone.'

'Why did Tenzin leave, how will you manage?' He asked.

Bee just shrugged her shoulders, empowered and devastated at the truth that she had just voiced.

'Ah, so this was a pity proposal. Kabir, you know I will find a way. And, next time when you do propose to someone don't lead with "if it is my baby". It will be taken as a conditional proposal.' She laughed, feeling consumed by the light of conviction that was new and welcome after so many dark days.

'Now that you put it like that, it does sound rude and cringe-worthy.' Kabir said, accepting his mistake with grace.

'Just my luck; why do men want the love of their women to the exclusion of all others?' Bhavya asked.

'Are you saying women don't? Come sit here, the light is right. No, angle your head a little lower.' The two seamlessly slid into their role as friends.

'Women...hmmm...I don't know.'

'That's because you barely have any female friends and I think you are a man in a woman's body. Also, insecurity isn't gender specific.'

'Insecurity...that's what it is. Love me best and only me.'

'You will see it in almost all relationships, even between a mother and son.'

'I see this every day, with Dheeraj and Ma. Wait till he marries, Ma is going to really have a....'

Kabir let her voice fade into the background, as he concentrated in capturing her essence on the white canvas. Her vitality suffused in him a need to prove himself, to her and to the world. She was the only one who saw the best in him and he wanted to succeed for her, to prove her right.

He did not know what love was but he had been ready to let his dream go for her. He knew what she said was true. He would probably come to resent her in time for taking him away from his dreams but being in her presence was like standing in the winter sun. The warmth was incomparable for one knew it would not last but one kept hoping for more time.

The sun, however, kept its own time, rising and setting as it was meant to.

# 36

## *Mirk*

### Partially or totally dark, gloomy

(Language: Archaic English, Origin: Old Norse)

Bee remained thoughtful for the rest of the day. She did what was necessary, called the clinic to set the date for Kabir to give the sample on the way back to the *Haveli.* Calm had settled over her after her cathartic conversation with Kabir.

Noorie's journal called to her, as if asking her to lay down her troubles as she navigated the intricacies of her life.

*Can a heart break again…and again and still be called a heart, an organ that gives life? Why do I feel that happiness does not suit me? The mere inkling of happy days and my destiny slams the door shut on them.*

*The beautiful ghazal, that I had written and sang for Hamad, brought a shower of applause, repeated calls for an encore that I coyly declined. Along with the appreciation came the clink of several hundred asharfis.*

*They wanted me to continue, but I knew he waited for me.*

*I flew down the hall to meet him, after Ammi nodded permission. My feet stopped their flight when I saw Rumi playing in the corridor outside.*

*'Why is she outside? You know a lot of drunk men come this way.' I asked Fatima.*

*She looked from me to the closed door of my room, not answering my questions, her eyes sliding away. I nodded understandingly and told my heart to forget all these small slights. After all, today was a big day.*

*'Take Rumi to your room and let her sleep with you tonight.' I told Fatima who rushed to pick up the busy child. As I watched her*

*walk away with Rumi who smiled at me and waved, it felt like a premonition, like I was watching her like this for the last time.*

*Fatima was more of a mother to Rumi than I ever was. I only played with her in between the riyaaz, the mehfils and the social whirl that was an everyday affair. It was Fatima who soothed the child when she cried, Fatima who had stayed up nights with her.*

*While I collected the appreciation of the men crowding the brightly lit kotha, she selflessly enjoyed the unconditional love of my daughter.*

*Shaking my head at the life that I was living, I took a deep breath and entered the room that had been readied for tonight under my supervision.*

*My anklets chimed a passionate note as I entered the room to see him lying on the bed decked in rose petals, the big dark man with scars on his face, my soul mate. I sat lightly next to him, not wanting to disturb his sleep. The hope of a beautiful night swimming in my eyes, I traced his sun-beaten face. Skin as dry as leather stretched over prominent cheeks and a tense jaw.*

*'Even in sleep you remain wary, my solider,' I whispered only to see his eyes snap open. He took in my bent form that leaned above him. From my sparkling maangteeka, to my large nath, to my shivering breath, his eyes drank in my face as if he could not get enough of looking at me.*

*After a few sand grains had slipped from the hourglass, I moved to get more comfortable, only to have his hands grip my arms and pull me to his chest.*

*'Don't go anywhere, Noorie,' he said, his voice heavy with... something. His tone had my heartbeat drumming with dread.*

*'What has happened? Did Baz Bahadur refuse to give you the jagir after all?'*

*'No.'*

*I straightened and wondered why then was he not ecstatic at this fulfilment of our dream.*

*'He has given me the jagir in Dilli near the Chowk but....'*

*'But?' I asked, my stomach falling away.*

*'My wife and her family have played a cruel joke on us. They were aware of my feelings for you and the fact that I was planning to take you as my second wife.'*

*I listened, not wanting to hear the rest. He got up and went to stand at the window looking out into the opal sky. His back to me, he repeated the incidents of the court and the games that people had played to separate us.*

*He said his wife had cited honour and moral platitudes and the King had agreed to give him the jagir only if he promised to marry no one else. He would be given a Haveli and a thriving trade to look after.*

*Once Hamad's wife had left the court, placated, the King passed a second farmaan. He gave Hamad the responsibility of spreading music and noble etiquette in the Chowk under the banner of Baz Bahadur. In closed quarters he told Hamad that his wife's father was an important member of his court and he could not displease him.*

*Then giving Hamad his blessings to keep me with him, as his personal whore, he added to the purse for Hamad to build a house for me nearby that would cater to the King and his interest in mausiqui and dance.*

*In other words, he could not make me a respectful woman but could continue to share me with all the others who would bid for me, even the King, if he found me appealing enough. He could become my pimp with the blessings of the King, if he so wanted. I wanted to shout, scratch his downcast eyes out.*

*Once a whore always a whore; I was not good enough to sit with or have a simple meal with.*

*I could not even cry hearing the underlying message that he was conveying to me. He was getting his dream on a platter. Would my feelings and wants come in his way or was I ready to sacrifice my dreams for the love that we share?*

*'Come with me, Noorie, I promise I will look after you. Always.' He said, gripping my hands in his.*

*'I will be a whore for the rest of my life.' I said.*

*'Not in my eyes or do I not matter?'*

*'You are the only one who does. But Rumi....'*

*He got up from where he kneeled before me and again turned his back to me.*

*'Let Rumi stay here, Fatima and Ammi will look after her.'*

*'What?' I said, disbelief making my voice shrill.*

*'Only till you are settled, we will call her and Fatima...even Ammi to Dilli. Just...after some...' His words faded away as he saw my miserable face and came forward to hold me.*

*'It is only for a little while; please say yes, I will refuse the King if you don't come with me, Noorie. It has taken us so long to get to this place. I cannot live without you!' He kept repeating the words that I had been dying to hear as he kissed me, as he held me in his arms, as the clothes melted away, as we became one.*

*The words that once had the power to move me to tears of happiness at the blessing that was Hamad sounded manipulative and false that night. My happiness was tainted by doubt and his inability to consider the sacrifice he was asking of me.*

*Morning came and he happily went to give the news of our departure to his Ammi, leaving me with a hole in my heart. I had already agreed, he did not have to convince me any further. A vacuum that no amount of blessings and envy at my good fortune could fill took the place where once my heart had thudded in my chest. He has left asking me to wait for his letter to begin my journey to Dilli.*

*My God has fallen from his pedestal.*

Letting the tears come, Bee curled her fingers and tried to curb the sounds emanating from her throat turning her face into the pillow. She did not know for whom she was crying or for what.

Was she crying for Noorie or herself, she wasn't sure. In her mind their stories had merged. The ultimatums that went against the love they had envisioned, hurt pride. Or was she crying for that part of herself that believed that love existed despite all odds?

*So where is the hitch? Why do I recoil every time I even think about giving in to Tenzin's demand to cut off all ties with Kabir? To anyone else, this is not even a viable point of contention. Why is it for me?*

*And, what of this baby, will Tenzin be able to love the baby if it is Kabir's? Will he not look at the baby and only see it as the physical validation of an error in his judgement? He had made it clear that he never wanted to become a father. How will he be able to deal with being the father of another man's child?*

Drying her eyes she went back to the journal.

*Somehow, the news has spread like wildfire through the Mandi. I think it was Shafquat Mian who has leaked it. I was hoping to leave quietly but the whole town is buzzing. I knew it would not be long before anger erupted at what others might perceive as good fortune.*

*Chirag came today, initially cajoling, showing me the negatives of the move and when I told him of Hamad's condition, he fell silent. His silence was fraught with disbelief and a disappointment...in me. That was as painful as a deep cut. He didn't say anything after that; just got up and left, even though I went after him to explain. I knew there was no explanation I could give that would make any sense to a soft heart like his.*

*Uff! What am I saying; it was because of his kind that I am in this predicament. Sometimes I amaze myself at my ability to forgive.*

*Now I cannot see anything beyond the move.*

*We shall finally be together.*

The knock on the door had Bee spring up in fright.

'Bee *di,* there is phone call for you, some clinic in...' said Fanny.

Bee shot out of the room and rushed to pick up the phone. She saw her mother standing near the door of the kitchen.

'Bee?'

'It is okay, Ma,' she said to pacify her worried mother.

'Hello.'

'Yes, this is she.'

'Yes I had.'

'What time again?'

'Okay, thank you. I shall be there.'

'Yes, yes, okay bye.' Bhavya said before disconnecting the call.

Bee knew she would have to lie; there was no way she was going to tell her mother that she had been asked to come to give swabs for the paternity test. She turned and her mother pounced.

'Bee, what is going on? This has gone on long enough. Is there a problem? You can tell me. We will get....'

'Ma...Ma...everything is fine, there is a test that determines if the baby has any genetic defects, problems with the child's brain and things like that. We just thought we would get that done to be sure everything is alright.'

'Why do you need to think the worst will happen to you? All that is God's will. Now you cannot do anything about it. We never thought of these things when I had all of you. Why do you do this, invite trouble?' Uma said.

'Ma, I...it is better to get it done.'

'But for what? Does Ten-sing know?'

'Yes Ma, he has already given the sample. Look, his family is unknown; I just want to know if there is something I should be worried about.' Bhavya said, feeling awful lying to her mother repeatedly.

'Oh, yes then it is okay.' Uma said, naively yielding to her daughter who obviously had the permission of her man to do these complicated tests.

'I can come along with you.' Uma said, before turning back to her work.

'No, no. It will only take twenty minutes; it's just the commute that will take time.' Bhavya said remembering Noorie's words.

*Once a liar always a liar.* Of course, Noorie had used it in a different context. Then she realised her mother was still talking.

'Could Darshana not do it?' Uma asked wondering why she was hearing about this for the first time today and why did Bhavya want to visit another doctor when Darshana, their family doctor, had been taking care of every one of them since they were babies.

'No Ma, it is very precise and you have to be trained for it. Also, I don't want you to tell her.'

'Why? She is your doctor...gynaecologist, she should know everything. Bee, you should not hide anything from....'

'Ma, just stop, you are talking of a time when mothers were unaware of what was happening with them. I don't want her to know. It is just a test and not even a prick is needed.' Bhavya said her voice stern.

'Okay, as you wish.' Uma said looking at Bhavya, knowing there was more than she was letting on.

'I mean it, Ma; I don't want you discussing it with Aruna or anyone else.'

'But why?' Uma pushed.

'Because I just don't, can you just for once do what I ask of you?' Bhavya shouted, much to the surprise of them both.

'Bee....'

'For God's sake, it is my life; just let me be, stop interfering.' Bee said rushing back to her room to cry her guilt at lying to her mother, at being a bitch to everyone, at taking the love and patience that her parents were showing in their silence and throwing it back in their face.

*What is wrong with me? When did I become this selfish person*, she thought as she cried at her inability to get the reins of her life in her hands.

She got up and walked out slowly. She found her mother sitting on the dining table with Etti, Gina and Fanny next to her who glared at her in tandem.

'Ma...Ma, I am sorry. Please forgive me; I don't know what has gotten into me.'

Uma looked at her with injured eyes, making her feel worse. Bhavya sat next to her mother taking her hands in hers and did not know where to start.

'I...am losing it, Ma, I am not sure what to do and I am taking the insecurity and indecision out on everyone. I am sorry; I did not mean to shout at you. I know you and Dad and everyone,' Bee looked at her sisters, who were listening to her intently, 'have been patient and waited for me to make up my mind for the last three months and I am just in a limbo, unable to move forward and unwilling to go back.'

'Do you want to leave Ten-sing?' Uma asked.

'I...I...don't know.'

'But why? You both love each other; you are going to have a baby together. If you leave him, this baby will be a basta...' Uma stopped, her eyes welling.

'Ma, sometimes love is not enough. To carry forward a lifelong commitment, friendship and trust is required too,' Bhavya tried to explain as best as she could.

'And the baby will be mine, not a bastard, never a bastard!'

Uma simply looked at her daughter and said nothing more. Nodding her head, she got up and walked into her room to shut the door quietly.

Bhavya looked at her younger sisters who were watching her in an odd way, then got up too. She knew she would have to leave soon.

'The test you told Ma about is done with amniotic fluid, not swabs,' Etti said from behind her.

Bhavya did not turn around. She paused and walked back into her room. Closing the door, she sat on the bed, her head swirling with the lies that were piling up, the hurt that she was causing.

*Now the end is near, I shall get the results and move forward with my life. This sitting on my hands is not doing anything but causing everyone pain,* she thought.

# 37

## *Akrasia*

## Lack of Self-control

(Language: Greek)

*Today is the day*; Bhavya woke up with the vivid thought after another troubled night. She had gotten used to the constant tension that was in the air. With Aruna's delivery drawing closer, the *Haveli* seemed to hold its breath as if fearing any sudden movement.

She spied her parents having a whispered exchange near the kitchen. Her mother was trying to placate her father who was sounding distressed. He was still wearing his walking shoes which meant something had happened during his morning walk.

'What is her plan, Uma? What does she want to do with the baby?'

'She will figure it out…I know you are worried but…you have to…it is a big decision Arun….'

'Someone asked me if she was married, what could I say? I had nothing…no answer….'

'People always say things. You know that, Arun, don't let it affect you…we have to stand firm for her, support her at this time, in spite of what we may believe….' Her mother stressed, it looked not for the first time.

'I know. I know…you are right. I do…support her decision…she is showing now, the baby…Uma…what will we say to everyone if she is unable to resolve her issues with him?'

'We will cross that bridge when we get to it. Right now our priority is Bee. She knows how we feel but she also has to know that we are with her….'

In that moment Bhavya reeled in the knowledge that her parents would always support her but not always agree with her. And she alone should be responsible for the decision or consequence of her actions.

She let it assimilate, the surety she felt in that instant. It seeped into her very soul, freeing her from any lingering doubts she had. She would find her way and on her own.

Her vision cleared and she knew what she wanted to do.

'…what has he done that is so wrong, why won't she tell us?' She heard her father say.

'I will move out but I will not allow you to push me to take a decision before I am ready. You will not guilt me into going back. My problems with Tenzin are my own and I do not want to discuss them because…' Bhavya said, her voice devoid of any uncertainty as she stepped out of the shadows to face her parents. '…in my world just keeping a woman is not enough. A man has to step up and be emotionally involved in my life as well; he has to be my friend. The days of considering your husband as God are over. Tenzin is not without fault and I shall not close my eyes to them just to keep my relationship going.'

'Oh, so he should do everything. What are you doing?' Arun countered, embarrassed at being overheard.

'Accepting his lack, Dad, loving him despite the fact that he is not as perfect as I would want him to be.' Bhavya answered softly, putting her hand on his arm.

'And, you are Bee?' Uma questioned her daughter.

'No, I am not, but the price he asks to be with me may be too high for me to give.'

'What price, what are you talking about? If you give half information, how are we supposed to help you?' Arun asked, leaning forward.

'And, did I ask for your help? All I did was come home to sort myself out. That seems to have taken too long.

I wonder if you had this same conversation with Aruna when she came back.'

'How can you compare your situation with hers? Rafi had beaten her black....' Arun defended.

'Oh, so my bruises don't show on the outside hence they are not important? It is okay, Dad, you have made yourself quite clear. Thank you.'

'Ma, I am going out.'

She walked out stopping to collect her bag from the room. Dheeraj met her outside and laying a hand on her shoulder, handed her the car keys.

'Bee *di,* don't let him ruin this for you. I stand with you, whatever you decide.' He said softly.

She nodded; his kind words stuck like a stone in her throat. She got into the car and sped away. She had no idea where she would go. She stopped the car at Kabir's flat. Large sobs formed and were seeping out.

She fell into his arms as soon as he opened the door. They sank to the floor where they stood as she lost all semblance of control and let her hurt, fear and uncertainty rush out in heart-wrenching sobs.

Kabir just held her, murmuring soothing words on her head, not asking what had caused this volcano to burst.

As she tired and wound down, he said, 'It's a boy, is it?'

The giggles erupted, she did not know what she was laughing about or why but she knew he was the only one who could make her put her troubles in perspective.

She sat up wiping her eyes, 'Sorry, I wet your shirt.'

'Oh darling, that is the least of my worries. Feeling better?'

'Yes, thanks.'

'Anytime, my shoulder is always ready.'

They fell silent.

'Any long-distance phone calls?' he asked.

'No.'

'Bee! You could do what he wants.'

'Yes, but I am not asking him to give up anything.'

'Aren't you, Bee?'

'What, you too?'

'No seriously, you are asking him to give up his long-held belief that men and women cannot have a platonic relationship.'

'I think that does not apply to us.' She smiled sardonically.

'Then what is the problem? Find your happiness with him, Bee. Forget this childish *zid*.'

'I can't. You don't understand. The baby....'

'Give it up for adoption...there I said it.'

'Kabir!' She stood up, her hands going around the baby.

'Why not, it is causing so much pain. I get your worry. That Tenzin will not be able to love it as much if it is mine. I cannot keep it, so go ahead.'

'Don't...just don't...I will never....'

'Why?'

'I love it already, that's why.'

'Is it even one yet?'

'That's enough, Kabir! I am not asking anything from you. Just be my friend,' she said.

'I can't see you destroy your life for...me. Bee, you mean everything to me. Your presence in my life is...more important than...but this cannot be more important than your happiness.' He explained.

'The question is of my happiness, Kabir, not yours and not Tenzin's.'

He fell silent.

She saw his table was littered with her sketches; her face was everywhere, laughing, thoughtful, smiling, reflecting, frowning, a clown face. She could see the ones he had done from memory and the ones he had made her sit for. Spending hours, talking, as he captured each change in her expression.

*Love can be myriad in its forms, never complete, always searching for fulfilment. One would be lucky if they found the one that was the missing piece to complete the jigsaw that was life.*

'Look, it could all be moot anyway. The date and time for the test is fixed.' She walked to his table and scribbled the details along with the address. 'Be here. Let us not say things that will come back to haunt us.'

She left him standing in the centre of the chaos that were his own wants and needs.

A man with the echoes of his muse.

# 38

## *Salient*

### Very important or noticeable

(Language: English, Origin: Latin)

Not wanting to go back to the *Haveli*, Bee went to the mausoleum instead. It had stared drizzling by the time she reached the entrance. She dashed into the inner sanctum and sat in the alcove, the pigeons cooing in the carved *roshandan* overhead.

A misty wind perfumed with the smell of petrichor rose, soothing her frazzled nerves. The clouds were thick but she found the light was enough to read. Getting comfortable, she stretched her legs on the stone bench on which she sat as she read about the woman that lay in the grave before her.

> *After four weeks of waiting, the letter finally arrived. My love has asked me to join him. He has written that he already has the foundations of my house laid close to his Haveli. I shall not be far from him in this lifetime or any of the others.*
>
> *Sometimes I think of what I am giving up to deserve his love. Chirag wonders why I am the only one doing all the giving. He does not understand that this is the way of love. True love demands sacrifice. He tries to dissuade me from leaving everything I know and that is familiar but I laugh his arguments away. I know he too is selfish; he only wants me to stay for his pleasure. I have accepted that nothing comes for free, not happiness, not love and certainly not friendship.*
>
> *At least not for someone like me.*
>
> *Does that mean that I am hard-hearted?*
>
> *Why can I not be happy for the life ahead and simultaneously feel sad at leaving? Why can I not rejoice at a future with my*

*love and also feel devastated at my child being torn from my arms? My heart aches at the prospect of leaving Rumi behind to be brought up by everyone else except me, even if it is for a few months. And, yet, I am aware that she would be better looked after in the comfort of what is familiar than what is new with me.*

*These questions slash at me not letting me fully embrace my dreams coming true.*

*I have so much to do and yet I sit here writing my thoughts. I find I can be myself here in this moment, without the masks that I have to wear. Or, maybe I am just vain, maybe I want my life to account for something. I want someone to read these pages and hopefully understand why I have done what I have done.*

*The clothes are packed in wooden chests; Shafquat Mian and Fatima have promised to bring Rumi to Dilli once I send word. My jewellery and money are rolled and sewn in the seams of my gharara. I finally sit in the palki that will take me away from this place, the only home I care to call my own.*

*All of Panna Mandi watches the procession that looks like a bidaai, a bride leaving her home for faraway lands to make her husband's home prosper.*

*Only this one does not change my status from a young daughter to a beloved wife. My eyes well up as I spot Rumi playing in Fatima's arms, unaware that her mother is leaving, maybe she does not even care. After all it is Fatima who she cries for if she steps away for even a moment.*

*I have to admit that though I love Rumi with all my heart I am not as good for her as Fatima. I cannot nurture a life even though I have given birth to her. I know this with an unflinching certainty. If it is a lack, I cannot escape it.*

*Yes, Rumi will blossom into a beautiful, strong woman under Fatima's love and Ammi's grace. And, I shall call for them soon so she grows up before my eyes.*

*I feel a ripping in my heart, as I am unable to see all that was familiar even as I stretched my neck as far as I could. The girls who accompany me are new and young. Their enthusiasm excites me to look forward to setting up my house.*

*I wonder where Hamad will meet us.*

*She actually left her child for her love,* Bhavya thought, looking at the wet grey stone that stood alone and lonely in the midst of the courtyard, that was a replica of the *Haveli,* just smaller.

*The handwriting is wobbly, did she write this as she was in the palki?* She wondered.

Then, leaning her head back, Bee could not help thinking of how the journey from Malwa to Delhi would have been for Noorie. What would she have felt, a young woman who was leaving everything behind only on the promise of a love that she would not be allowed to even call her own?

Bhavya began reading again turning to the next page.

# 39

## *Sarang*
## The feeling of wanting to be with someone until death

(Language: Korean)

*These months have been trying if I were to put it mildly. We arrived at the gate of Dilli where Hamad was waiting for us. I wanted to run to him, wrap my arms around him and never let go; I was finally before the man I loved, ready to embrace our life forsaking all others.*

*I kept sitting in the shade of the palki for he had not offered me a smile, despite seeing me behind the purdah. Oh, I know he could not raise eyebrows here in the place where he was the authority.*

*The story, he told me later, that he had circulated was that I had been sent on special request to make art; music and dance thrive in Dilli. It was a great honour and hence my kotha was being constructed near the Chowk, next to Hamad's Haveli.*

*Men are gullible enough to believe that their stories are believed and their honour is intact. Women know better. It was a well-known secret that I was Hamad's mistress. Everyone just nodded, either because they feared him or had some work they needed done from him. I let him assume that he was fooling everyone while facing the backlash of this very assumption every day that I lived in his Haveli.*

*The Haveli is like the Chaand, pearly white marble, cool to the touch, shining on the night of the full moon. When I first saw it, I realised that this Haveli has lived for centuries, and would live to see many more when we would be just ashes and dust.*

*It has seen so much and it was in its destiny to bear witness to my history. I shall call it Chaand henceforth, mera Chaand.*

*I told Hamad that I wanted my house to be black in colour. He tried to dissuade me with arguments like black was too dark a colour, getting the stone would take more time, too hot in summers. But I was adamant. His Haveli and mine had to be two halves of a whole.*

*Had Chirag been here he would have understood, even appreciated the irony and the romance.*

*But, one can't have everything....*

*So I gave up friendship for love and hence I have to employ all the ways I can to get him to agree to what I know is right.*

*Anyway, he led us to the Haveli where his family resided. His wife and her brother watched us as we entered the courtyard. He does not have children. She is barren, he had told me. He had left her alone since she told him that she did not want him to touch her.*

*I wondered why someone would shy away from being held, for Hamad was a gentle lover. He liked to touch and be touched. But, to each his own I suppose.*

*Of course, she knew of our love and though she did not want him, she did not want to share him either. Besides the taunts and snide comments, the petty ways of showing that she was the wife and I the whore, she made sure that she flayed my heart by bringing up Rumi in every conversation.*

*It took all my restrain from slapping her smug face these last few days. I finally told Hamad to let me move into my own house for I was unable to bear her jealousy anymore.*

*He reluctantly agreed, more to maintain the peace of his house than anything else. The fact that we were unable to spend even a few hours alone added to the simmering tension.*

*Ten months have passed since we arrived in Dilli and I have finally moved into my own house with a sigh of relief. Not only me, but the girls too had started fretting due to the inactivity and the constant disapproval. Confined to our wing of the Haveli, the inability to move about freely was suffocating.*

*Riyaaz constantly interrupted, stale food, lack of water and mainly the absence of respect sapped the will of the girls. They would lie around listlessly. I finally insisted that Hamad let us move. We were making do in the Haveli; we could easily live in difficulty here as well. The added advantage of the absence of disapproval brightened their young faces.*

*An octagonal foundation, it is a replica of the Haveli, just smaller. The workers had to work day and night to have the front of the house ready in a fortnight after I lost my patience with his wife and her coterie.*

*Oh, but what a house my Hamad has built for us! I call it Chaand Raat. The black onyx marble sourced from the mines of the Punjab province near the west of Hindustan is unique and exquisite. I fell in love with the stone that would imitate the starry skies that we used to look at from the terrace of Panna Mandi. The flames of the lamps extinguished by veined hands, the opal black of the skies had glittered with millions of stars. The sight was so breathtaking that the rays of the sun waited for us to feast on each other under this carpet of diamonds before beginning their soft walk across the skies.*

*Tomorrow is going to be the beginning of many such nights again. I have to get the house ready for him. No more hurried caresses, rough embraces in hidden corners of the Haveli or finding excuses to be in each other's arms in the late pehers of the night now.*

*I shall make our dream come true.*

*So Noorie found her ever after, at least someone was not disappointed, Bhavya* thought before turning the page.

*It has been exhausting. So much to do and such little time. I wish I could write of the hectic days and love-laden nights that have become the routine. There is nothing more I could have wanted from life.*

*A thriving house and business, esteem, currency, gratitude, praise and most of all the love of Hamad has filled me to the brim. After the initial hiccups the house that everyone now calls 'Chaand Raat' has become the hub of the Nawabs and the nobility.*

*The greatest fankaars, maestros of ghazals and shairs of repute and ustaads of instruments all vie for an invitation from 'Chaand Raat'.*

*I carefully select the right mix now that I am more aware. Earlier I used to take Hamad's help. Though he loves to sing and writes erudite and heart-rending poetry, he wishes to remain anonymous. He says it is not mardana to do all this. I laugh uproariously at his words.*

*But, hearing him hum a ghazal as we watch each other breathe, his face free from its daily worries, nestled on my bare breasts, feels like paradise.*

*There can be no heaven when one is separated from their soul mate.*

*Now I understand why people are ready to die for their love, wage wars, lose their minds. I used to wonder what makes two unknown people come together and then decide they were incomplete without each other.*

*Now I know.*

*But, where there is love and happiness how can there not be jealousy and the need to wrest away that happiness?*

*Hamad's wife has started showing her true colours, inciting the maulana and the priest. She says we bring disrepute to the neighbourhood.*

*As if her own tantrums are very pious and helpful to the downtrodden! Though Hamad tries to placate her she demands that I be removed from within the city limits like garbage.*

*Arre! The other day she brought some women with her and started angrily shouting at us. Asking us to do our dirty work outside, saying that we were misleading the young boys to partake in alcohol and flesh trade.*

*What rubbish she spouts, everyone knows she is just jealous. Since I came, Hamad is happier and she cannot tolerate that. She does not allow him to meet me, checks on him constantly. But I know my Hamad; he will not stand for her ugliness for too long. He will give her an ultimatum, to shut up or leave.*

*Her noise has resulted in the awakening of the sleeping dogs of the self-proclaimed keepers of the moral police. They warned him politely about the ill-effects of this blatant display of affections for a prostitute. What it meant was that do what you need to but under the cover of darkness.*

*My Hamad was so offended that day; he wanted to break their heads. It took me hours to make him see reason. These people have the backing of the King. What is the point of posturing before these dogs?*

*Unhappy at having to bow down before the people he did not consider worth talking to, he remained in a foul mood that week, especially when he saw that they were keeping an eye on us. He had to stop coming to me at will. That left us only the heavily attended mushairas and the nightly mehfils where I could only look at him. It was as if the whole world had suddenly decided that we should not be together.*

*Unable to sleep, I had taken to talking to the softly glowing ivory walls of the Chaand, his Haveli. It soothed me strangely, even though the girls thought I am losing my mind. I whispered my longing and heartache to the walls that are far away but somewhere within them sleeps my Hamad, my love, my soul.*

*Then last week he suddenly appeared behind me as I stood at the jharokha as dusk turned the sky mauve. One minute I was alone murmuring my agony to the universe and the next he was holding me in his arms.*

*My clever lover had a passage dug that connected the Haveli and Chaand Raat so that we could keep meeting in secret.*

*The sweet joy of uniting after a long separation is like that first sip of clear water after days of being parched.*

*And, we drank our fill.*

*He told me how precarious the situation was and why he had to stay distant in public. He had proclaimed his undying loyalty to his wife in court because of the uproar that was in the air about us. It amazed me that these fanatics use whatever they can to get what they want. Kill, rape, pillage in the name of faith and honour. And, that was what he was forced to do by the machinations of the religious zealot that his wife had become.*

*The King had just shrugged his shoulders, his focus on the ongoing war with Akbar looming dangerously close, and Hamad had to toe the line. My proud man was seething at this insult to him and to me. But he kept silent, agreeing with their demand of severing his relationship with me, except a public and professional one.*

*Oh the irony! I wanted to laugh.*

*I fumed in silence too, the questions I wanted to demand answers to, bubbling in my head. Why did we not leave? If he loved me all he had to do was tell me to pack my bags and we could go anywhere and live a simple life. I did not need the good life; I only needed him, his respect and his trust.*

*I knew why I did not ask him these questions; it was because I was scared of his answer. What if he realised that I was not worth the effort? What if he felt that he did not need me in his life anymore? What if he chose his life outside Chaand Raat and not me?*

*I hugged him tight, not wanting to ask anything.*

*When could I send for Rumi? I missed her and had not seen her in months. What if she forgot what I looked like?*

*Chirag's letters that arrive intermittently tell me of a girl growing under the tutelage of a teacher that he has arranged. His letters also hint at his growing fondness for Fatima.*

*Now, for the last couple of days, things are back to the way they were. The days go by in the rush to ready the house for the evening, riyaaz and waiting. And the nights bring with them the thrill of the tryst, the excitement of defying the world, the satisfaction of knowing that my love is reciprocated.*

Bee found herself unable to read any further. She snapped the journal closed.

*Why is Noorie fooling herself? Hamad does not love her as she does him.*

'Withholding even the hope of a commitment, making her leave her child in the care of others, letting his wife dictate his life and love...what kind of man does that?' She said aloud.

'Why don't women see this?' She said through clenched teeth.

*Because we love them with everything that is in us,* a soft voice whispered in her ears. It spooked her, the words.

She collected her things and drove back to her sanctuary, the *Haveli*, Noorie's *Chaand*. She would be hard-pressed to see it as anything else except that from now on.

# 40

## *Koi No Yokan*

## The feeling of meeting with someone that falling in love with will be inevitable

(Language: Japanese)

On seeing Bhavya walk in Uma heaved a sigh of relief and told her daughter that she was staying put and that was that. Bhavya smiled but did not commit to anything.

Five years back she would have walked away from her family, in fact she had been estranged for two years, a cold war with her father in retaliation to his unjust, angry accusations at Aruna's situations. Now, she was old enough to realise that decisions taken in haste or when one is emotionally labile usually lead to further complications. She gave herself time till the results of the test were in hand. Post that she would be compelled to lay her cards on the table.

However, today she felt compelled to climb to the first floor of the *Haveli,* her bare feet soundless on the stairs. She stood at the railing watching the glowing mausoleum. From a distance, it looked pretty but like any other tomb.

Now that she knew of the lives that it had held within, the love that must have thrived within its dark exterior, the heartache that it had witnessed, she could not help but look at it with new eyes.

*I wish I could speak to Tenzin, he would find this so interesting and thrilling, the nerd,* she thought, smiling. His absence was more acute these days; it had been a month without any contact. *Does he not miss me then?*

On days like this, she wanted to forget her pride and go back, to her own house. Eat at her own table.

Maybe compromising on this one thing would not be so bad.

*And, would you forgive him, if you went back? Would you not feel you gave him a part of yourself when you did not want to?*

'But that was never the battle, was it? The fight was to stand for what I believe in. Why am I forgetting this again and again?' She said, clutching at her hair.

'You again,' she heard Gaurav say. 'Lady, you need to get some sleep.'

'Yeah...yeah.'

'All these midnight trysts, someone may get the wrong idea.'

'As long as we are sure, does it matter?'

'Yes, it does, Bee,' he said, realising that there was a duality in her words.

'Why?'

'Because one lives in a collective. Some things are sacrosanct.'

'Like, like what...you don't cheat on your spouse whatever the provocation. And if you have you don't justify it.'

'Is that what you are doing, Bee?'

'No.... I did not cheat on Tenzin, Gaurav.' Bhavya said, clarifying without missing a beat.

'I...I know you wouldn't but the baby...is at the crux of the matter.'

'Yes, and giving up a part of myself, my right to choose who I interact with, who I let into my circle.'

'Is this person harmful to you in any way?'

'In what sense?' she asked.

'Drugs, alcohol, wild parties and the like?'

'No, quite the opposite—art, culture, ability to get where I am coming from, a deep appreciation for all things spontaneous and so much more. I just like being around him, it makes me happy.'

'I hope it is not me?'

Bee grinned at her friend shaking her head in the negative.

'Shit, and here I thought I will have impacted someone's life.'

'Gaurav….'

'Just kidding! Do you want my two cents?'

Bhavya nodded.

'Your problem from what I can gather is twofold. One fork is the choice that you have made to have the baby out of wedlock. That I cannot and do not wish to comment on. It has more layers than I know and I would not like to get in the middle of it. The other choice is the between yourself and a readymade pigeon hole.

In my view, people marry a person and then spend the rest of their lives trying to fit them into the mould of the person they actually wanted to be married to. They do this with the knowledge that pretence can only last for some time. Eventually, not being true to oneself only leads to resentment and bitterness,' Gaurav said.

'A mould…seriously I choose the best minds to be friends with. I completely agree. And therein lies the problem….'

'But, what do I know; I have yet to fall in…hmmm.'

'Can't even say the word, can you?'

'And put it out in the universe? What if it finds me?'

The friends laughed at their silliness, much to the discomfort of a pair of thin, gently sloping ears eavesdropping on them.

Tenzin missed her presence, her quirky habits, even the irritating ones. There was the absence of non-stop chatter; no one who rushed to hug him when he entered the door. He missed her smell, her skin, her physical presence. He missed her.

He looked around the apartment. This is how he had lived for forty years, not a thing out of place.

Till she had come into his life like a whirlwind.

Throwing his ordered life into chaos, albeit a beautiful one, she had moved around the pieces of him, and try as he may he could not put them back together. They just did not fit anymore.

*I wonder if they have taken the test. What will they do? What if the baby is his? Will she…and if it is mine? What will I do then?*

Becoming a father had never been on the agenda. He did not want to be responsible for another life. Or was this reverberations of his own insecurity, as Bhavya had accused? Maybe, but he could not see himself playing the role of a father.

*Pah la* always had the answers but he could not seek his counsel on this matter, since Bhavya had not spoken about what the reason for their separation was, letting everyone assume what they would. He could not go behind her back and discuss the reason for them living apart. What would he say?

The tall man standing at the kitchen island sighed. There was no way out.

If *Pah la* could hear his thoughts he would laugh and shake his head, 'That was not our way,' he would say. Their way was all about sacrifice, service and inner peace—the three goals of Buddhism, to alleviate suffering, to find a solution, a nirvana.

Tenzin found himself repeating the ways he had been taught coming easily to him, as if they had always been pulsing under his skin. Burning of the incense, donning the robe, unrolling the coir mat, chanting his mantras as he sat with eyes closed, facing the Buddha.

He could hear *Pah la's* voice in his head instructing him, to imagine that they were the 'Other' person, someone who has the same needs as them. They too wanted to end their own struggles and find happiness. The idea was to inculcate compassion and understanding.

He envisaged Bhavya sitting before him as he took a deep breath, inhaling the throbbing hurt he had caused her, and then exhaling the white light of happiness into her. He did not know how long he sat, wanting to fill the illusionary Bhavya with the white of happiness and contentment. In the process of this give and take he found the strength to look within himself. What he wanted. The ultimate truth, as *Pah la* would call it.

Eyes closed he cleared the mists of doubt and found the green valley of his dreams.

# 41

## *Laminscate*

## The infinity symbol

(Language: English, Origin: Latin)

When clarity arrives, it does not see time or place or favourable situations.

Clarity did not come to Bhavya with the force of a sledgehammer. Instead it came like mist, sweeping a green field, enveloping her in its denseness without a whisper. Soundless in its presence but oh so beautiful, so still.

It started out, small, with her going with Kabir to give their samples at the hospital. After their samples were collected, Bhavya and Kabir were shown into the doctor's cabin. She was politely informed that it would take a couple of weeks for the results to come. Nodding she asked for the amount to be paid.

The doctor coughed, cleared his throat and looked at Kabir who had been strangely quiet the entire time.

'Ummm...actually, we have already received the fee for the test. It got transferred, your hus...ummm...the other gentleman, paid in full when he came to give his sample.'

Bhavya was taken aback, but remained silent.

She drove towards Kabir's apartment to drop him off. She didn't know if she felt relieved or miffed at Tenzin's unilateral decision. They had finally agreed to split the cost between them. He was to pay the first instalment and she the final. Why did he need to override what they decided? Always!

She knew some would ask why did she have to be contrary on every little thing but it was not about the money. It was his backing out of what they decided as a team. She did not like being blindsided like this and he knew this. Plus, it personified a lack of respect for her as an equal partner. She did not want a saviour for crying out loud, she could take care of herself.

'Is everything alright?' She asked a subdued Kabir, who asked her to come up.

'What will happen if the baby is mine?' He asked once they were inside his apartment.

'Why do you ask?' She said, as he dumped the bag on the floor thinking, and here comes that conversation.

'No, I mean what will be expected of me?' he asked, pacing before her. 'I…I…had applied for a scholarship in the States, for a Master in Fine Arts.'

Bee wondered how to let him off easy for she knew where he was taking this.

'You got accepted, that's great, Kabir. Congratulations!'

'Yes, thanks, but what if….'

'Okay, look, don't worry about this so much. You go and do what is your calling,' she said, and then ached when she saw the relief flood his eyes at her words.

'Kabir, you have been worried about this? Why didn't you talk to me?'

'After the last time, I had convinced myself that I would go back to the family business and take care of you and the baby even if it was not mine. But, when I held the acceptance letter in my hand, all that slipped away and what was left was this hollow, selfish man who felt caught up in the situation between you and Tenzin,' he admitted, bluntly.

She looked at him and saw him for the young man that he was, a man with flaws, who believed that he was something that he was not.

'I am sorry. Really.' He said unaware of her thoughts.

'For what?'

'For leading you to believe that I….'

'You did what any good man would have done, Kabir. Look, both of us know that commitment requires love and friendship. One without the other is bound to end in misery.'

'So...what will you do now? Go back to Tenzin?'

'We will see, but first you tell me about this program,' she said and let him ramble on about his well thought-out future plans of creating a name for himself in the art world.

Emotionally exhausted, Bee crept into the *Haveli,* only to be faced with a frantically waving Fanny, telling her to avoid crossing Dad's study. Bhavya stood still for a moment listening to the agitated voice of her father and the calm voice of Suresh Uncle.

*Most likely discussing what to do with me,* she thought, then gestured to Fanny to tell her the details later once she had finished eavesdropping. Fanny grinned a big yes and continued standing there unrepentant.

She did not want to meet her mother's accusing eyes. She had already cornered her once, snidely remarking that all her kids were making their own decisions, what was she needed for, then. Therefore, she was avoiding her for the moment.

A phone call to the human resource consultant proved to be the first dent in her plans to break away. They were not going to be many people looking for a pregnant creative head in an advertising agency.

*Shit, what now?* She thought looking at herself in the mirror.

She spied the journal on the table and picked it up to finish Noorie's story. Her life would have to wait to be sorted.

She skimmed the pages that were filled with the details of how Delhi, now her home, was changing before her very eyes. Her trysts with Hamad become shorter and mundane. The happiness and novelty of being the reigning *tawaif* turned to a business and profit-making cycle that she soon lost the zeal for. After trying to hold on to the position with all her might, age ultimately took away her looks and her admirers. Some men who were admirers of her voice and *ghazals* still came to listen to her but with other younger courtesans reaching their prime everyday Noorie slowly became obsolete. The pages very rarely had Hamad's name mentioned as she carefully read the entries. Some pages were torn out, ripped out as if in anger. She read the bits she could, constructing the passing years from the torn pages.

'No…no what happened to you? Did he stop visiting, what happened to him?' Bee muttered, her voice heavy, flipping the pages again and again. She took a deep breath and started reading the last remaining intact pages.

*The reality of a man, or any person, only emerges when they are in a crisis. Nothing lasts, not beauty, not love. Only friendships and regrets last for a lifetime. With stars in my eyes I had built a dream. A dream that I did everything I possibly could do, to fulfil. And even though I did get what my heart desired, I remain unsure if this is what I had wanted.*

*Would it have been better if I had stayed with Rumi, who does not remember me except what she is told by Fatima, now her mother in every sense of the word? Chirag, her mentor, has made her a shaira to be reckoned with.*

*Adept in art and history, she teaches in a local school. I cannot imagine that my little girl is already a woman. Has it really been that many years?*

*Pata hi nahi chala, where time slipped away.*

*Ammi passed away recently and her kotha is now in the hands of others. I should feel happy that she left a few of her belongings, including her book of poetry and her Koran, to me. Hamad got them back for me, his face crestfallen. We sat together silently thinking about the days in Malwa, Ammi's booming laugh, her sparkling eyes. I wish he had taken me along. But his wife was going with him for the burial so I could not.*

*It is my lot in life, I suppose, to always be considered after someone else. I have made peace with it. I did not fight and just gave him a dua to whisper at her kabr.*

*Hamad also gave me her jewels, so many shiny trinkets. The green wooden box took the three of us to lift and hide, so heavy it was.*

*Hamad's wife has yet another reason to be angry with me now. With Ammi leaving all her jewellery and money to me, she feels slighted.*

*What consequence will I have to face for Ammi's generosity, I shudder to think.*

*I am filled with emptiness, the decisions I have taken, the lines I have crossed in the name of love haunt me on most nights. But, I am used to this now. I only wait for the day when Hamad will realise that I have given up everything for him and come back to me.*

*The old Hamad, my love, who used to sing to me, hold me close; make love to me gently till the stars faded.*

*This hard man is unrecognisable. He does his duty by me but duty was not what I had wanted from him.*

*He cannot forgive the words that I uttered in anger at his constant mistrust. Can he not see that I have been repenting for years now, closing my doors to everyone but him?*

*He is aware that if I had wanted riches or possessions I could have snapped my fingers and so many would have gathered to take me away from this monotonous existence. But he only remembers my words; he does not see the compromises that I have made for him.*

*Some days I want to shout at him, when he visits to hand over the money for the month and to ask if I need anything.*

*The days when I used to demand he face me, goad him with slurs to make him react, have passed. After he started sending the servant boy I gave my word that I would not create a scene and begged for him to visit.*

*Now, his back to me, he stands rigid, steadfast in his anger, not looking at me, as he had promised he would not, so many years back.*

*Why does he fulfil this promise when he did not fulfil the others that he made to me? It is easier to trample on me because I remain his constant.*

*Haven't I been punished enough for wanting more?*

*Apparently not, it seems, for he will come again and ask the same question and I too shall answer as I have been doing for years now.*

*'Do you need anything else, Noorie Begum?' He will ask his head bowed.*

*'Yes,' I shall say from behind the purdah.*

*'What?' He will ask with his voice heavy, as the servants will walk away after storing everything in the kitchen.*

*'You.' I shall whisper to his profile, as he turns his head to catch the word.*

*'That I cannot give you, not in this lifetime,' he will reply, his head bent again, I know his eyes would be closed.*

*Then nothing else.*

*'We thank you, Mian for your generosity and your alms.' I shall say my voice raised.*

*He will nod, hand over a bag of asharfis to one of the old girls and stoop low to cross the threshold of Chaand Raat.*

*I shall rush to the door, to watch him walk away, his shoulders relaxed, his body swaying and hum the ghazal that he loves till he is visible no more.*

*He knows I will wait for the next month to roll by for the visit and the conversation that sustains me, keeps me alive.*

*Sometimes, it feels that I will be waiting at this threshold forever. God forbid.*

Bhavya turned the page to find it empty; she flipped the pages to see if she had missed any side note.

'What...how could she stop writing?' She said as she marched to her father's study.

She opened the door without knocking and found him bent over some blueprints. He was alone, not that she realised it. Noorie's plight and her questions had overpowered her better sense. She slammed the soft leather on his table.

'What happened to them, why did she stop writing?' She asked, bent forward in an aggressive stance.

Arun leaned back in his chair, watching the death grip with which she was holding on to the soft leather.

'*Tsk*, Bee, you will spoil the pages, when will you learn to take better care of the things given to you?'

'Can you stop the Bee bashing for a minute and just answer my question?'

'What? Give it to me.'

'Where is the rest of it?' Bhavya asked her father, frantic to read, what had happened to turn Hamad against Noorie, how would their story end.

'What?' He said absently as he pulled the journal from her hand. She watched him as he caressed the leather before wrapping it in the green velvet and putting it back in the secret drawer in his table.

The green of the dulled velvet triggered a memory of watching him stroke the cloth between his fingers since she was a child.

'Her story. What happened to her?'

'I don't know.'

'What do you mean you don't know?'

'Just that.'

'Dad?'

'I checked the archives. There was sixteenth century ruler of Malwa, Miyan Bayezid Baz Bahadur Khan who was in love with Roopmati. There is written record that Akbar, through Adham Khan, was successful in winning his throne. But there are only personal records that talk about a Hamad Bahadur Khan, who was given this *Haveli* and the *jagir* of the Chowk. That he got the Chaand Raat constructed. There is mention of Noorie Begum, a famed courtesan, in the times but her details are very sketchy and almost non-existent.'

'So they erased her from history as well. Poor thing....'

'It was the times, Bee.'

'It is apt that you would take their side, all men are the same,' said Bhavya with brimming eyes, then ran out of her father's study.

## 42

## *Oneirataxia*

## The inability to distinguish between fantasy and reality

(Language: English, Origin: Greek)

Arun knew where his daughter would go. So he rolled the blue prints before stowing them carefully, giving her time to get the grief he knew she was feeling out of her system.

He strolled down the path that he could traverse blindfolded, above the ground and below. He went to the tomb rain or shine, whatever it took. He owed her that much at least. He walked past the soft grass that covered the *Chaand Raat* on all sides now. The dying sun made the bands of white in the onyx glitter. He went to the inner sanctum where he found his daughter sitting near Noorie's tomb.

*Oh this girl has a heart so soft, so easily bruised! How can I help but worry for her? Agreed, my worry usually comes out as anger, but she knows that she is loved. She had hardened and guarded her heart well, even developed a thick skin in time, but she is helpless when it comes to the people she loves,* he thought, looking at his daughter unable to fathom what went on in her head.

He wanted to shake her and tell her to move on with her life, take a decision and stop this waiting around. Another part of him wanted to rescue her from whatever demons he knew she fought.

'Bee...what are you doing?' he said to break her out of the trance-like unawareness.

'Dad....'

'What has happened, why are you sitting on the floor? Are you alright? Is it the baby?' He said, checking her dazed eyes.

'No, the baby is fine.' She said, closing her eyes to his worry that added another brick of guilt that seemed to be cutting off the air from around her.

'Don't sit there, come.' Arun said, as he pulled her up to walk over to the stone bench in the alcove that was opposite the grave.

'Why?' Bee asked.

'Do you see how strange that wall is?'

'Yes, it is circular like a pillar,' she said, looking at its misplaced addition to the courtyard that was otherwise a perfect octagon.

'It looks rough, and unlike the other smooth walls of stone. It is made of bricks, the old kinds; why is it here?' She asked; sweat breaking out on her forehead.

'Some say that Noorie was immured by the order of the wife of the Subedar who lived in the *Haveli*. Hamad.' Arun said, walking forward to touch the wall.

'Oh, is that how she died then?' She asked, not wanting to step forward.

'I don't know, these are only stories, one can never tell how much has been twisted to suit the people telling the story for applause,' Arun said, looking at the wall in agony, the line of sweat snaking down his back.

'She gave up everything to be with him,' Bee said, looking at the grey stone covered with dust that were her mortal remains.

'Yes, but she knew what she was doing. When she left her baby, when she decided to come and restart her life with Hamad. She was aware of the life it would entail. She chose that life.' He said.

'He had promised to bring her daughter here...' Bhavya murmured.

'But she did not ask him to do so, did she? If this was her end, is it not better that her daughter remained away?'

'They had a fight, what about?' Bhavya asked her father.

'I only know as much as you do Bee.'

'Dad?'

'I think about her admirers.' He said caressing the grey stone, clearing away the small leaves from the headstone.

'Oh, so it is okay for a man to live with a wife but he cannot abide that the women can have friends or admires of the opposite sex?' She lamented.

'He was not without fault I suppose. Who is?' He said softly.

'But to not look at her when she obviously loved him....'

'Don't judge him too harshly, Bee, we don't know what he was going through, who he was protecting, what was going on in his life. From what she writes, he took care of her and the people who were dependent on her. Giving them food and money to survive.' Arun said.

'He had to; he had made her close her doors to the people who could provide for her.'

'She did that on her own, Bee. She made her choices and he made his. You cannot blame others for reaching where you are because no one can force us to choose right or wrong. We do that ourselves, most times. When things go right, we are ready to take the credit then why do we shy away from owning the wrong moves?' He asked his thoughtful daughter.

'They were all choices we made consciously, why blame others?'

'She must have regretted her choice then.' Bhavya said.

'Maybe...maybe not. I did not find her bemoaning her love for Hamad in her words, did you? Maybe their love dulled or became mundane but it never went away. And regret, Bee, regret is such a disease. Why do we forget that when we made the decision to do the thing we now regret, it was the path we wanted to take more than anything else? So, why repent or regret now?'

'You mean we should own our choices and move on, good or bad?' Bhavya asked again.

'Yes, I do. I will say learn from the story what you can but don't go into the what ifs. Also, let the baby come, we will take a call then about your moving out. If you need to feel useful, come to the shop. Put your skills to use there. Dheeraj is at the end of his rope.' Arun said to his shocked daughter.

'Now let's go home, Uma will be worried.'

They stood looking at the lonely grey stone, then turned to bend down to pass the threshold. Arun turned once to smile at the emptiness, then walked away. The air shimmered and the seeds of white shone brighter near the threshold until the father and daughter turned the corner.

'You need to be more careful, Bee, this is not some foreign country that you can roam around alone...actually you should not be roaming around at night anywhere in the world, but especially here. The times are not right, Bee. Come now.' He said brusquely, picking up the pace as she lingered wanting to say so much but unable to put words to his concern.

'Bee...' he tried again when he saw her fallen face, liquid eyes that she tried to cover with her curls, pulling the strands back with her fingers.

'I just wanted some air, Dad,' she said.

'It's fine, I...okay, but next time will you tell Dhee...or Suresh or even the *chowkidar* to accompany you.'

She nodded.

'Or you could tell me, maybe....'

'You?' She asked startled.

'I mean if you feel okay coming here with me.'

'Why do you come here so often?'

'I don't know. From the first day I stepped into the *Haveli*...I wanted to rush to... Anyway....'

'Dad...tell me...' Bhavya said, wanting to know more.

'It's nothing, I...just...nothing. Now stop this. It is May and hot, why do you wear this shawl. It is tattered and looks about to fall apart. Tell your mother to buy you a nice one this winter.'

'I like this one. It is Ma's. You gave it to her when I was born, as a gift.'

'She told you that?' Arun asked.

'Yes.'

'Oh.' He did not know what else to say, his heart happy that she kept the shawl, knowing that it symbolised his affection and happiness at her birth.

Both father and daughter ran out of things to say, the emotions pulsing around them, making them both uncomfortable and awkward.

'Bee.'

'Yes, Dad.'

'You are the only child I have who is not scared to fight bare-knuckle. That you have taken from me. When the going gets difficult you don't back down, you fight as dirty as it takes, to win. I...I respect that about you. Your passion, your conviction, your enterprising attitude, these I have lost along the way.'

'Dad...what....'

'Let me finish. Why are you moping about here?'

'What, are you asking me to leave after just ordering me not to?'

'No, you know what I am saying. I will find a way to get you out of trouble but you say that you haven't done anything wrong. Then why are you running? Stand and fight and know that your father shall be standing right next to you. This hiding does not suit you, my Jhansi ki Rani!'

'You used to call me that....'

'Yes, I know.'

'Why did you stop?'

'You grew up, did not have time for our fun battles anymore.'

Bhavya nodded, squared her shoulders and sniffed. She knew the days of inaction were over for her. With or without Tenzin, she was going to blaze her own path with a little help from her family, for now.

Noorie's life had made sure she understood that bit of her future....

They walked slowly back to the *Haveli* in silence, lost in the questions that fired their hearts.

# 43

## *Peiskos*

## The feeling you get when you sit in front of the fireplace and enjoy its warmth

(Language: Norwegian)

Arun and Bhavya walked into utter chaos. By the time they strolled back into the driveway, it was already dusk and the lights were shinning brighter as if in celebration, lighting the foyer of the *Haveli*. They hurried in, wondering about the taxi that stood waiting at the door.

Bhavya's eyes adjusted to the mayhem inside and it took a moment for her to process what she was looking at.

The whole house had converged in the hallway, ready to go out. Dheeraj was checking his pockets absently. He then picked up the car keys from where they were usually kept. Ma was talking to Tenzin as he carried a bag for her as they came out of her parents' room while Suresh Uncle was counting wads of cash in a hurry.

*Wait back up*; she looked at the montage again.

'What are you doing here?' She said aloud, stopping everyone in their tracks.

Tenzin stood motionless, just taking in the vision that stood before him. The red shawl barely covered her shoulders, it was hot in Delhi but he knew the shawl was more for comfort than actual use. Her hair was slightly longer and she was looking at him with shock and maybe some irritation. Her body was still slim but her face was softer, fuller. What hit him was the swell of her belly that was suddenly visible. How could it have increased to that size in one month? His eyes refused to move from her stomach until her hands covered her belly. He looked up, meeting her annoyed eyes, knowing that his own were filled with awe.

*Was he wrong in coming here? No, she would have to use the words she loved so much and tell him that. She would have to make him leave,* he thought with determination.

'Bee…' Uma said.

'What's wrong, Ma? What is happening?'

'Aruna *di*…she is on her way to the hospital. The baby is coming.' Gina answered excitedly.

'Oh wow!' Her eyes popped open as she too turned around and made her way out of the door.

She spied Tenzin standing near the taxi, separate from the melee, his eyes tacit, watching her. A strange bubble rose in her throat. She did not want to call it happiness for that would defeat the decision she had reached.

Loaded in two cars the family reached the hospital talking over one another. Tenzin helped her out even as she noticed the distance Gaurav and Etti maintained, especially recently. Along with her body it seemed time too had slowed. Or was it that all these emotions were floating on the surface, always within reach to be found by anyone keen to look and she hadn't cared to look till today?

While she was observing all this, Tenzin was observing her, the changing expressions, the frowns, the half smiles, and the sadness.

'You haven't said anything much since you got back, are you feeling okay?' Tenzin asked.

'Yes, thank you,' she said and moved ahead.

They went to Aruna's room and found an anxious Bhuvan holding his daughter close.

'Here, let me have her,' Fanny said, taking Tara from him. She nodded coolly at JD who had driven them to the hospital and heard Sweety Auntie's laugh from inside.

JD, Sweety Aunty and Singh Uncle lived in the apartment below Aruna and Bhuvan's. They were practically family just as neighbours should be.

'*Arre puttar*, you are an old hand now at this, just bear down, the second baby slips right out like butter.' They all heard Sweety Auntie's booming voice.

'I...need to get my mother out of here. Uma Aunty... could you...' JD said feeling out of place, his eyes constantly pulled towards Fanny who was playing with Tara.

*She is forever lost to me.*

'How is she?' Uma asked Bhuvan, ignoring the boy who had broken her daughter's heart.

'Fine...the doctor is with her...and Sweety Aunty. She heard us rushing around in the apartment and called to ask if everything was okay. Tara wouldn't stay back with her, so we all came.' He said his throat dry.

'All will be well, Bhuvan, don't worry. Let me go in and check,' Uma said, and then enveloping everyone in her look, she ordered.

'All of you will stay out and I mean that!'

Arun and Suresh found their seats near the TV and switched on the news channel. Etti and Gina surrounded Fanny, closing ranks and moved to a far corner to keep Tara busy. JD wanted the earth to open up and swallow him whole.

'Faced with so much antagonism I would want to tuck tail and run too,' Gaurav whispered to Tenzin, who stood on the side lines observing everything, sifting through all the undercurrents that were swimming in the waiting lounge. He was enjoying this play immensely. Unaware of the details of JD and Fanny's story, he did not comment, but felt bad for the poor boy.

For once he didn't feel out of place, different, freakish. Everyone knew everything or at least some form or version of what was going on in everyone's life. It was a joy to see the lines intersect...separate...converge. He wanted so desperately to stay…be absorbed, as they had accepted Suresh and Gaurav.

His eyes out of their own volition went back to the one he could not seem to resist looking at.

*Always slightly away from everyone, slightly separate. Bee, a part and yet not one,* he observed.

'Who wants tea?' Gaurav asked.

The chorus of affirmations and raised hands had Gaurav rushing off to get several cups. He took along JD to get him out of the heated glares being thrown his way from the corner where the girls stood.

Bhuvan's mother and sister Sona joined the fracas. Dheeraj perked up and sat next to Sona, talking excitedly. She only looked at him with a faint smile. Bhavya lowered herself to the chair, her body aching from the effort of smiling, greeting and looking happy. Bhuvan's mother walked up to her, hugging her close, asking about the baby's due date.

Tenzin did not approach Bhavya after her brush off in the parking lot but kept her in his sights. He watched her fend the questions with ease, finding it impossible to get through to her.

How long he stood and how many cups of sweet milky tea he gulped he didn't know…and he didn't even like tea. He just knew he could not have left Bee even if his life depended on it.

Finally, Bhuvan came out and announced that they had given birth to a healthy baby boy. Loud congratulations followed and Tara proudly proclaimed that since Santa had granted her wish early did that mean she could ask for a puppy now since Christmas was some time away, making everyone laugh.

Much joy and jubilation followed. Tenzin bent over the baby cradled in Uma's arms and felt a curious elation come over him as he looked at the little, pink infant. He didn't realise when the little bundle was placed in his arms or when he cradled the helpless baby closer to his warm chest. The moment the little one rubbed his scrunched-up face on his chest, Tenzin knew he was in love. The ooohs… and ahhhhs…of the others who were keenly observing this byplay faded in the background as he imagined holding his own child in his arms and felt a wave of gratitude overwhelm him.

He raised his eyes to Bhavya's liquid gaze, the awe and wonder in them clear for all to see. Then he gave his full attention to the squirming baby in his arms.

*What was I thinking? I am the most idiotic fool that has been born this side of the Atlantic. He is the ONE. And, I was busy looking for faults when all I needed to look for was his intent. I know his heart, how big it is,* Bhavya thought as she stood stunned at what she had seen in his eyes, an ocean of love that did not cull on the basis of birth or blood.

All masks wiped off, she had looked into his heart that loved her without asking for much. He had made the journey…twice…to reach out to her, how could she let that go unanswered?

Tenzin noticed how Bhavya's smile kept slipping as if she couldn't wait to get away from everyone even as she hovered over her beaming sister and the sleeping baby. Her mind was not in it. Her hand kept going to her back, rubbing it to ease the ache lodged there. Her eyes followed Bhuvan and Aruna, how they were almost one unit and he could see her face become sadder, her smile dipping further.

Finally, when he could not take it anymore, he delivered a hasty congrats to the new parents and then taking Bhavya by her hand, he dragged her out of the room.

'I am taking her home.' He threw the words back over his shoulder.

# 44

## *Aurora—Dawn*

(Language: English, Origin: Indo-Greek)

She snatched her hand away when they reached the corridor.

'What the hell? What do you think you are doing?'

'Not here, Bee...this is a hospital.'

'Okay...but stop manhandling me, I am not your wife.'

That made him take a step back.

'Okay...please step into the car.' He said arms out.

'And who do you think you are to take me home? If I want to go I will, I want to stay with my sister,' she said, her hands folded over her swollen belly, her face set in obstinate lines.

'Shut up, Bee, both of us know your lower back is giving you trouble. All you want to do right now is lay yourself in the bed and sleep the night away. Everything is under control here.' He said, his patience fast eroding.

She sat in the car with a grimace and then promptly burst into tears.

'Why...what...why are you crying? I will take you back, Bee, if that is what you need. Please stop crying. What is the matter?'

'I don't know, Tenzin. I don't know how to...to be a mother. I am going to suck at it and you...you keep a distance...as if what I have is contagious.'

'I don't...that's not true.'

'Did you say anything to me, even two words since you came?'

'I just arrived and you were not home, and then Bhuvan called. Where was the time?'

'Just tell me where to sign, I will.'

'Sign what?'

'Divorce papers.'

'We aren't married.'

'Oh yes, we aren't.' She said, and burst into loud tears again.

'Bee, what is wrong with you? In the time I have known you I have not seen you cry…well, except once. Why?'

'It is this damn baby; I have no control over my emotions anymore.'

Tenzin sat quietly, not knowing what to say, how to make her believe that she was the most important person in his life. She had always been the talker in their relationship.

He started the car and drove back to the *Haveli* slowly. He tried to practice what he would say but everything sounded cheesy…superficial. His brows knit he wondered if his lack of voice would lead to him losing her.

Bhavya, on the other hand, fought to control her emotions. Embarrassed, she fished for a napkin to wipe her eyes in her purse then used the offered handkerchief.

*Who would give her a handkerchief once he left?* Her eyes welled up again, but she held back the tears telling herself to grow up.

They reached the *Haveli* just as dawn was about to creep onto the far horizon. The sky was turning an intense grey. The air was sweet scented with *champa* flowers that were blooming on the trees that lined the driveway.

The ivory-white *Haveli* shone like the moon in the darkness against the Prussian blue of the sky. They kept sitting in the car, watching as the first rays reached the sky, the stars started fading, the streetlights flickered off. They kept sitting together with nary a word exchanged between them. Bhavya shifted, trying to get more comfortable in the compact car her brother was so possessive about.

'Bee, I think you should lie down.' Tenzin said.

'Hmmm...in a minute. Since I came back in March, I have not had a moment of peace. There is always someone talking, something that needs doing. There is too much movement, too much chaos. This is nice. I think I am getting old.' She said with her eyes closed, her voice heavy with sleep, her head resting on the back of the seat.

'Bee.'

'Hmmm....'

'I did not talk to you because I thought you didn't want to be with me. I realise that you are never going to be happy to settle for one person. You will need different people to fulfil different aspects of your many-faceted personality. I will never be the only one. For me that was the definition of love...still is, to be the only one. You are that one for me.

But, I get that this is not the definition of love for you. For you, it is the ability to choose. That was what I was taking away from you. And I...am sorry for that.' He took a deep breath.

She looked at him, wanting to rush in with platitudes, tell him he was such an idiot but then didn't, only listened.

Tenzin grew quiet as the words dried up. He realised Bhavya had yet to say anything to him.

'What about the baby?' She asked finally.

'I did not come here with a set plan; I just came because I could not stay away. We will figure it out, I guess. When are the results due?'

'The doctor said a couple of weeks.'

He nodded.

'So, what now?' She asked.

'Now it's up to you. I realise that marriage to me is a lot to take on. Why would any sane person want to mess up their life with me? The baby…I thought I could let you walk away, could watch the baby grow from a distance. But Bee, watching Aruna and Bhuvan and the kids…I couldn't…I cannot do that. I will try my hardest to be as good a parent as I can but don't remove me from the periphery. I want to be with you when the baby comes… but I am willing to settle for whatever you decide. You are the bright star I wished for, the one that shone only for me as I looked out into the dark night. The lodestar that guided my next move as I navigated these troubled waters I call life. I wouldn't know how to survive without your light to…' He stopped.

Bhavya knew her next words were important, crucial even. This proud man was laying his soul bare and words said casually at this time would affect their future. So with utmost care she formed the words in her head, then articulated what was in her heart.

'You are in my heart, Tenzin, flaws and all. I love you and that is all that matters. *You* matter. But I cannot be less, even for you. I am what I am, rough around the edges, moody. I love life and I cannot live in a controlled environment. I like change, taking risks, doing things that I can, experiencing life as it comes, with a question rather than a sigh. It is too ingrained in me to be changed.

The difference between us is that I see the end and have the trust in myself that I shall be able to remove all the obstacles that come in my way and you…you count the obstacles and give up. I obviously fail more than you do but…'

'…You live more than I do too.' He finished.

'We both are right in our choices because they lead us to the way we choose to live our lives. These are the paths we have chosen. As long as our paths intertwine it should be alright. I tried to convince you to see my way of having fun as the only way to live and you did the same. I was wrong in that and for that assumption that you were rigid

I will apologise. You are not rigid, only your idea of fun is different. It took me a while to get that. You never stopped me from living my life and I did not appreciate that. But, I see no point in saying all the right and beautiful stuff now and then later wonder if we did the right thing by coming together.'

'Are you saying you want a break...?' Tenzin asked.

'I am saying that you will have to accept me as I am and I shall accept you as you are.'

'Can it be that easy?'

'Of course not, but we have to start somewhere. Look, think about it, you may have missed our life together due to this separation and hence you are...' Bhavya felt duty-bound to caution.

'You know me better than that, Bee.' Tenzin said.

'Yes, sorry.'

'What if the baby is Kabir's? Will you still feel this way; you were so against being a dad.' She asked.

'I was, yes. Truthfully, I was scared that I would turn out a failure. I have *Pah la* to call a father and he is my mentor but it isn't like the father and son relationship that I used to dream about, as a boy. I know I never told you but I left the orphanage to look for my parents, to reconnect or at least find out why they abandoned me.'

'Oh okay....'

'After I started working, I was finally able to trace them. The private investigator gave me my mother's address and I went to meet her. I still remember how nervous I was, unsure and yet thrilled to finally end my quest. We met in her house and I asked the requisite questions, the answers to which she gave very sensibly without the emotional outburst I was expecting, dreading and secretly hoping for. I am the result of a young love that was not yet ready to add responsibility to their repertoire. My father, a young Casanova, had abandoned my mother after bringing her to Leh on the pretext of infiltrating the struggle. Patriotic fervour as a seduction ploy, can you believe it!

And, she being too young to do anything beyond having the baby, ergo me…just got rid of me, the best way she knew how to before going back to her family in Tibet.'

'Do you blame them?' She asked softly.

'Not anymore. I did go through a rough patch when I found out. She wanted nothing to do with me. Her family had married her off to another and he did not know about me, so…anyway long story short, I wanted to avoid failing my kids at all costs.'

'Why did you not tell me all this before?'

'It made me feel small, insignificant like I was… unworthy.'

'Tenzin, yes, parents are the first influence but don't forget you are an individual with a thinking brain. You can refuse to follow what you feel is wrong. We choose to become the kind of people we are; no one, not even our parents, can be held responsible. We can't change everyone, but we can change ourselves,' she said.

'So, if you feel you have the potential to be a good father, here is your chance…take a chance, you just might surprise yourself,' she said, holding his hand.

He nodded, understanding, relieved; simple words said with inaudible conviction can work as bridges across troubled waters.

He squeezed her hand and sat looking at the *Haveli* that glimmered in the soft, misty light of dawn.

'It is going to be madness once Aruna comes here with the baby,' Bhavya said.

'Bee, you are blind as a bat to the kind of blessing you have unknowingly received in the big, loving family that you have. They are your greatest strength and you keep them at arm's length. They will stand with you no matter what. And that…that is the sum total of their love for you.' He said, looking at her.

'And, what of us?' She asked.

'Let us try for acceptance despite our differences.' He meshed his fingers with hers. When she did not extricate her fingers from his, he pulled her closer and wrapping his arms around her said, 'Bee, let's go in.'

'Hmmmm....'

There was silence for a minute, then Tenzin turned towards her more fully.

'You forgot to get the keys again, didn't you like last time when Tara was born? I cannot believe this. If this is not *déjà vu* I don't know what is but I am not waiting in the car this time. I am going to break a damn window, I am telling you. Waiting for six hours in the car once is enough in the name of love. I have paid my dues for God's sake....'

She squeezed her eyes closed, letting the giggles sneak out. It started as a gust of wind exhaled then as he continued his triad it increased in volume and intensity until she begged him to stop.

'I am going to pee in Dheeraj's car if you don't stop talking, I swear it, Tenzin. Don't make me laugh anymore.' She said her hands around her baby.

'Yes, I know you are laughing too.' She said to her tummy.

'What?' Tenzin looked at her.

'He is laughing, kicks when he wants to tell me....'

'Can I touch your ummm...?' He asked hesitantly.

She took his hands and placed them around her stomach. His big, warm hands trembled on her skin as he felt the ripple inside.

She looked at his bent head when she heard his breath hitch.

'Tenzin?'

'God, Bee, I am a father! A father. I didn't think I would even have someone love me and you have given me this gift of...' He closed his eyes, unable to continue. 'You make me want to trust myself, Bee, only for you...I would... will you....'

'Don't say something that you don't believe in, Tenzin. I don't want nor need a marriage certificate to tell me that we are a unit, that we belong to each other. Let's do that when we are both ready. Not because of the baby, not because of what people will say, but for us.'

Their arms came around each other. Soft, unhurried. She touched his face; he kissed hers and everything that was in the air seemed to fall back in place with a soft sigh as if the universe had only been waiting for them to iron out the wrinkles in their life's fabric.

'I love you...Bee...your astonishing capacity to love... will you be my partner, the mother to my child?' Tenzin asked tenderly.

'I was always your partner...yes to the mother part.' Bhavya said, smiling at the laugh that rumbled out of his chest on which her ear was pressed against.

'Oh and the choice is between waiting here for at least six hours with me in your arms or driving all the way back to the hospital to get the keys.' She said between kisses on his smiling mouth.

Tenzin laughed. 'Life is never going to be dull with you around, Bee.'

'That's a given,' she said, closing her eyes hearing his heart beat her name.

Bee...Bee...Bee...Bee....

# Epilogue

Bhavya lay wrapped in a kaftan, lightly snoozing, almost aware of the re-run that was playing on the television and the soft tapping of Tenzin's fingers on the keys of his laptop.

The chill in the air was welcome after the humidity of the last month in Delhi. Here in Paris the air was still crisp. Her mind fogged with a restful languor, she thought back to the exhausting last few weeks in the *Haveli*.

Enveloping the baby and Aruna with adoration and love the family came together to celebrate the joy that permeates hearts when a baby is born.

She smiled remembering the unadulterated delight that came over Tenzin whenever he had picked up the baby.

*I am so glad I recognised that in him at the hospital when he first held the baby. How could I question his capacity to love children?*

It had also meant they got some time to themselves. They would stroll dreamily at the mausoleum as Bhavya told him Noorie's story. He had been fascinated with her life. They had spent hours going through the journal again, discussing, dissecting and enjoying their shared views. It was like finding an old friend and realising how much they mean to you.

*'He may have his flaws but they will never be the inability to love you,'* she whispered, rubbing her swollen belly.

The baby kicked as if in understanding making her grin.

She exhaled a gratified breath closing her eyes, a beatific smile lighting her face.

*I think I love him more now than I did a year back. Is it because I know he will make a good father, or that he was willing to accept me as I am, without preconditions?*

Bhavya opened her eyes thinking about Kabir, her smile slipping a little. She was still getting used to the e-mails from him that spoke volumes about the status of their relationship now.

Tenzin remained silent on this matter. She knew it would take effort from both their sides but they would make it... because in the end they needed to be together.

*Anyway, the choice was not between Kabir and Tenzin, it was always between our differences and our ability to include, to bend, to accommodate. In this bending and shifting we have gotten more intertwined, it seems,* she smiled thinking of their love that had become deeper and more intense since they had reconciled their differences.

*I think I finally believed in him when the envelope with the results came from the clinic,* she thought looking out of the glass window.

How happy everyone had been to know that she was going back with Tenzin, that they had sorted out whatever had been troubling the two. Most likely, hoping for wedding bells to ring in a few months. And, Bhavya had promised to take the decision when they were sure, completely sure.

The phone rang making her jump, disturbing the peaceful cocoon that she had created for herself.

'Sorry, sorry, I will take it in the other room, you rest,' Tenzin said, as he shot out of the chair with an apologetic smile.

Bee smiled back, sleepily wondering if she could ask him to make tea for her. Then sighed and roused herself to put the kettle on.

As she went to get the plate of biscuits, she heard Tenzin on the call, murmuring about some bank transfer. She spotted the envelope that had arrived a few days back lying on his desk. She had been dreading this envelop from the clinic. Despite his assurances of not bringing up the past, she knew people reacted differently to situations when they were faced with the reality of the circumstances.

She had handed over the envelope to Tenzin, silently watching his eyes for any sign of discomfort.

He had smiled and laid the sealed envelope back in her hands simply saying, 'I don't need to see the result, Bee, you have a look if you want.'

'But what if....'

'I don't care. The baby is yours and that is what matters to me.' He said and hugged her.

She had had to blink back tears.

But, as a precaution, she had left the envelop on his desk just to see if he meant it. Since that day the envelop had been gathering dust.

She hummed as she added the tea bags to the cups. Then filling them with hot water, she walked to the door that was slightly ajar. She was about to swing it open with her foot when she heard the words:

'Thank you, Doctor.'

She leaned forward to listen to the rest of the conversation.

'Yes, we got the report. No, no it does not matter, the baby is ours. Please be rest assured that she will be taken care of. No we do not want to look at options for adoption. As I said... the baby is ours....'

There was silence as he listened to whoever was on the other side.

'Thank you for your concern but we are good. You have been very accommodating and discreet for which both of us are grateful, however, the baby is mine and Bee's and that is what matters. Goodbye.'

*Love did not need a piece of paper to make its existence known,* she thought as she opened the door wider.

*The baby's cries reach me, making my heart throb. They named him Rumi.*

*Can there be any doubt that he remembers? I know he does.*

*Arun frequently paces his study, a caged animal, the frown making an appearance on his high and proud forehead on such nights when there are things troubling him. All I want in this moment is to go to him, wrap my arms around him and comfort him as I know his wife never will.*

*She is the sensible one, the one who carries his name like I never did or ever will. But I know he needs me, I saw it in his eyes then and I see it in his need to visit me every day, rain or shine, now.*

*How strange, that the one who is our partner in life may not necessarily be our destined soul mate.*

*I, who can hear his heart, am not allowed to call him my own and the one who can touch his soul refuses to do so.*

*Oh! The irony.*

*I, who left my homeland, my family only to follow love when he moved to change his city, was relegated to the corners and the one who had no interest in the man, only the position, was celebrated.*

*What a tangled web we weave. The small slights, the disappointments, small wishes unfulfilled and yet I wait, for the One to find me, love me as he had once.*

*Will my wait be never ending? I fear it just might be....*

# Acknowledgments

This book is an ode to geographic distance. I wrote it in Delhi, it was beta read by Sakshi Nanda in Belgium and edited in Kolkata by Indrani Ganguly to come full circle.

Hence, let me begin by saying a big thank you to Sakshi and Indrani who were invested in the characters from the word GO.

Dipankar Mukherjee, the publisher, cannot be thanked enough for his focus and for always having my best interest at heart even when I didn't.

I end by thanking all my friends who have surrendered their lives to my inquisitiveness answering my million questions that sometimes may have been intrusive. I love you and wish you find the happiness you deserve.

My creative process is incomplete without my other half Chandeep and his support. He is my sounding board, my bull-shit detector and my human hard drive. I am blessed to have him with me every step of the way.

This book goes out to all of you.

Harshali Singh
2018

# About the Author

Harshali Singh is a New Delhi-based author. She has completed her tenure as a member Judge at the Consumer Forum recently.

An academician with a decade of experience of working with pre-primary age group in different capacities ranging from Operations Head to the Curriculum and academic head, she, as a teacher trainer conducts workshops to enhance proficiency in advanced teaching methodologies.

She is a trained Occupational Therapist from the Institute of the Physically Handicapped and also holds a Bachelor's degree in Education as well as an LLB degree.

While handling these demanding jobs she managed to take out time for her passion, that is, painting and also held an exhibition of her exclusive, vibrant paintings at the India Habitat Centre in 2014.

*A Window to Her Dreams,* a contemporary adult fiction is her first novel, published by *Readomania*. It is the first book in a series of seven books.

*The Anatomy of Choice* is the second book of the series.

Harshali can be reached at:

Email: harshalisingh@gmail.com
Twitter: @harshalisingh

# Glossary

| | |
|---|---|
| Ammi | Mother in Urdu |
| Apni | Our |
| Arre puttar | Oh my child |
| Asharfi | Gold coin |
| Beta | Son in Hindi, term of endearment |
| Bidaai | To see off or send off. It is particularly used in the context of a girl getting married off and leaving for her husband's place. |
| Buri nazar | Evil eye |
| Chaand | Moon |
| Chaand Raat | Night of the new moon |
| Chhatris | Elevated, dome-shaped pavilions used as an element in Indian architecture. The word *chhatri* means 'canopy' or 'umbrella' |
| Chikankari | A delicate and artfully done hand embroidery that originated in Lucknow, India |
| Chowkidar Bhaiya | Gate keeper |
| Dayra | limit |
| Diwan-i-Arz | Officer in Department of Military under the Delhi Sultanate |
| Dua | In the terminology of Islam, an invocation or prayer |
| Dusht | Wicked |
| Fankaar | Artist |
| Farman | Royal charter |
| Gen la | Teacher in Tibetan Language |

| | |
|---|---|
| Gharara | A traditional outfit from Lucknow worn by Nawabi ladies. It's a pair of wide-legged pants having ruche at the knee for flares. Worn with a mid-thigh length kameez and dupatta |
| Ghazal | A lyric poem normally set to music |
| Hookah | An oriental tobacco pipe with a long, flexible tube which draws the smoke through water contained in a bowl |
| Hunr | Skill |
| Jagir | A grant of the public revenues of a district in northern India or Pakistan to a person with power to collect and enjoy them and to administer the government in the district |
| Jharokha | A type of overhanging enclosed balcony used in the architecture of Rajasthan and Indo-Islamic architecture |
| Jhoola | Swing |
| Kabr | Grave |
| Kotha | House of ill repute, whore house |
| Lakeer | A line |
| Maangteeka | An ornament worn on hair parting that adorns the forehead |
| Mandu | Or Mandavgad is an ancient city in the present-day Mandav area of the Dhar district. It is located in the Malwa region of western Madhya Pradesh, India |
| Mansabdar | Rank of a government official |
| Mardana | Masculine |
| Mausiqui | Urdu word for music |
| Mehfils | An evening of courtly entertainment poetry or concert of Indian classical music and dance, performed for a small audience in an intimate setting |
| Meri jaan | My heart |

| | |
|---|---|
| Mian | Mister, landlord |
| Mushaira | Poetic symposium |
| Naach-gaana | Indian dance |
| Nâng-miy | Family in Tibetan Language |
| Nath | Nose pin |
| Nawab | A Muslim nobleman or person of high status |
| Nazm | Urdu word for poetry, verse |
| Ngay bu | My son in Tibetan Language |
| Nizam | Hereditary title of the ruler of Hyderabad |
| Noor | Light in Arabic |
| Paan | Betel leaves |
| Paandaan | A small box, usually of decorated metal, used to hold *paan* or the ingredients for making *paan* |
| Pah la | Father in Tibetan Language |
| Palki | Palanquin |
| Pata hi nahi chala | Did not come to know… |
| Peher | One division of a day under the system where a day (and night) is divided into eight parts, one part consisting of three hours |
| Purdah | The practice in certain Muslim and Hindu societies of screening women from men or strangers, especially by means of a curtain |
| Rajma | Red kidney beans |
| Riyaaz | Practice |
| Rooh Afza | A non-alcoholic, rose-based squash |
| Roshandan | Skylight and ventilator |
| Saaz | A musical instrument |
| Shah | Monarch |
| Shair | Poet |
| Shaira | Poetess |

| | |
|---|---|
| Shehzada | Prince |
| Sheikh | An Arabic leader |
| Shukrana | Gratitude |
| Solah shringar | The term literally translates into 16 adornments that have been defined by the Hindu scriptures as mandatory parts of a woman's ensemble. These constitute: *bindi, sindoor, maang tikka, kajal, nath,* earrings, necklace, *mehendi, baju bandh* or armband, bangles, *haath phool,* cummerbund, anklet, toe ring, fragrance and hair accessories. |
| Subedar | The governor of a province in the Mughal and the Maratha Empire |
| Tanpura | A long-necked plucked string instrument |
| Tawaif | Courtesan |
| Thaap | Beats in music |
| Ustad | An expert or highly skilled person, especially a musician |
| Vaid | Healer |
| Zamindar | A collector of the land revenue of a district for the government during the period of Mughal rule in India |
| Zanana | The part of a house for the seclusion of women |
| Zid | Recalcitrant, obstinate |